# AND NO QUARTER

# AND NO QUARTER:
## An Italian Partisan in World War II

### MEMOIRS OF GIOVANNI PESCE

**Translated by Frederick M. Shaine**

OHIO UNIVERSITY PRESS 1972

# CONTENTS

# Introduction by the Translator

Giovanni Pesce, whose code name was Visone, wrote one of the most gripping eyewitness accounts of the downfall of the Italian Fascist regime and of the liberation of Italy from German occupation during the period from July 1943 to May 1945. He saw it from the streets as a partisan in constant peril of his life. The Partisans' opportunity came about as follows.

On the afternoon of July 1943 King Victor Emmanuel III of the House of Savoy summoned Benito Mussolini, who had been Duce of Fascism and Prime Minister of Italy uninterruptedly since October 1922, to the palace and dismissed him from office. The officials of the Crown, the Army, and a few within the Fascist Party itself, had already for some time been plotting and maneuvering to seek a separate peace with the Allies and to appoint the former Army Chief-of-Staff, Pietro Badoglio, Prime Minister with powers to conclude peace. The King had been hesitant—fearing the fall of the Monarchy which Mussolini, whom he did not like, had preserved. But the Fascist Grand Council of Italy itself had in the early morning hours of 25th July, on the resolution of Dino Grandi, a former Foreign Minister and a power in the Fascist Party, voted by 19 to 7 to express no confidence in Benito Mussolini. So Victor Emmanuel acted. In the palace courtyard the Carabinieri (Italian National Police) arrested Mussolini as he left the audience with his King. He was taken under guard to the island of Ponza; Badoglio became Prime Minister.

Badoglio's policy was to seek peace with the Allies; to release all political prisoners (of whom Pesce was one) and all allied prisoners of war; to consolidate all Italian national groups dissenting from Mussolini and, with the help of the Allies, to end the German occupation of Italy. Throughout Italy, mass anti-Fascist demonstrations and loud public rejoicing in the streets celebrated Mussolini's downfall from office just as shortly before this time the Sicilians had greeted the invading Allies as liberators. It was triumph for the Italian Anti-Fascist National Front which had, as early as March 1943, succeeded—even as a disorganized underground resistance and at enormous cost in lives—in paralyzing the whole heavy industry in the cities of north Italy by strikes in favor of Italian withdrawal from the war.

Those of the Fascist Party who remained loyal to Mussolini were powerless to release him, to re-establish his government or to maintain order in the rear of the German armies still engaged with the Allies as far south as Naples and beyond. The Germans knew that the King and Badoglio were likely to secure an Armistice with the Allies (it was signed on 8 September 1943). Heavy German reinforcements began to pour into Italy to counter the Allies landings at Salerno (9 September 1943). By October the Allies had entered Naples to find that it had already been liberated from the German rearguard by the Italian underground in four days of heavy fighting.

The King and Badoglio had, simultaneously with the publication of the Armistice in September, taken refuge with the British Headquarters at Brindisi in the far south. Mussolini, still under arrest, had been transferred by Badoglio's regime first to LaMaddalena, an island near Sardinia, and after 6 September to a ski resort hotel at Campo Imperatore atop the 9,000 foot high San Grasso mountain in the Abruzzi.

The German Reich and High Command was anxious as ever to preserve both *de facto* control and the appearance of a *de jure* Italian government behind its own lines. Therefore it dispatched an Austro-Hungarian, Colonel Skorzeny (of the SS and subsequently acquitted as a war criminal for deeds around Bastogne) to arrive on 12 September with a small force of gliders on the San Grasso range. Mussolini was flown on to Adolf Hitler's headquarters in East Prussia.

The fruits of these consultations in East Prussia between Hitler and Mussolini were: a new Italian government (under Mussolini) to be called the Italian Social Republic (RSI) with its seat at Salò on the western shore of Lake Garda; a military force to support the RSI under the command of Rudolfo Graziani, a former Viceroy of Abyssinia, with the assistance of veterans of Mussolini's 1922 march on Rome, such as Farinacci, Pavolini and Buffarini-Guidi. The duty of the corps was to assist the occupying German forces in rounding up "dissident Italian elements" behind the German lines and to render such other duties as might be required to throw back the invading Allies.

So in September of 1943 the lines of battle in Italy were clearly drawn to reinforce the informal anti-Fascist Front of March of that year. The Liberals (PLI), the Christian Democrats (DC), the Republicans (PRI), the Socialists (PSI), the Communists (PCI) and the more recently formed Action Party (Pd'A), comprising all anti-Fascist opinion from right to left, were temporarily of one mind and intention. The Socialists and the Communists had already shown themselves to be the more effective militants against the German occupation. All these anti-Fascist parties now formed themselves into a Committee for National Liberation (CLN) with Ivanoe Bonomi, a pre-Fascist Prime Minister (July 1921 to February 1922) as their leader.

At this point Pesce, released from a Facist prison camp, with several thousands of others had begun to strike where it hurt the Germans and the Fascists most, in the streets and railroad terminals of North Italy.

During 1944, the Allied priorities in effective weight of men and material in the European theatre were directed to the Normandy Invasion and the Invasion in the South of France. The Allied advance in Italy was slowed and the Allied Commander, General Alexander, considered, as did Churchill, that Italian activity behind the enemy lines should be subordinate to the needs of Allied strategy. It was also feared that the strong Communist element among the Partisans might turn the war into revolution. As the Allied Armies moved closer to the Northern cities, however, the more confident and brazen the Partisans became and the more desperate the German reaction and the fury of Mussolini's Fascist Republican Blackshirts.

In this larger setting the personal campaign of Giovanni Pesce against Fascism, its fanatical supporters and their Nazi allies, takes place.

Pesce had been at war or in prison since he was eighteen and his active experience of combat had begun as a Young Communist and as a Loyalist Volunteer in the Spanish Civil War from 1936 to 1939. But in Spain against Phalangists, Fascists and Nazis he had fought another kind of war as part of an army under regular command and, despite all the privations and improvisations of the Loyalists, in organized units in attack or defense. As a partisan in North Italy he was alone or, at best, with a small group of un-uniformed youngsters behind the enemy lines. Their tactics were to hit and run, to scatter, changing identity and address, forever on the prowl, forever conspiring from one end of an enemy city to the other, into the countryside to strike by surprise and back to the city to uneasy hiding.

Pesce's life had begun in the despair that marked the working poor of the industrially backward and depressed areas of Europe and which nourished both Communism and Fascism to clamor for state dictatorship. When he was six his starving family had fled from total destitution in Italy to the grinding horrors of the mines of a French company-town. Their pitiful earnings were mortgaged to the truck store before they could buy either food or clothing. His father died in an unsafe mine. Pesce himself started work there while he was still a child. He lived with men who saw the only hope of betterment and justice in a Marxist revolution and in a loyalist victory in Spain. He joined the Young Communists. He was recruited to fight in the International Brigade. Proficient as a soldier, he was invalided for wounds. When the Spanish Loyalist Government collapsed he was in France. Instead of granting political asylum the French returned Pesce and others to Italy. He remained a political prisoner in Italy until he was liberated by the Allies. Once freed, Pesce made his way to the North of Italy.

Pesce's partisan group, called Gappisti (GAP, Gruppi di Azione Popolare), was made up of small groups of young men, mostly in their teens, who were usually organized under the aegis of a Communist activist. These groups operated mainly in the large cities and their environs.

Pesce recounts his activities as an organizer and trainer of these groups, his attempts to arouse in them the spirit of camaraderie and a desire for freedom from the German occupying forces and Fascist government. He describes his own feelings of isolation and utter loneliness as he fights and conspires alone with little or no communication with others. He displays an almost super-human courage in the face of the enemy. He writes of stark incidents which involve all phases of aggressive underground activity—assassinations, treachery, arson, explosions, railroad derailment, work stoppages, revenge, roundups, ambush, secret codes, passwords and disguise. We move with him stealthily in alleyways of towns, in crowded railroad terminals of large cities, to isolated hideouts hidden in the hills, to lonely farmhouses for secret assembly. We witness his plea for firearms; we sit with him as he outlines a plan of attack on a German barracks; we shake with him as he lies in fear; we stand with him before a group of youngsters as he chastises them for carelessness and lack of precaution. We grieve with him over the death of a fellow partisan.

Pesce's account carries us through April 25, 1945 "the day of the last historical fact of Italian Fascism," for it was then that Mussolini departed Milan for the last time with a motor convoy and proceeded northward, eventually following the narrow, twisting road along the western shore of Lake Como, headed towards the Swiss frontier, in company with an entourage of Fascist officials and his mistress, Claretta Petacci.

But, he never did reach his destination, for on April 27, while seated in the rear of a motor lorry disguised as a German Army sergeant, he was stopped and recognized by a partisan band outside the village of Dongo, near the Swiss frontier. There the Fascists who accompanied him were assembled on the lake shore and shot. The following day, Mussolini and Claretta Petacci were lined up against the wall of a villa in the small village of Giulino di Mezzegra, south of Dongo, and were riddled with bullets. On April 28, their corpses were taken down to Milan and hanged upside down by the heels in front of a gasoline station on the Piazza Loreto, alongside those of other Fascists, for all to see.

"And No Quarter" is the dramatic episode of one man in the Italian partisan movement during World War II. A similar chronicle can be recounted by thousands of other Italians, who represent a wide range of political opinion.

It is estimated in some quarters that as many as 200,000 had participated at one time or another in the Italian underground during World War II and that possibly 40,000 had been killed. This is Italy's little known but proud picture of heroism during the dark days of Fascism and warfare on Italian soil.

I am especially grateful for the source material provided in "Mussolini's Enemies, the Italian Anti-Fascist Resistance," by Charles F. Delzell, Professor of History, Vanderbilt University; "Mussolini, A Study in Power," by Ivone Kirpatrick, former Permanent Under-Secretary of the British Foreign Office; and "The Brutal Friendship," by F. W. Deakin, Warden of St. Antony's College, Oxford University.

# CHAPTER 1
# *On the Run*

When they let me out of the political prison of Ventotene,[1] my aunt and cousins let me come to their home at Acqui.

Acqui was, and still is, a little town of old Piedmont. The houses were decorous, but not pompous; the streets were just wide enough to let horses and carriages pass each other. Old gentlemen of a nineteenth-century elegance sat around barroom tables. The town had a tranquil air. The war seemed far off.

People talked about the 25th of July and the downfall of Mussolini[2] as though it had been a distant earthquake. I could think only of the joy it had brought to us who had been confined at Ventotene. But those people in Acqui spoke with a sort of nervous pride of their own accomplishments. Sometimes I smiled; they seemed to go everywhere on tiptoe, to whisper in undertones. "Is it all right, doctor?" "With your permission, your honor?" That earthquake had not really shaken Acqui.

But people were fighting and dying only fifty miles away. It was hard to believe, among hills green and yellow with thistles, with beautiful grape arbors and rich fields of corn. The summer weather was beautiful. Gratefully I learned to know my aunt and cousins for the first time. I took part in conversations which brought back the faces of my mother, father and brothers.

---

1. Translator's note:Ventotene: an island off Naples, where over 1,000 political prisoners, mostly members of the PCI (Italian Communist Party), were confined. The author was a member of the Italian Communist Party.

2. Translator's note: The day (1943) that Mussolini was deposed by the Fascist Grand Council.

After the rocky squalor of Ventotene, I felt a yearning for open fields, a burning desire to walk along country paths, a longing to rest in the shade of the trees, to listen to the chirping of locusts in the bright noonday heat. After so many months pent up on that little island of barren earth, restlessly assaulted by the sea, I felt free life around me again.

Sometimes, in the afternoons of that summer of 1943, I slept for several hours in the open. I would dream of Ventotene, the hard, cruel confinement. Then I would waken and fill my eyes with wonder at the beautiful countryside of rolling hills, with grapes ripening in the sun, corn growing to golden maturity. Once again I had found my land, and I knew it—the place where I had been a little child, the paths which my young mother and father had known before their exile.

Farmers ploughed their fields. The rich brown earth would yield a second crop after this early corn was harvested. And in town the streets were semi-deserted. In their quiet, one could hear the distant rumble of columns of military vehicles, somewhere out of sight beyond the horizon.

The war's tragedy came to me vividly when I visited an old couple on a farm, people who had known my parents. They were there all alone.

"Where are the children?" I asked.

"Gianni is in Africa, Pietro in Russia," they answered sadly. Emptiness hung around them in their house, and I felt that it was the same emptiness that I felt among the hills, on the streets of Acqui. So many good young men were gone, nobody knew where or to what fate.

That evening I returned to my aunt's house, on a little square across from the church. A hot supper and kind attention helped me to shake off a feeling of claustrophobia, one result of my imprisonment.

"Don't tire yourself out," I was admonished. "You did not rest today."

I began to visit several bars. I began to speak Italian again. Though I had been educated in French schools and had something of a foreign accent, I could use my native tongue, and I could understand it. I was able to talk with an open heart to my companions in the bars, the few young men who had escaped the draft and some of the oldsters. The talk was about the war, and the hopes for peace.

"What is Badoglio[3] going to do? How will it all end?" These questions were asked over and over, with no certain answers. I began to understand what my neighbors were thinking.

I had been back in Italy for four years; but nearly all that time had been spent in confinement. Among fellow prisoners at Ventotene and in jail at Alessandria, I had learned several valuable lessons in the art of secrecy. I had spoken little, but I had listened much and had learned something. Now, free to walk and talk and sleep without dread, I was making up for those years, and I studied this little town, that seemed to be living on its tiptoes.

Acqui had an aura of serenity in a time of tragedy. It had not lost its ancient calm, its atmosphere of another time. Its reserve and apparent timidity hid a strength and courage which would face up to any adversity. This realization grew upon me as the days passed.

On the afternoon of September 8, as I walked out, I found myself striding vigorously. I had regained my health and appetite. I walked a long way and as evening fell, I came to the top of a hill and looked down upon the town. Rain had fallen the night before, and twilight brought a chill into the air. A sudden shiver went through me. The sunny days, limpid nights and star-sown skies had made me forget that this season, not yet spoiled by war, could not last forever. The days had been beautiful, the air full of light and fragrance. I had sniffed the odor of wisteria twining the walls of old farms, the odors of threshing, the intense-smelling odor of new-cut hay. I had thought of the coming harvest season, the crushing of grapes, the harvesting of grain. I had gazed at happy pigs, drowning their snouts in troughs of wet mash, growing fat.

That sudden coolness of the evening made me remember other chill days and nights, spent in the mountains of war-torn Spain.

---

3. Translator's note: Marshal Pietro Badoglio (1871-1956) Chief-of-Staff of the Italian armies and Prime Minister (July 1943-June 1944) of first government after fall of Mussolini which negotiated the Armistice with the Allies (Sept. 3, 1943).

I remembered the nightmare winters of the war. Back home I trudged, less happily. As I lay down to sleep that night, I said aloud, "The summer is over." I woke next morning to loud noise.

My room looked down to the Piazza del Duomo. The severe, blocky outlines of buildings in the background were softened by the shape of the fourteenth-century cathedral, which had undergone restoration. Narrow streets led into the Piazza del Duomo, and these were crowded only on Sundays and market days. Rising that morning, I heard a commotion, and I knew that something dramatically strange was happening.

Up to my window rose a sudden wave of excited voices, a tramping of thousands of feet, a crescendo of shouting. I looked out, and gasped. The streets and alleys were filled with soldiers, vigorously changing themselves into civilians.

Swarms of young men were throwing off their gray-green army jackets and clutching civilian clothes. One dashed into a large entrance hall, another scrambled in at a window. Women were coming out, fetching clothes belonging to their husbands and sons, handing these things to the soldiers escaping from their uniforms and what the uniforms meant.

Hurrying into my clothes, I rushed into the street. Excited neighbors answered my questions. The Germans had blocked the roads into town, and these Italian soldiers were running from them. That previous evening, the announcement of the Armistice had been broadcast, and things had fallen apart. The Wehrmacht suddenly had become an army of occupation. Germany would not let Italy fall.

I knew I must get out of Acqui. Back at my aunt's house, I quickly gathered some necessary things, for a journey to Alessandria. If I could get there, I could make contact with the Party. Off I hurried toward the railroad station.

Someone was shouting on the street. "The Germans have surrounded the barracks!" he cried. "They have captured all soldiers who were left inside!" At once I turned my course toward the barracks on the Via Cesare Battisti. Others were running along with me.

The old burnt-yellow building came in sight. German soldiers in olive-colored uniforms blocked the entrance, with levelled rifles. A crowd was gathering. Many women were there, some with babies in their arms. I came within twenty yards. I could see the faces of the Germans, hard and tense, under their steel helmets. Shouts rang from the windows of the barracks, then came a harsh rattle of gunfire from the courtyard.

Ten or twenty of us had come close, halting in a compact group. Several Germans fired rifles and pistols over our heads. Then a moment of silence, and some of the people ran. I peered at the barracks, and the hands and faces of the imprisoned soldiers behind the bars of the windows.

In the open space before the building, a group of Germans had mounted the roof of a truck. An officer rasped an order. Back from a window came a warning shout. The men inside bobbed out of sight as a burst of machine gun fire struck the gutters and roof. Back came howls of defiance and execration.

The crowd around me thickened and stirred. Someone pushed my shoulder from behind, and I pushed the man in front of me. We began to move forward, as though in a planned, concerted advance.

The Germans saw, and began to back away. One of them shouted something, and an officer barked an order. Machine gunners moved toward the barracks entrance.

Then we rushed.

It was a human avalanche. Men and women alike struck the cordon of German guards, knocked men sprawling. I saw men wresting weapons from the hands of the fallen Germans. We surrounded a group of them, and they dared not fire.

Now, I told myself, something must be done. I gestured this way and that, to several men who looked able-bodied and resolute. They came with me to push open the doors of the barracks, and we rushed inside.

"Go out the opposite way!" we yelled at the soldiers inside. I could hear shots behind us, and the screams of women. A quick backward glance showed me that the Germans were surrounded, herded helplessly together.

The Italian soldiers hurried to escape. Some of us pushed our way into a large room, where rifles were stacked. We grabbed them and handed them through the rear windows to men on a back street. The escaped soldiers ran along the row of houses, and again I saw women handing civilian clothes from doors and windows. Acqui seemed to be transformed into an immense dressing room.

I felt better, happier. I had taken part in the first rebellion against the Germans, but there would be more rebellion. I forgot about fleeing to Alessandria. I could do something here at Acqui.

First, I would try to find the young men, the boys, who had arms in their hands. I knew none of them, but they had seemed cool, reliable, the sort of fighters that could form a nucleus for a larger force. Where to begin my search? Already, patrols of Germans were moving along the streets. Townspeople bobbed out of sight wherever they could find hiding places.

I found myself in a warehouse, with a group of others. Among them was an Italian captain, still in uniform. He sat on a box in a corner, his head hanging in dejected humiliation.

"Were you in the barracks just now?" I asked him.

He nodded dully, his eyes fixed on the floor.

"How did the Germans take you by surprise?" I tried again.

"They came to the barracks at dawn."

"Didn't you have any information or orders from headquarters?"

He glared up at me, as though my questions angered him. "We had heard nothing from headquarters for at least twenty-four hours," he growled. Then he cursed under his breath. He looked nervous, with all of us watching him.

Just then a red-haired soldier caught the attention of the others. He had been given a handsome wedding suit, elegantly cut. He had even put on patent leather shoes. "How can I find a ride in a truck with this costume?" he demanded.

I turned back to the captain, who spoke readily now, but bitterly.

"Maybe the war will end now," he said. "I've had enough of being kicked, slapped and insulted. To be beaten like a fool, by four Germans!"

"The war isn't finished," I said. "Germany is still fighting. There is much for us to do."

"Perhaps," he granted. "But how, and with whom? I was an officer in the army, but now the army has melted like snow in the sunlight. If I could do something definite—yes—but what?"

Women were calling to us through the window, to say that the Germans had gone away. We went quickly out of the warehouse. The captain and I walked along the street together. He was the only uniformed figure in sight.

"I couldn't decide whether to ask for civilian clothes," he said. He stopped in front of a bar, and shook hands. "If there is anything more to do, we'll see each other again," he said, and turned to enter the bar.

I gazed after him. Probably he would decide to find his way home if he could. But I felt sure of what I would do. I had done such things before, I had started doing them in Spain in 1936, in the bitter battles against the Fascists. I walked in, looking for those youngsters from the barracks who had taken arms with them when they escaped.

In this way, during the week that followed September 8, 1943, the partisan life began for me.

I found my fugitives in the hills. Among them were several I knew, and we organized ourselves as a hard-nosed irregular force of fighting men. Later this group developed into the first partisan division, led valorously by Minetti. Some of the soldiers from the barracks joined us. Soberly we began to plan.

At first we were too few to fight the Germans. They flowed through the land in huge, efficient columns. We cut telephone wires and carried out small sabotage actions. We had to hide, gather strength and become dangerous. We set up secure, hidden billets and headquarters. During that first week we wanted fiercely to strike back, but there was not even a minimum of organization. Ceaselessly we argued possible strategies and tactics of partisan warfare.

Scouting in Acqui, Visone, Strevi, Ricaldone, Cassine and Gartosio, we saw hurried, excited people on the streets. Young men in civilian clothes strode the pavements with a step that hinted of army training. Often they wore their army shoes; borrowed civilian shoes belonged, after all, to other soldiers far away, perhaps trying to come home.

Several of our force departed. "If we must fight, it's better to fight near our homes," they said. But others came, asking cautiously about our organization. Some joined us. We did not yet know what we would do, but instinctively we saw ourselves as a new army, self-organized and self-sustained, formed to fight the Germans without quarter, with our own method and our own blood.

To help us organize and operate, I volunteered to go to Alessandra and make contact with the governing organization of the Party. I bought a ticket and boarded a railroad car. Sitting down, I heard the stationmaster blow his whistle, heard the responding blast of the engine whistle. The train chugged away. It seemed absurd to me that the train still functioned after the State had broken up, the army dissolved, the world turned upside down.

The air in that car was stifling. It was a warm day, and not many windows could be opened. It was an old car, grubby and dilapidated. Clouds of smoke, from cigarettes rolled from scraps of old newspaper, made a fog. Odors of sweat and mould hung heavy.

Most of the passengers seemed to be soldiers in civilian clothes. There were a few old ladies, dressed in black, breathing heavily, holding bundles in their laps. I wondered if they were not mothers, going in search of vanished sons, in barracks up north, or perhaps in the hospital at Alessandria. Perhaps they would find sons or husbands, lead them home, hide them before the Germans drafted them and sent them away.

These passengers talked. They told gloomy stories of battle and death, of miraculous flights from danger—all the talk was about the war. Some jabbered incessantly to others who listened dully. Importantly the talkers swore each other to secrecy, "or you'll be finished." Sly ones sat quietly, perhaps thinking of black market profits, or waiting raptly for a miracle. But all were afraid of road blocks.

A tanned young man told his companions how, in his barracks, a group had struggled to freedom through a pipe that ran along a half-filled ditch. Several had almost suffocated inside the pipe and had had to be dragged out by their companions.

Another, who looked as if he had been a man of importance, lectured us. "I tell you," he said loftily, "they are now busy sending people to Germany. We're insane to let ourselves be found aboard a train. As soon as the Germans catch their breath, they'll begin to search, left and right, everywhere."

Silence fell. Nobody felt optimistic enough to say anything. We felt, sitting in that box of iron and wood, that we were caught in a trap, the sure prey of a German platoon waiting at the next station.

Here and there the train stopped to let passengers off. When we reached Alessandria, the compartments were half empty. The women could rest their heavy bundles on empty seats. I was happy to see no Germans waiting at the station.

Quickly I went away to find the directors of the Party. In Alessandria I did not find the excitement and restlessness I had left at Acqui. At the center of town, great crowds had gathered at the food stores, but the side streets were almost deserted. I entered a dreary cafe and ordered a cup of coffee.

The old man in charge did not seem to hear me. He picked up a coffee pot and carried it toward a table at the rear.

"Hurry up," I called after him, but he only frowned, then went to a table where a man sat, wearing the familiar, hated black shirt of a Fascist. This customer stared disdainfully at some old men playing cards in a corner. He and the proprietor whispered stealthily together, and the Fascist laughed. Not until then was I served with a cup of coffee. I drank it, and it tasted rank and bitter.

"Is it possible," I asked myself, "that these Fascist fools are coming back into circulation so quickly?"

Leaving the cafe, I moved swiftly to the quarter of town where the Party director lived. More people seemed to be walking on the streets. Men in civilian clothes, obviously fugitive soldiers, spoke to women on the balconies above their doors. They seemed quiet, assured. So far, the German motor patrols were keeping to the central zones.

I reached the house I knew. Several young men loitered at the entrance, perhaps on guard duty. Inside, my old friend, Comrade Camera, greeted me affectionately.

"You find me just as I'm about to leave," he said. "The Germans will be scorching the earth here, and it's up to me to change my address."

I spoke hotly. "The situation in Acqui pleases me very little," I said. "There are a few old followers of Bordiga, but they do nothing. I've remained steadfast in my purpose for twenty years, dreaming of ways to overthrow Fascism. But they haven't moved a finger to help me."

"Patience," Camera comforted me. "I know the situation well. One person wants only to talk, another feels he must move. Our first task is to consolidate all our forces. We need all the help we can find, to fight the Fascists and Germans, and we must show it can be done."

My irritation left me as he spoke.

"And don't worry," he urged me. "Plenty of those strong young fellows now escaping in civilian clothes will eventually join us old good-for-nothings of the anti-Fascist struggle. They'll be there when the time comes."

We agreed to keep in contact. I would go back to Acqui and try to meet with other groups who would help us in the struggle for freedom. We came to the door. There he walked away, with the young men who had waited at the door.

I knew that as soon as the Germans got their hands on the police archives and mobilized the Fascist police and the Black Shirts, the hunt for anti-Fascists would begin. It would go hard for any they caught. But Camera would transfer his headquarters to a better hiding place. From there, he would direct the anti-Fascist forces of Alessandria.

Back at Acqui, I passed an almost sleepless night. It seemed to me that the Party was already mobilized at Alessandria, was ready to operate secretly and efficiently. But here, there was no organization. I felt baffled and disappointed.

In the square I met one of the Bordighiani. He talked eagerly about the successes of the Red Army, and told about exciting broadcasts of Radio Moscow and Radio London. "Better times are coming," he assured me as we parted.

I kept in touch with my comrades hidden in the hills, but the contact men seemed spiritless. I had no sense of enthusiasm or organization in the group. Inertia seemed to overwhelm us. Meanwhile, the Germans were occupying the area, taking over its government, and rounding up thousands of young men who might help us and sending them away to Germany.

My burning desire for action tormented me. I was glad when, at last, I heard there would be a meeting of representatives of various anti-Fascist factions. They wanted a member of the Communist Party to attend. Would I come?

I hunted up an enthusiastic old comrade, and set up liaison contact with various Party cells. We decided to call ourselves and each other by battle-names. If one of us was captured, he could not inform on the others.

On the day of the meeting, I went to the office of the manager of the Garibaldi Theatre, in the center of Acqui. A group of men, of all backgrounds and ages, gathered there.

I winced to hear them introduce themselves by first and last names. The atmosphere had something of archaic, eighteenth-century conspiracy, with no regard for the rules of secrecy. A stout gentleman, wrapped in timidity as in a cloak, began the discussion by turning to a neighbor, a man with an air of conscious authority.

"How do you think this thing will end, Advocate?" he asked.

The advocate replied optimistically. With Italy having surrendered, he said, Germany, too, would cease to fight. The Allies would take over, promptly and efficiently. But others broke in, offering their own conjectures. There was no search for a common course of action. I felt that we were gaining nothing, would remain helpless in the face of the oppressor.

"Gentlemen, may I have permission to speak?" I asked suddenly.

All faces turned toward me. Dolefully, I reflected that diplomacy had never been my strong point. And my Italian was imperfect, I had a French accent, they would think me a foreigner. I would be unable to speak eloquently and effectively.

But I began, and with no verbal niceties.

"The hour for discussion is past," I told them. "The moment for action is at hand." I went on to propose the formation of a central group, made up of representatives of all factions, to form and coordinate their forces for combat action.

As I spoke, I felt that I had truth on my side. But, when I finished, the others sat gazing at me with cold eyes. Some of them seemed even disgusted at my outbreak.

"We would have preferred someone more tranquil and conservative as a spokesman for the Communist Party," said someone at last, with a courtesy that seemed as cold as ice.

I left the room, trying hard not to show my disappointment and fury. There was but one course left open, I told myself. The Party must act, boldly, even desperately. Then, surely, the other anti-Fascists would join with us.

I determined to make contact with Fillak[4] and with other

---

4. Walter Fillak, born in Turin June 10, 1920, university student at the

young anti-Fascists I knew who, like me, felt ready for action. But my plans were to be changed drastically.

One night, I returned to my aunt's home in the old building in the Piazza del Duomo. Usually the only noise in the quiet evening was the light tolling of the rectory bell. I walked across the resounding paving stones. Inside, I felt almost faint as I went upstairs and got ready for bed. It was about eleven o'clock.

Then, on the floor below, a sound of tramping feet and a loud knock at the door.

"Does Giovanni Pesce live here?" shouted someone. "Where is your nephew?"

"He is not here," my aunt stammered.

"Open up, quickly!"

They were storming in. I heard furniture crashing as they flung it about.

I grabbed my clothes and cautiously opened the balcony shutters. The little street extended in front of the house from one end of the Piazza to a junction of narrow alleys. Shadows moved down there, but I dared not hesitate. I sprang from the window, barefooted, clutching my trousers in my hand. I ran to one of the alleys, diving into its darkness as into water. Behind me I heard the loud shouting of the men who had come to arrest me.

I finished dressing and headed through some gardens toward the railroad station. An empty freight car stood on a siding, and I crept in. A friend worked in the railroad yards. If I could find him, he would help me.

Two hours passed, and he came through the darkness. I called him to me. In whispers we agreed that police headquarters files had fallen into the hands of my enemies, and that all anti-Fascists

University of Genoa, founded a Communist cell in the winter of 1940-41. In 1942, he was arrested for the first time by the O.V.R.A. Freed after July 25, 1943, he was in Turin in September, 1943, where he organized disbanded military operatives into groups. He was also Partisan at Pian di Castagna (Acqui), vice commander of the 3rd Garibaldi Brigade in Liguriaj, he was instigator of numerous actions in Genoa. Political Commissioner in the zone of Cogne (Aosta Valley), and Commandant of the VII Garibaldi Division, operating in the Aosta Valley, in Canavesano and Biellese. Captured during the night of January 29-30, 1945, in Sace (Ivrea) with members of his command who were eventually shot after being ambushed by a German patrol which was led by a spy, he was hanged at 3 P.M. on February 5, 1945, on the Alpetto Road near Cuorgne.

were being arrested. My comrade fetched me an old jacket and a pair of shoes that fitted fairly well. At dawn the freight car was attached to a train that rolled me away toward Turin.

"On the run," I told myself. "I'm leaving Acqui, really on the run."

## CHAPTER 2

# *Political Awareness*

Everything had begun for me nineteen years earlier, when I was six years old, arriving in Grand Combe, near Nimes, France. It was a cold November afternoon in 1924. My mother got out of the train with my little brother Gino, six months old, in her arms. I followed with two-year-old Gilfredo. My father was there, and picked Gilfredo up and held him. I dragged down our luggage, packages and bundles. My father and mother hugged each other with the little boys caught between them.

I looked around curiously at my first coal miners. Their smudged faces were like masks, blending into the grubby black of their clothes and caps. The yellow light from a lamp struck brightness from their eyes. We gathered up our possessions and tramped along the street to the house my father had rented.

I dragged bundles into a big room. I saw two beds, a table, a few chairs. The bare walls were caked with coal soot.

"And the children," my mother said. "Where shall we put them to sleep?"

My father stood silent a moment by a dull window pane, his hands in his pockets. "I don't have a penny left," he confessed. "I wanted to buy more furniture, but I sent you all the money I had for your railroad fare."

"I still have a little money," said my mother. "We didn't spend anything on the train."

They bought a second-hand crib for Gino, and a few pots and pans. Gilfredo and I slept in one of the beds.

A few days later, my father and mother had one of their rare arguments, about where I would go to school. My father favored the public school, perhaps because the consul, the mine owners and all the officials wanted the miners' children to go to the Catholic school. But my mother insisted that I must have religious training, and she won the debate. To the Catholic school I went.

I was fairly happy for the next three years. I was not really aware that we were poor, that I lived in a slum. While my father mined coal all day, my mother made a home out of that dull, bare room. She plastered the walls and hung bright muslin curtains at the window. One holiday we hung a simple ceiling light, on an iron plate enamelled white. We called it a chandelier. It spread clear radiance through our home.

My playmates at school were mostly children of immigrants, like me. Only a few of them were French. The others were Italians, Germans, Poles, Slavs, Algerians. Those Algerians were poorer even than we, and lived in wretched wooden barracks. We spoke different languages, but we understood each other as we played the games all children play—cops and robbers, hide and seek, jump rope. Some of the fair-haired, rosy-skinned little Polish and Slav girls made sharp contrasts with the background of soot that covered the walls, the pavements, our clothes. I never saw a truly white shirt while I lived at Grand Combe.

One winter day, I entered the house to find my mother kneeling before a sacred image on the wall. She was deeply religious, but I had never seen her like this; she prayed and wept simultaneously. I stood watching her, holding my bag of books. I thought of the gate to the mine, through which I had seen injured miners carried on stretchers. Suddenly fear clutched my heart. I turned to run out again, when she rose and walked over to Gino's crib. I followed her and looked at my baby brother. His face was flushed, and he gasped.

"The doctor says it is bronchial pneumonia," my mother said. "There is nothing we can do."

That night my mother and father sat together by the crib. I lay in bed, beside the sleeping Gilfredo. For hours I watched the lamp, with its shade made of a newspaper. I fell asleep at last, and woke up too late for school. That day we carried Gino to the cemetery, in a little coffin made of raw wood.

Next day I carried a note from my mother to the teacher. He read it, silently, with no expression. Fiercely I wished I were big enough to hit him in his blank face. That night after school, I did not go out to play. For several days I sat at home.

My father seemed wearier each night when he came back from work. He said that the section foremen demanded more coal. Some of the overworked miners were becoming sick, and several seemed to be dying. I heard him say a baleful word to my mother. Silicosis—a terrible sickness that eats the lungs of men who work at the bottom of mine shafts. Eventually my father too, was sick. It was bronchial pneumonia, the disease that had killed little Gino. He lay in bed for almost two months. There was no meat on our table, and very little bread.

I was ten years old by then. One day my mother drew me aside.

"We'll remodel the house," she said. "We'll open a canteen, where miners can come to eat. I'll do the cooking. You're a big boy now, and you can help me."

Resolutely she did what she said. We set up a large room, with tables and chairs for customers, and two rows of shelves stacked with bottles and plates. At a large coal stove, my mother did the cooking; always the same things, stew and polenta. That was a thick mush, made of yellow meal from Italy. She made it in a great copper boiler, stirring it with a wooden spoon. After the customers left, I helped her wash dozens upon dozens of plates, knives and forks and glasses, and fold away bright-colored tablecloths.

Much of Grand Combe was made up of brick or wooden barracks, long streets of them, separated by partitions. The living units were but eighteen feet long—eighteen feet in which to suffer every day, in which to rest, to collect one's thoughts, to remember, to try to hope. Often I wakened at night, to hear angry voices and blows in some nearby cubicle. In one eighteen-foot room as many as eight men tried to live. Some would go to bed as soon as they got there, exhausted from work. Others mumbled, drunk with a mixture of fatigue and wine. Some snored, some talked in their sleep, some wheezed with silicosis. Often such roommates quarrelled and fought, made desperate by day after day of perilous work, brutalizing fatigue, threats of losing jobs or expulsion from France. On pay day, company guards came to the canteen to meet the miners, subtracting from their pay sums advanced for food or clothing. Very little remained of a miner's pay when he got it.

A man who came in hope, with wife, children and sometimes parents, found himself a prisoner. The tradesmen, kindly at first, grew relentless when payments were due. They took the pay before it came to a miner's hand, forcing him deeper and deeper into debt, driving him to new and baffling desperation. Often they came with wagons to repossess furniture, while wives stood protesting and little children cried with fear.

My father still hoped for security. He left for Morocco, where, he said, things would be easier. We could join him there. But he could get work only as another sort of miner, digging for sulphur. My mother kept the canteen at Grand Combe. I had come into my teens and I went to work in the coal mine. Soon I joined the Communist Youth Organization.

The two things really happened together. Even before I became a miner, I knew what the life was. With boys like myself, I sorted coal from the slag and rock in the open area around the mine entrance. Mining was degradation. It left a man crippled, broken down, barely able to drag himself to bed or to the inn.

Payday came twice a month, and then Grand Combe showed its worst side. Madness exploded in the streets, in the canteens, in the bordellos. Men drank up what was left of their pay, to feel alive for at least an hour, to forget exploitation, impotence, bitter memory, the cursed dust. Those same men, slaves of the coal, went into delirious frenzy. They drank and caroused, and late at night their wives and children would appear, begging them to come home. Angrily, the drunken miners would insult their wives, sometimes beating them and the children in the middle of the street.

Seeing such things, I swore I would not end up like that. I would fight to find a way out. A new breed of miners had come to Grand Combe, mostly from Italy. These were not dull professional laborers, but were workers, even intellectuals, fleeing from Fascism and hunting for freedom. Listening to them, I felt they spoke a new language, and it gave me hope. They said that things need not necessarily remain like this. Even though I was young, I felt that I did not have to escape to Morocco to find a good life. I was becoming a man. I would fight like a man, to win my proper place in the world.

Late at night, I listened to these men as they sat talking under the canteen lamp. They gave me pamphlets to read. One told about conditions in Italy. My world, limited to Grand Combe, suddenly widened. Fascism operated openly in many countries. It was at the root of the toil, privation, wretched living standards of Italian miners. Fascists were not only men in black shirts. They included men like Dr. Bernadon, who in 1932 was the candidate of the Grand Combe mine owners in the political elections. Later, even after World War II, Dr. Bernardon continued his infamous game. The Maquis "vindicated" him.

The French miners were best organized. Almost all were Communists or Socialists. I remember the election campaign of 1930, the crowded assemblies of voters in the large room on the square near the city hall, the meetings in homes, the discussions in the inns and canteens, the banners, the leaflets which we Communist and Socialist youths affixed to the walls and trees or distributed to the homes.

I was convinced that the election would change the world. I slept only brief hours each night and, in the morning before going to work, I delivered pamphlets, tied together packages of handbills, prepared glue and streamers. After dinner at night, when I felt dizzy from lack of sleep, I would duck my head in a basin of cold water to clear it. There were always meetings to attend, homes to visit, periods of duty at Party headquarters, flour and water to mix into paste, banners to display, posters to put up. Our nights were long, followed by days of toil, with black dust to mask our fatigue.

It was a thrilling period, that month during which I became a man. Election day saw the success of the Left, the defeat of the other parties. For us miners, it meant not only the victory of all the immigrants—Italians, Slavs, Poles, Hungarians, all who had helped and worked and finally had been able to vote. It was a triumph over Fascism.

My father could send no money from his job in Morocco, and six months after the election I applied for work in the mine shaft. My Party comrades and fellow union members were working in the shaft. I wanted to be with them. I felt proud on the July morning when I picked up my lamp at the mine storehouse. At the entrance of a tunnel a train of little cars was being made up. I got into one of the cars with three men.

At first it was like the Cave of Wonders at the festival of Santa Barbara, but without the gaiety. I was a man, I felt, among the best men I had ever known. The cars trundled for more than two miles into the tunnel. Here and there, the faint beam of an electric lamp fought with the darkness. We stopped at last, and I moved forward in a press of miners, to board an elevator cage. About forty of us stood wedged inside. The cage dropped down. I clung to the metal grill, my stomach turning sickly. We plunged into the earth for fully two minutes, at what seemed a headlong speed. Then we came to a jolting stop. The gate opened and we started the march into the long lower tunnel where we would work. We moved swiftly, for we were paid according to the amount of coal we broke loose and sent up.

It was like a great city, inhabited by moles. Between the roughcut rock walls of the principal tunnel ran tracks for the horse-drawn coal cars. Other tunnels branched left and right, growing narrow along the way. In some, one must walk at a crouch for two or three hundred yards. The air, pumped down to us from far overhead, was cold. Even so, we breathed as hard as though we were in the tropics.

We worked in twos and threes. One of each team used a pneumatic drill to break the coal from the face. His companions loaded the chunks on a mobile platform, which upended the coal into the waiting car. Sometimes there were barely two feet of space between floor and roof, forcing the man with the drill to lie on his back for hours on end. All strove to send out coal, more coal. We had no time to think of possible cave-ins. Halfway through the day, we stopped work for an hour. Wading across the soggy mine floor, we would find a dry spot to sit down, open our bags of food and eat by lamplight while the dusty air swirled like fog, and water dripped here and there. The heat, the eye-tingling fumes of the lamps, the hellish stink, were always with us. Mice scuttled between our legs, looking for fragments of our food.

I worked with Josef, the Pole. For eight hours I shoveled coal like a madman. Josef's drill seemed a part of him. He drove it into the solid coal, breaking loose layer upon layer of fragments, while I strove to keep up with him. I do not remember how many loads I sent away that first day.

At the end of the shift, I crept wearily to the elevator again. It soared upward with a load of us. Outside, the sun was shining. I felt overcome by the sight of it. I seemed to have been underground for an eternity.

A shower refreshed me somewhat. I looked at the bodies of other miners under the showers. They were marked with blue, in lines and patches. Someone told me that those were scars, made indelible like tattooing by the coal dust that worked its way into the wounds made by their work.

Back at the canteen, I was too tired to eat. I went to bed and slept heavily. I dreamed that someone was breaking my bones with a heavy stick. I woke later in the evening. It was time for a union meeting. Miserably I yearned to stay in bed, sleep again, forget Grand Combe, the mine, my work. But that meeting was important. Even then, I realized that the path through life led through a dismaying labyrinth. Even the first choice of an uncertain turning might be the most decisive. I got up and went out.


Even the hell of Grand Combe had to change as years passed. We miners worked long hours for low pay, under perilous conditions. Silicosis cut down more victims than cave-ins. Tuberculosis claimed more than fire-damp. But strikes, struggles, concerted demands managed to wrest something from the greedy grasp of the bosses. The great difficulty was to unite the workers.

Foreigners added to the problem. Poor men came from all countries to find work. They became miners, did the most unrewarding and dangerous of all things, because they had to. During the years of the worldwide depression, appeared some Italian Fascists, whose adored regime had given them nothing but their passports. Many were disenchanted with Mussolini and his promises, but others received food packages from the Italian consul, and paid for these with information about the anti-Fascists. Some such unfortunates, returning to Italy to visit their families, were arrested. Others kept in close contact with the Fascist regime through groups which, allied with the followers of Colonel De La Rocque, carried out acts of provocation against the French government.

This did not help with good relations. The French often showed their resentment against foreigners. Angrily, the French miners protested that the immigrants worked too hard and too fast, trying to earn more money but instead causing the mine heads to demand more production.

Payment at the mine was on a piece-work basis. The more coal one mined, the more he was paid. For a while a team might strain to send out more coal, and for a few weeks would profit. Then the management would increase the minimum requirement, and the bonus would vanish, leaving only the greater work load. New arrivals, inexperienced and needy, pressed for all they were worth. They damaged only themselves and their comrades. The wrath of the French miners, too, helped the bosses. Craftily they played it against the foreigners, until even the union members hated and mistrusted each other.

Thus provoked, the French blamed every friction, every difficulty on the foreigners. The Italians suffered particularly because of accusations brought against them by the Fascists. It came to a head in the summer of 1934, with a murder.

Etienne, a French bailiff of the local court, had been ordered to collect payments on some promissory notes, signed for the most part by Italians. On the morning of August 2, he rode his bicycle to the nearby desolate village of Mas Dieu, a huddle of wretched houses occupied by farmers and peasants. He did not come back.

Vanished—had he been murdered? Undoubtedly Italians had done it. Officers and volunteer searchers took up Etienne's trail. Several people at Mas Dieu said that Etienne had come riding up the single road through the village at 9:30 a.m. A shepherd reported seeing him at about 10 o'clock on a rocky footpath, but that was the last word of him. Days passed, with gossip growing more frantic. At last, an arrest was made.

The suspect was Albino Salvaris, an Italian who loved a woman who kept a tobacco shop in Mas Dieu. He had been heard begging for a loan of money. The police questioned him, and he appeared frightened and confused. A search of his home turned up a pair of pants and a shirt, stained with blood. Savaris insisted that he was innocent. Those stains, he said, were the blood of a woman, with whom he had been romantically, though somewhat roughly, occupied on August 2. He refused to tell her name.

Volunteer searchers helped the police explore woods, tunnels, cellars and wells. Their leader was Mario Frabiguette, a carpenter of Mas Dieu, who seemed particularly relentless and zealous. Under repeated questioning, Savaris told the name of the woman with whom he had spent August 2, and she vindicated him. He was released, but suspicion continued to oppress the Italians of the community.

But then, it was learned that Frabiguette was in debt. Etienne had been trying to collect two promissory notes from him, with a total value of 250 francs. Two neighbors testified that they had seen Etienne enter Frabiguette's home on August 2, and they had not seen him come out again. Investigation showed that Frabiguette had gone to Ales that same evening, had paid a garageman 6,000 francs, and had then passed the night among a company of prostitutes.

Under sedulous grilling, Frabiguette confessed. He had beaten Etienne to death with a club.

"During the night," he said, "the body was hidden in the middle of my workshop, among boards, sawdust and shavings. The next morning I dragged it to the basement. There is an old bread oven there, left by a former tenant. I levered the body up with a plank to the mouth of the oven. I could not push it in from outside, so I slipped a cord around its neck, wriggled myself inside the oven, and dragged the body through. I got out again and plugged up the seams of the door with wood and paper. I hid Etienne's bicycle in the loft, and left his leather purse in my parents' house."

Police had to drive back would-be lynchers as they led Frabiguette back to Mas Dieu. He stood impassively as Etienne's putrified body was dragged from the oven.

The case was solved. The motive had been greed, not political or national enmity. Frenchmen started to greet their Italian neighbors again. The Fascists sought new ways to cause ill-feeling.

"The French are pigs," the Fascists would say. "They turned their backs on us for days. They are as false as we are proud. Wait until Fascist Italy dominates this decadent France."

The militants of the French Right, too, incensed their people against foreigners. When, in October of 1934, Anton Pavelic's followers assassinated King Alexander of Yugoslavia and Barthou, the French foreign minister, at Marseilles, the Rightists tried to place the blame on foreign immigrants. The police searched the homes of several foreigners in Grand Combe, and held many for questioning. Bad feeling rose. We foreigners reacted furiously. Democratic forces joined us.

These were small, local happenings, important only to those who were caught up in them. Meanwhile, the Popular Front gained power, the Left gained elections in France, Mussolini sent his armies into Ethiopia, and, in Paris and London, political leaders still talked optimistically about accord with the dictators. We at Grand Combe heard of such things, but we saw simpler but infinitely clearer and more personal realities.

We saw stretchers, bearing the bodies of miners killed in accidents because their bosses would not relinquish a few days' profit to ensure safety; we saw the agitators of the Extreme Right, trying to stir up the French workers against the immigrants; we met agents of the Italian consul at Nimes and the Fascist Secret Police, trying to convince the Italian miners that their wretched condition was brought about by those who voted for the "unjust sanctions" and who disputed the "vital space" sought by Italy in Ethiopia. On both sides of every frontier, the Fascists strove to divide the working classes, stirring up hatreds and resentments among those who, though they spoke diverse languages, ate the same bread.

Storm was coming. On July 18, 1936, an announcement on Radio Ceuta said, "Serene sky in all of Spain." That was the cipher signal for rebellion against the reactionary owners of large tracts of land, the financiers and clergy, all of whom opposed the Republican government in Madrid. The revolt exploded simultaneously in Morocco and in the Canary and Balearic Islands. The rebels attacked old Castille, in Navarre, Seville and Saragossa. On July 19, the workers' militia of Madrid and the troops faithful to the Republican government left their offices and barracks to face the rebel forces mustered against them. On the same day, Moroccan troops arrived at Cadiz, led by General Franco, commissioner of Spanish Morocco. "Our fight constitutes not only a Spanish problem but an international one," he told a group of foreign correspondents. "I am convinced that Germany and Italy sympathize with our objectives."

His conviction was well founded. Almost at once, Italy and Germany openly intervened on his behalf. On July 30, twenty German Junker-type planes and twenty Caproni planes from Italy, assigned to transport Moroccan forces into Spain, arrived at Tetuan. Hitler, vowing he must protect the lives and welfare of

Spanish citizens, had already sent two naval formations into Spanish waters. On July 31, the London *Daily Herald* reported that twenty-eight airplanes loaded with munitions had left Hamburg for Spain.

The French Socialist government of Leon Blum proclaimed a rigorous neutrality, refusing even to release the arms and planes bought by the Spanish government prior to the outbreak of the revolt. While the dictatorships consolidated their attack, the democracies seemed to be blocking all resistance. Only Soviet Russia came to the help of the Spanish Republicans.

At Grand Combe, I witnessed the great popular rebellion against Blum's static neutrality. There were demonstrations, meetings, proclamations. The miners donated money, medicines, clothing and blankets for the Republicans. But such things were not enough.

We knew that we must take up arms and join the fight. If Fascism was playing its cards in Spain, we anti-Fascists must play ours, and at once.

"The fight in Spain is the fight between democracy and Fascism," said J. Diaz to the Cortez, and his words rang across the miles to Grand Combe. We hastily met and secretly organized a group of volunteers to fight against Franco.

I was eighteen years old, hardened by years of labor in the mines. I enrolled with the volunteers. My friend Carlo Pegolo and I would leave for Nimes on November 11, 1936, anniversary of the day when the world thought peace had come on Earth forever.

## CHAPTER 3

# *Death to All Fascists*

The train left Nimes for Perpignan, loaded with volunteers. They were of every age, party and condition, from everywhere. Some of us had joined impulsively, some premeditatively; but the train's departure signified for each the sudden end of a definite phase of his life. We stared from the windows at the houses, flying away faster and faster, between the Maison Carrée and the Roman amphitheater.

It was the hour when my mother's canteen would be filling up with miners. The canteen was no different from other sections of the barrack-like buildings. It had the same peeled, uneven walls, the same faded and unhinged shutters, the same look of desolation and abandonment outside.

As a boy I had imagined that all miners' villages had the same name, the same streets muddied by rain, dusty under the sun, briefly white and clean-looking from fallen snow; now seeming deserted, then overcrowded. I had never dreamed of villages, streets, stores and homes of any different character.

I had spent my childhood at the canteen. I had known the nighttime flurry, the daytime emptiness. My mother had worked there from early morning to late at night, always there, on her weary feet. A hundred bonds tied me to those four bare walls, to the smelly wooden partition behind which sawdust was stored, to the smoke-blackened ceiling, the cheap, stumpy glasses, the tables, the reddish glow of the lamp and the fluctuating shadows it cast in the big room.

And bonds tied me to the miners who came there. Their cigars and pipes were no less familiar to me than the intermittent creaking of the door when they entered. I knew each face, each voice, even though I did not always understand the language.

In that canteen I had grown to be a man, and had watched my mother become old. I had left it, and I had left her. Tears came to my eyes.

Pegolo poked his elbow into my ribs. "Are you sleeping?" he asked.

"Let him sleep as long as he can," said someone else. It was a Frenchman, sitting in a corner away from the others. His face was thin and hollow, his eyes looked hard and fierce behind his spectacles. On his finger was a wedding ring.

I rummaged a pack of Gauloises from my pocket and offered them around, as the miners did with newcomers to the canteen.

"*Merci bien!*"

"*Danke-shön!*"

"*Grazie tante!*"

We all began to talk. The train running in the night was filled with our discussion for hours. We wondered about the future, trying not to sound apprehensive. We talked about ourselves, saying who we were and where we had lived. "That's who I am," we said to each other. "Let's shake hands!"

Spain is thronged with castles. On every summit, on every hilltop loom the medieval manor houses, symbols of ancient power. Churches, convents, homes of the rich; once places for prayer, study and assembly, they had become forts, with towers, bastions and moats, to house the might of Christian nobles and Arabian emirs. Our first stop in Spain was Castello di Figueras.

At first the place seemed reserved and cold, with massive, monotonous architecture. But the people showed their true nature on the day we departed. They emerged from their shells as though they had been given a secret signal. Gathering on the streets, they swarmed to meet us.

We had formed on the street to march to the station, lean companies of volunteers without arms. Our only uniform was a red handkerchief at the shoulder. As we tramped along the tree-lined pavement, windows flew open and long-haired, black-eyed girls looked out. Men, women and children rushed in waves to either side of our column. They filled our arms with flowers and souvenirs. A thousand faces smiled, a thousand voices greeted us.

It was like that wherever we stopped. At Barcelona, Tarragon, Castellon, Valencia, at the foot of the Sierra Enguera, all the way to Albacente, crowds surrounded us, walking before, behind and beside us to the stations.

Albacente was where volunteers from fifty-two different countries would be mustered and trained. It was as cold as an Arctic winter there. We met Italians of the glorious "Gastone Sozzi,"[1] wounded in battle. There were French and German volunteers, and Poles and Russians, all there to learn to fight. Men of all sorts were drawn to Albacete, like ships to a harbor. There were workers, peasants, miners, politicians,[2] Communist militants, anarchists, Socialists, Republicans. We found men who had abandoned comfortable homes and thriving businesses to fight Fascism, along with simple farm hands and laborers from the Italian South, from Croatia, from the plains of Hungary. A professor from the Sorbonne and a miner from Grand Combe shared a mess-tin, a bit of

---

1. The "Gastone Sozzi" Company, named after the anti-Fascist martyr who was killed by the O.V.R.A. (Fascist Secret Police) in 1921 while imprisoned at Perugia, was formed by the first echelon of Italians who had come to Spain in August, 1936. The Commander of this company was Francesco Leone.

2. Translator's note: Including Luigi Longo, current head of the Italian Communist Party (PCI); Pietro Nenni, longtime head of the Italian Socialist Party (PSI); the Rosselli brothers, Carlo and Nello, Italian anti-Fascist leaders and expatriates in France, who were later assassinated by the French Cagoulards with the implicit approval of the Italian Fascist hierarchy (for eight years, Carlo published the anti-Fascist magazine, *Justice and Liberty* in France.) A crowd of over 200,000 marched in their funeral procession in Paris; Vittorio Vidali, a Communist Party activist from Trieste; Eduardo d'Onofrio, who was for a short time Italian Communist Party representative to the Comintern; Aldo Fedeli, Socialist, later appointed mayor of Verona by the liberating Allied forces in 1945; Giuliano Pajetta, Communist organizer of Italian emigrants in France, later incarcerated in Grasse; Osvaldo Negarville, later a member of the Executive Committee of Comitato Piemontese di Liberazione Nazionale (CPLN), a partisan group in Turin; Teresa Noce, wife of Luigi Longo (see above); Velio Spano, who had been an anti-Fascist youth leader in Egypt and Tunisia, and who returned to Italy with the Allies in 1943, where he then took an active part in the southern Committee for National Liberation (CLN).

straw to sleep on, a rifle for target practice. All these had left behind their sentimental ties, ambitions and passions, to fight, not for the Spanish people alone but for world freedom.

The new arrivals encountered veterans just returned from the front, in the taverns and barracks. Some were wounded and mutilated from proving themselves in battle. And women from all countries were there, to care for the wounded, make clothing, prepare bandages, to fight and die if necessary. One afternoon, I watched as the body of Hans Beinkes, the political commissar, was brought into town. He had fallen at Madrid on the first of December. The dead inspired the living.

From Albacete we went to Roda, eighteen miles away, to continue training. The commandant there was Picelli, and with him were Illio Barontini and Felice Platone. We fretted under instruction. Veterans of World War I argued that they were already experienced, while boys like me grew impatient of discipline and refused to heed the guard schedule or formation on the march. "We didn't come to Spain to waste time on useless drill!" we cried. Our officers and Malozzi, head of the Communist cell, stubbornly pointed out that we must face the well-trained, well-equipped battalions of Franco. As it was, the time for training was short. They needed us on the Madrid front.

We cheered on the afternoon when an Abyssinian veteran called the Moor and Marchini of the Gastone Sozzi brought us our transfer orders. Next day, December 14, 1936, we rode away on trucks that lurched on the rough roads of outlying districts. Peasants watched from their windows. Into Madrid we rolled, past the Prado, once the elaborate royal residence. The trucks stopped in line in front of a barracks where the militiamen of the Garibaldi Brigade were mustered. The Commandant was Pacciardi and the Commissar Roasso. I was back among Italians. It was like being at home again.

Next morning we rose at six, in cold darkness. We lined up outside. An officer read off our names and assigned us to companies. I found myself in the second company, in the machine gunners' section. My comrades were named Tomat, Faleschini and Cerbari. Two days later, December 17, we left for the front and the baptism of fire.

✿　✿　✿　✿　✿

I remembered these things seven years later in Turin, when the Fascists captured one of our leaders, Garemi,[3] and posted the news that he had died before a firing squad. People read the poster without looking at each other, lest they betray their horror. Spies were everywhere.

This was the terror. Turin had been the city of my childhood, of which I had dreamed for years. Now its citizens must feign submission, indifference. The nightmare of reprisals muffled mouths and dulled eyes. Even in their homes, people spoke only in whispers.

Bitterly I wished I was back in ragged uniform in Spain. I wanted the angry explosions of big guns about me. To rush into battle, to shoot at the enemy, to take a position or lose it, to avoid the cold thrust of a bayonet, to sleep in the cold night, wrapped in a threadbare cloak, to waken before dawn under a sky full of stars— a man could live or die as a man. It would be better than cringing in Turin, where the ugly fear of the firing squad hung in the air.

We met in secret. Columbi, who had organized the Communists in Piedmont, was a man of few words. Big, obstinate, laconic, he gestured sentiment away. He would organize two brigades of Gappisti, to shoot Fascists everywhere.

But two brigades—where would he find the men? Contacts were difficult and dangerous. Every meeting, every conversation with a comrade, might be the last one. At such times I felt the police right behind me. Was the comrade being followed? Would we be arrested together? If caught, I would be asked about the message system, liaison responsibility, the technical aspects of explosives, my comrades who furnished guns. We always asked questions of each other whenever we prepared a maneuver. To be a few seconds behind time could change everything, bring about failure. We spoke our doubts. Wouldn't the police intervene? Was this

---

3. Ateo Garemi, born March 6, 1931, was one of the most active fighters of the F.T.P. of the Marseilles region. He reentered Italy September 22, 1943. He was the first Commandant of the G.A.P. in Turin. With Dario Cagno, he participated on October 24 in the execution of the senior officers of the militia. Arrested, he and Cagno were condemned to death and shot. When the presiding judge of the court asked if he would ask for clemency, he responded, "I do not ask for clemency; I have completed my duty as a proletarian, as an Italian, and as a Communist. I am calm, and death does not scare me. It is you who fear, you who will die in humiliation, as do all traitors."

building the right meeting place? If one waited, his hand went to the butt of his revolver, his eyes were on the alert for danger.

Fear was upon us. It was useless to hide our fear from ourselves. It pushed at us, and our planning was that much more nervous and difficult.

After the meeting I returned to my lodgings at Number 3, via Brunetta. That neighborhood seemed strangely peaceful. Trees still grew along the street, though in most parts of the city they had been cut down. Home owners had moved away, but every week or so returned to tend their gardens and put their rooms in order. That was one chief reason I had chosen Number 3. Few eyes could follow my movements there, and if I lived quietly and did not go out alone at night, I might escape suspicion. I valued the narrow streets and bush-bordered secondary lanes. If I had to hide, there were clumps of evergreens and deserted gardens.

Looking out, I saw a woman with a large purse on her arm, walking slowly from door to door and ringing bells. Almost nobody answered, because most of the houses were empty. She seemed to be selling small articles—cakes of soap, balls of yarn. Her face was familiar, but I could not remember where I had seen her. She rang the bell at my door, and I opened it.

"Marco is not well," she said, handing me a piece of soap.

I gave her a coin, in case someone was watching. She had given me a code message. She turned and walked away, and I closed my door. Inside the wrapping of the soap was a note, telling me to be at a certain street corner at a certain hour that evening.

I went out and met another comrade, who asked for a light for his cigarette. He whispered to me my orders: I was to kill.

The man I would execute was Aldo Morey, marshal of the Fascist militia and a personal friend of Mussolini. He was responsible for arresting and deporting over seventy patroits and partisans. He had distinguished himself by the number of captures he had made and the cruelties visited upon his prisoners. He was one of the symbols of terror and danger to anti-Fascists.

Returning to my quarters, I found my comrade Antonio. He and I were the first recruits of the projected partisan brigade. We talked about my assignment, no more talk than was needed. He agreed to go with me as a lookout. Then he left, and I lay down.

I had slept in Spain, under the earth-shaking bombardment of Huesca. But now I could not close my eyes. The soft wind brought sounds of war. I heard cadenced, marching steps; the track of a heavy military vehicle biting into the asphalt; and, farther away, a single shot. As dawn drew near, I heard airplanes overhead—German, by the sound of their motors. And every quarter hour, the bell in a church tower rang. That measure of time was the only normal voice in the fear-dominated city.

At daylight I rose, mounted my bicycle and rode to Antonio's lodgings. He was sleeping peacefully, but got up and came with me.

As we cycled through the streets, I saw barricades blocking the way. Republican militia and German soldiers stood guard. We approached a store where Marshal Morey often came. Observing all obstructions, all possible ways of escape, we rode away again.

I did not have to be told of the danger of my assignment. Once I shot the Marshal, I must run. The people in the store would spread the alarm, perhaps enemy troops outside would hear the shot. My one hope would be to lose myself in the excited crowd that would gather.

"Have you seen the Marshal?" I asked Antonio.

"He has the face of a tyrant," said Antonio, and not a word more.

Back at my room, I tried to think of every possible aspect of what I must do. Next day I would seek Marshal Morey out. I felt fear, anger, tension, all mixed with a deep hatred toward the enemy who forced us to fight like criminals. This was utterly different from the direct combat I had known in Spain.

Lying on the bed, I stared at the ceiling. I would be alone in this perilous adventure. I knew the object of my attack, I could plan how to strike, but I could not rationalize how the enemy might strike back. At last, just before nightfall, I walked out.

I came to the banks of the Po and stopped to look at the water. This great river, I told myself, was one of the few things that remained normal, like the tolling of the bell in the tower. Gazing at the flowing current, I thought of the river as a great natural force, moving according to physical laws, attaining its level. It was a majestic, solemn, potent movement.

Again I considered my assignment, my struggle against the

sense of fear and loneliness. We partisans, I thought, were so many separate rivulets, prevented by enemy pressure from flowing together into one great, powerful river. Unity might come, but under the whip of terror, Turin seemed an eloquently gloomy contradiction to any hope. The terror—could anyone escape it? That was my duty, and the duty of those like myself, to strike back against the terror, rekindle hope in hopeless hearts.

I hurried back home, to avoid any questioning by patrols in the street. I read, ate, and put my few possessions in order. I took special care to destroy any document that might compromise any comrade, if I were killed or captured. Into the fire I threw some notes and memorized a few addresses and telephone numbers before burning them, too. After half an hour, I tested my memory, and found it held the things I wanted. At last I went to bed and fell fast asleep. When I woke, the sun was already high.

But as Antonio and I rode toward the center of the city, I felt apprehension and confusion again. A sense of desperate aloneness gripped me. I alone was charged with the responsibility of destroying an important cog in the machine of terror in Turin. And the city ignored Antonio and me, seemed absent and indifferent. I looked into the faces of men, women, babies, I glanced at Republican militiamen and helmeted Germans. We saw a bakery, with people rushing to get in, ration cards in hand, before the ovens stopped baking. Women looked anxious to return home before an air alarm drove them to shelter, away from their families. I noted the faces of children, plaintive and old-looking.

Antonio, moving ahead of me, stopped at a street crossing. There was the store we had located the day before. I stopped in front of it and leaned my bicycle against it. Cautiously I looked this way and that. No militia, no Germans. I walked into the store.

There he was, leaning on a counter, talking to three women. Another woman, perhaps the proprietress, stood beside him. I felt for the revolver under my coat. As soon as those women moved clear, I would have a fair shot at him. I stood near the entrance, with an uncomfortable sense that people were staring at me.

"May I pass?" asked a man, entering behind me. I moved aside to let him walk into the store. Again, a maddening indecision came upon me. The Marshal began to move away. I took a few steps and leaned against the doorpost. Stooping down, I pretended to pick up something. Don't do it, I told myself. Don't do it. Fear held me helpless.

I went back outside, feeling as though I had made a frantic, dangerous escape.

"The Marshal wasn't there," I lied to Antonio, despising the lie as I told it. "We'll come back tomorrow."

Riding home again, I thought of what had happened, what I had done and what I had not done. Fear had mastered me; but it had done so gradually, not in a sudden, paralyzing incident. I blamed it on that sense of being alone, of being hounded by the hosts of the enemy.

Barca came to my lodgings that evening. "Now, Ivaldi," he called me by my battle name, "where do we stand?"

He was one of those men who seem at ease even in the most difficult situations. He was an artist at getting through the inspection and search parties set up at block posts on the street. No crisis seemed to dim his resourcefulness. Again I told the lie.

"Marshal Morey was not there," I said. "Perhaps he will be there tomorrow."

When Barca left, I didn't feel like eating my supper. I lay in bed, drowned in shame. Barca and Antonio had trusted me as the battle-tried veteran I was. I knew what it meant to fight, to fear and fight fear, to fight the enemy and the fear together, and win. At last I slept, and dreamed of war in Spain, of Madrid; of hunger and bombardments, of the stirring strains of the International, sung by Madrid's citizens. They had greeted us as saviors when we came. Again I left with my comrades for the front at Boadila del Monte,[4] in a freezing gray dawn. We passed the shattered, burned houses, the strings of fugitive old women carrying babies and dragging their possessions in rickety little wagons. I could see the wounded, the blood and dirt on their bandages.

Then we were at the front, passing first aid men with stretchers, drivers with ambulances. A command rang out, and we threw ourselves flat as bombs rained down upon us. A lull, and we counter-attacked.

We charged. I knew what battle was, I was in the thick of it. A contorted, terrified face loomed before me. Two hands lifted

---

4.  Boadila del Monte: was the first front where I participated in battle.

in submission. He was an officer of Franco's colonials, his pride and arrogance gone, terror clutching him.

✿   ✿   ✿   ✿   ✿

Then I woke in the darkness. Still I seemed to see the face of the captured officer. No, it was the face of the Marshal, a face swollen with pride, fiercely scowling, then suddenly cringing in the moment of peril. I sat up in bed. The Fascists felt smug and secure in Turin, under protection of German Panzer battalions, the SS and the police who crammed prisoners into torture chambers. They thought we were helpless, paralyzed. They were mistaken.

I had run from the store because I feared being alone, because I had no comrades rushing with me to the assault. I had missed the fierce shouting from hundreds of throats. In this new war, silence reigned. No banners fluttered, no friends or enemies stared at deeds of valor. Yet, war was the same in all places. The adversary had the same face, too—an officer of Franco's army, a commander of Fascist militia, or just a common, stupid soldier. I must advance alone against the enemy, fight terror with terror.

At dawn I met Leone at the Piedmont Regional Command. The sun was bright, but the air was icy. I told my lie yet again, but without anguish this time. I rode my bicycle to Antonio's house, and he went with me again on my mission.

We headed into Corso Francia, among a rush of buses and street cars. Crowds of shabby, bundled-up pedestrians moved on the walks. Here and there stood details of enemy troops in green-gray or olive uniforms. The store—there it was again.

Antonio posted himself as before, to cover my retreat if need be. I dismounted from my bicycle and entered. There was the Marshal, with no one close to him this time.

"You won't kill or torture any more," I heard my voice saying, and he whirled toward me as I whipped out two pistols and shoved them almost against him.

He stared in blank, startled amazement as I fired. Then, abruptly, he doubled over and fell forward. Before he struck the ground I had run out and mounted my bicycle.

People were running into the store, yelling to each other. A bus stopped and passengers jumped from it. Away I rode, around a corner and along another street toward the outskirts of town.

As I rode, truckloads of Republican militia roared past me toward the store. They had heard the news, they were hurrying to the scene. None of them glanced at me, the sober, solitary man on the bicycle. Nobody knew that I had brought retaliation upon them.

## CHAPTER 4
# *How a Bomb Is Born*

I kept to myself for three days, in a mood of critical self-consciousness. I still lacked the experience to lead an assault in the city. Risks were manifold: we must organize to the utmost, keep secrecy and make the most of opportunities. My task was to be methodical, calm and decisive.

Then, one day, came a stealthy knock.

"Who is there?" I asked, and the voice of Dante Conti answered me from outside. I let him in, and with him was Ilio Barontini, a legendary fighter at Madrid and Guadalajara. Commanding the Garibaldi Battalion, he had scored a dramatic victory over the Fascists. He was one of the few of us who had fought as a partisan against the invaders of Ethiopia. Smiling, he embraced me heartily.

"He will stay with you for a few days," Conti said as he left.

Barontini besieged me with questions. How many months had I been in Turin? How were we organized? What was our plan of action? How had I coordinated my activity with the general struggle of the masses? Had I gathered a minimum of technical apparatus? Barontini brought into the open my apprehensions, weaknesses, doubts and uncertainties. For two days straight we discussed a thousand details. At last I shouted my exasperation.

"We don't have concrete plans, manpower or organization," I cried. "I can't accomplish this all by myself—I don't even know how to make bombs."

He smiled. "If the bombs are your problem, that will be quickly resolved," he assured me.

"And the fuse?"

"Now I shall teach you something more. Take notes, even if it is against the rules of secrecy, so that you'll know how to construct a fuse of very slow combustion which won't burst into flame and which burns silently. You cannot buy them anywhere. Take a plain piece of thread which is used in a wick, preferably of white linen, because it creates less odor and, furthermore, throws off less smoke. Dissolve eight grams of bichromate of potassium into one hundred grams of water; let the thread soak in it for ten minutes. Then take it out and let it dry in the dark. Take forty threads of this material; make sure they're dry, in whatever length necessary, and bind these forty threads with the treated thread, thus making a small cord which will burn at the rate of half a centimeter a minute.

"It certainly seems easy," I commented.

"It *is* easy," Barontini agreed, "if you have a friend who is a metalsmith."

I interrupted him, impatiently. Barontini took a pencil and a piece of paper and made a drawing as he talked. "Take any kind of pipe, large or small. It could be made of iron, cast-iron, bronze, even of aluminum; cut it into 10, 20 or 40 centimeter pieces. Attach a cover to one end, made of the same material as the pipe, and then bore a hole in the center of the cover, about 6 or 7 centimeters wide." While Barontini talked, he continued to draw, and a bomb was born right before my eyes.

"The end of the pipe without the cover," Barontini went on, "is threaded for a few centimeters in depth so that another cover can be screwed on. The explosive is placed in the pipe, and the fuse with the detonator is passed through the hole in the other cover so that the detonator is merged in the explosive. Finally, you screw on the second cover, and the bomb is ready."

"Will it be powerful?"

"As powerful as you wish, according to the diameter and length of the pipe, and the quality of the available explosive. You can prepare a bomb of ten kilograms, or twenty, which is capable of destroying a barracks. You only have to try it. Go to your friend the metalsmith, construct the bomb, and then experiment with one of the objectives you wish to blow up."

"Certainly, I'll do it," I answered. . . . "If they will agree!

However, I cannot do it all by myself. There are no men to help me, nor is there any organization to which I can turn. Liaison is not established; there are no technicians, nor are there any arms."

Barontini allowed me to let off steam, smiling and remaining silent while I talked. Then he turned on me: "Arms, arms! And your bombs? Aren't there perhaps some very powerful arms available among the people for waging war in the streets, in between the houses? You don't have technicians? Why don't you become one? Learn first to make explosive bombs, and then, the incendiary type! You need more than bombs? Go out into the street in the evening with a hammer, a club, a knife, or whatever instrument you choose that can kill. Take the arms away from a Republican, a German, another Republican, another German. We will have arms for you and for the other comrades who, today, are flowing into the ranks of the Gappisti."

I was overwhelmed and amazed by the quiet self-assurance of this intelligent man. He inspired a great respect, but I didn't want to make it appear obvious.

"The Party," I interjected, "Won't the Party help me?"

"You are mistaken," exclaimed Barontini, "You are really mistaken. You are the Party, we are the Party, and we are all helping one another, together with all the other parties lined up against the Fascists. All of the Italian people are involved. It is a battle in which everyone's help is needed. Isolated factions are not only useless, but are often dangerous. You must always bear this in mind."

I was speechless. Barontini gave me answers which I had certainly always known, but which I had never been able to explain to myself. Everything suddenly seemed simple.

Barontini, who had gone out in the afternoon, returned that evening with a package. "Here is your first bomb, I have prepared it myself. It wasn't difficult."

I knew when I would use it. The action which I contemplated was very clear in my mind, detail by detail, second by second.

Two days later I met with Andrea and Antonio. Under my arm I carried a bomb, carefully packaged, with the fuse protruding. Andrea and I pedalled along a street, then left our bicycles to walk toward a cafe that faced the railroad tracks. It was frequented by Germans and Fascists. Antonio came to join us.

"There are thirty Germans inside, most of them officers," he whispered, "and there are many Fascists."

Andrea and I walked close to the cafe. Under a window, Andrea lighted a cigarette, leaning toward me as though to protect the flame from the wind. He pressed the lighted end of the cigarette to the fuse of my bomb. I saw it flicker into flame. At once I set the package on the window sill. We walked away, fighting to keep from running. Mounting our bicycles, we rode off along the street. Behind us came the sudden lacerating, deafening explosion of my first bomb.

When I reach home, Barontini took one look at my face. He saw that the mission had succeeded. "Bravo, *muchacho!*" he cried, catching me in his arms.

On January 4, 1914, the German headquarters issued a proclamation to "all citizens who love order and justice." It was an invitation to collaborate with the Nazi forces, and it threatened grim retaliations against any who resisted. Barontini was unimpressed.

"The French partisans are inflicting damage on the German invaders," he said. "These threats of reprisal won't frighten us. This is war, and if they can retaliate, that's part of it. We'd be wrong to stay inactive, hoping for the Allies to come."

His voice grew stern, confident. "We must strike everywhere, in the mountains, the cities, in the heart of Turin where the Nazis and Fascists have flattered themselves they are safe. If we spread panic and terror and force the enemy to keep big forces for defense and search, we help the Allies on all fronts. And we'll instil in the populace a feeling of trust in us and distrust of the Germans. The Germans will discover that they are increasingly vulnerable on this front that has no limits, that menaces them from all directions."

He talked for hours, and as I listened I grew calm and assured. "Waiting," he said, "will serve no purpose. But fighting brings the hour of liberation closer by a day, a week or a month."

We had gathered some recruits for the Gappisti, but they wanted to engage in riskier, more effective actions. They left to join the resistance in the mountains. Again I was alone with Antonio, a brave boy of nineteen.

"When you are alone, you are still a party," Barontini had said. His words strengthened my trust and confidence. But as the new year progressed, the Germans occupied the capitals and nations of central Europe. Hundreds of thousands of captives were dying in extermination camps. Driven to action, Antonio and I killed a Fascist sergeant in the street and escaped. But we *must do more than isolated killings.* Above all, we must enlist more men. We found some willing to go on strike, distribute leaflets, join the forces in the mountains, even overpower and disarm isolated German or Fascist soldiers on side streets. But almost none were prepared to join the Gappisti in decisive, relentless, explosive action.

Early that January, Comrade Bessone (Barca) brought me orders from headquarters of the Garibaldi Brigade. "You must not participate personally in the operations, but you must organize, enlist and train the Gappisti." I groaned. Who was there to train and organize? Antonio and I comprised the Gappisti in Turin.

Meanwhile, the enemy furiously pursued the mountain brigades in Val di Susa, Val di Lanzo and other valleys of Piedmont. It was our duty to hack away at the enemy in Turin. Perhaps we could convince them that a large partisan group operated there. Then the enemy command would be forced to keep part of its troops there, out of battle.

We agreed to act as the brigade we were. Two German officers had brought themselves to our attention by their harsh zeal. One evening, I started to town. Antonio would wait at a previusly designated point.

Corso Vittorio Emanuele was crowded with laborers, clerks, office workers. Truckloads of Germans and Fascists in uniform rolled back and forth. Horns, the bells of street cars, the whistles of locomotives resounded. I walked slowly along in the frosty gloom, my hands inside my coat, touching two pistols. Suppose I was stopped, asked for my identity card, searched? If I went home and did nothing, I would only be obeying my orders. But the Brigade must attack. Yonder I saw the other half of the Brigade—Antonio, waiting near the cafe where I was going.

Four Fascist officers strolled by. I almost drew and fired at them, in my overpoweringly tense mood. I wanted to do something to show that I could act. But those were not my two Germans. I followed the four into the cafe, and watched them hail a group of prostitutes. Two more men entered, the German officers I sought. The Fascists sprang to respectful attention. Out I went, and waited outside. I tried to tell myself that the cold night made me shiver. An interminable, nerve-racking half hour passed.

Then they were coming out, my two Germans. I wished I were somewhere else, anywhere else. They strode toward me, talking. I fixed my eyes on the Iron Cross on the breast of the nearest. As they came almost upon me, I whipped out my pistols and fired. Down they went and, standing over them, I emptied both weapons into them.

For a moment the throng on the street stopped, thunderstruck. Then they began to run. Two more Germans rushed out of the cafe, Luger pistols in their hands. I aimed and pulled the trigger, but both my guns were empty.

Instantly I darted away, around the corner of via Gioberti. Throwing myself to the pavement, I fed a loaded magazine into one empty pistol. Behind me came the thunder of pursuing feet, and then I saw the Germans. I fired at the first, and again and again. Down he went. I sent two more shots at the other, who dropped his pistol with a yell. He stooped for it, and I fired yet again and saw him crumple.

I felt no fear now. Shots rang from around the corner on Corso Vittorio Emanuele. Again I ran, some fifty yards, reloading as before. Then I ducked under an arcade as a group of uniformed Fascists and Germans came running into sight. I fired into the thick of them. Several dropped, the others turned and ran. I, too, sped away, to join Antonio. Gratefully we lost ourselves in the crowd.

On the following day, Barca appeared at my door, grinning. He handed me a newspaper. The headlines screamed news of an assault by "bandits" against several German officers. At 8 p.m. blackout had been ordered. And a reward of half a million lire, about $10,000, was offered for any information leading to the capture of the "bandits." Fifty citizens had been imprisoned as hostages.

"Who did it?" demanded Barca.

"It was I," I told him, and he gazed at be dumbfounded. Then he went out again. The Liberation Committee of Piedmont would be meeting that afternoon to discuss the problem of Nazi retaliation. Would the Committee approve or disavow my initiative? It would be known, at least, that a Garibaldino, a Gappista, had killed the Nazi officers.

✿   ✿   ✿   ✿   ✿

I spent *that evening* in memories of the battle of Guadalajara. Toward the end of December, 1936, orders had come to leave for the Mirabueno front. The Garibaldi Battalion, which had no guns at the first encounter with the Franchists at Madrid, was now completely equipped. It was still dark when we left early the next day. The trucks ran through the suburbs of Madrid, along the Guadalajara road up to Siguenza, then to Brihuega. We camped for the night and left again the following morning. In the villages and hamlets, the people were busily gathered around dilapidated carts and trucks, rushing to evacuate the zone around the Front. Peasants were at work around the manure pits. We got off the trucks to proceed on foot, loaded with arms, ammunition, and bundles, walking past vehicles and marching of militia. A few hours later, we reached the battlefields of Mirabueno, where we joined the fighting forces. The Franchist colonel who commanded the zone was surprised by our advance, and fled quickly, leaving behind his wife and children. Mirabueno was already in our hands when the Republican planes arrived. The Polish volunteers attacked the new Franchist positions.

On January 3, two companies and the combat troops of the Garibaldi Battalion joined in the "Dombrowski" maneuver; on January 5, two other companies made a bridgehead on high ground in order to protect the flank of the Polish formation.

Despite the broken ground, the advance through the woods, ravines and low ground proceeded speedily. Picelli[1] marched at the head with pointed gun. Suddenly he shot at a Fascist patrol which had come into view without warning. Picelli always marched at the head of the troops. Pacciardi[2] and Roasio[3] had often

---

1. Picelli, Communist deputy, was organizer of the anti-Fascists' armed resistance by the people of Oltre Torrente at Parma.

2. Translator's note: Randolfo Pacciardi, longtime head of the post-war Italian Republican Party (PRI), leader of the Garibaldi Battalion in the Spanish Civil War.

3. Translator's note: Adrian Rossetti, born in Mongrando October 13, 1894, a bricklayer by profession, was one of the founders of the Communist Party in Biellese. Having emigrated from France, he was among the first to go

said to him, "You must command, but not risk your life at every step." He reached the high ground. All at once, his machine gun jerked upward in his hands, and he fell over, lifeless.

In the evening between January 6 and 7, we were relieved by the regular Loyalist troops, and we moved toward Guadalajara. We got there in time for an aerial bombardment. The Fascist bombs destroyed homes and killed old people, women and children. Beyond the city we set up a bridgehead at Colmenar Viejo, near the Escorial.

Frontal attacks by the Franco forces had not captured Madrid, but the city remained under a semi-siege. Only at the west the capital maintained communications. Guadalajara was the key point for entrance to Madrid, and Franco gathered thousands of men to conquer this decisive position, supporting them with tanks, artillery and planes. The focal point of his attack was France Road, from Siguenza to Guadalajara to Alcala de Henares. If Madrid was totally cut off, the city must surrender.

We knew that Franco planned to hit our defenses on the plateau between Siguenza and Guadalajara, where any attempted withdrawal might be obstructed and destroyed. Therefore, we determined to engage his forces at Brihuega, where we could bring up reinforcements more readily.

They attacked at 7 A.M., March 8, 1937. A murderous artillery barrage preceded the advance of the Fascist infantry. All day long the outnumbered Republican forces at Mirabueno and Las Vienas held their ground, then counterattacked at Alaminos. The enemy, who might have broken through our defenses in a few hours, remained nailed to his positions. Next day, when our infantry ran out of ammunition, the Fascists succeeded in capturing Alaminos. We counterattacked with the bayonet, but were pushed back toward Brihuega, where a road descended from the plateau toward Guadalajara. Franco's generals exulted in their certainty of victory.

My company was ordered back during the night of March 9. Unhappily we heard that the Fascists had repulsed our regular troops, driving them back to Brihuega and threatening to open the way to Guadalajara.

---

to Spain in 1936. He was political commissioner of the second company of the Garibaldi battalion. Injured, he was cited for his courageous role in the battle of Guadalajara.

We rode trucks in the cold darkness, bouncing as a gale of wind struck us. We rode for an hour, when it began to rain. The thunder and lightning was like a bombardment of artillery. The trucks stopped two miles from Brihuega in the morning, and we climbed out of them, wet to the skin, to assemble on a great estate belonging to someone called Don Luis. "Fifty thousand Italians are up ahead," we were told. "Fascist troops, sent by Mussolini to help Franco."

"Well, then we'll settle some old scores," said a comrade, and others nodded grimly. I listened. I was only eighteen, and had left Italy at the age of six. I had no experience of living under Mussolini's dictatorship. But others in the company had known, at first hand, persecution by blackshirted tyrants. They had been imprisoned, beaten, starved. At Grand Combe, Fascism had existed only in a deceptive, insidious form. Now we would encounter it openly, in battle.

"It's a clear matter," I heard someone say. "Either kill or be killed."

I marched with the others, a machine gun on my shoulder. Suddenly I was aware of activity all around me. A motorcycle appeared on the road ahead of us. Then an angry shower of bullets crackled around us. Ilio Barontini, commanding the Garibaldi Battalion in place of Pacciardi, ordered us into position.

We machine gunners set up our weapons and crouched, waiting. Barontini walked from group to group, coolly repeating his orders. "The Fascist army is just ahead," he said. "Its advance will be upon us."

That motorcyclist had vanished. He must have been an enemy scout. Through the morning came the enemy, moving cautiously in open order through the fields to the front. We opened fire, brought down several, and saw the others take cover behind little stone fences that bordered the fields. They returned the fire, but it was disorderly and inflicted few casualties.

I told myself not to waste ammunition. I fired short bursts whenever I saw targets. Big guns began to roar from behind the enemy, and shells exploded in the woods about two hundred yards away. Then they fell silent. The infantry attack must be imminent.

We hurried to set up our defenses in more orderly fashion. De Ambrogi, commanding our company, told me to set up the two heavy anti-tank machine guns at the edge of the road, almost in full view of the enemy. Hurriedly I scooped a shallow hole in the soft earth, down to rocks below. I would have to stay there, come what may.

Six hundred yards to the front, around a curve of the road, appeared a tank. It was like a gigantic monster. I felt trapped, helpless, as a second tank followed, then others—six in all. The Fascist infantry was up now, firing as it advanced.

"Open fire!" shouted Faleschini, second in command of the company.

My machine gun jumped as I fired. My bullets struck the first tank. Then, as I shifted my field of fire, a burst struck the infantry.

Instantly they were back behind the walls. The leading tank stopped, advanced a few feet and stopped again. Both our heavy machine guns poured bullets into it. We had disabled it, and the others were blocked behind. The Fascist infantry was now retreating, firing as it went. The other five tanks drew back, out of sight around the curve in the road.

Violent rain started, churning mud in the little holes where we squatted. The enemy artillery opened on us again, then fell silent as the infantry and tanks surged back. We flogged them with gunfire, drove them back as before. By evening we had repulsed four murderous assaults, had held our position under five bombardments.

While the last siege of shelling was in progress, in the dim evening, I heard the sound of motors. It grew louder, and in the shadows I made out the shapes of two motorcyclists, evidently scouting us. They stopped a hundred yards away, without seeing us. I heard them talking to us. Through the sights of my machine gun they looked small, grotesque, in the deepening shadows.

Then they saw us, and wheeled around to flee. I squeezed my trigger. Others also opened fire. One motorcyclist fell in the mud. The other held his hands high and came hurrying toward us.

Our resistance had surprised the Fascists. We were outnumbered and poorly armed, hastily positioned, without strong reinforcements in reach. That night we lay in the mud, pelted by rain, cold, tired and hungry. At about two in the morning, rations came to us. I had never eaten so savory a stew, or drunk so warm and delicious a wine. After eating, we felt strong and ready to fight again. We even slept a little, under the lashing rain. At dawn, we glared toward the road. Eerie shadows moved in the cloudy light, making us start nervously.

At full daylight, tanks again, ten of them this time, and thousands of infantry.

Through the slits in the first tank's armor, we saw light flash on the guns. We fought as before. Under our fire, we stopped the leading tank, blocking the way of the others. It blazed up like a torch. Men of our assault units rushed from their holes, carrying grenades. They ran across some hundreds of yards of open ground, crouched behind a stone wall, then charged again, belaboring the second tank with bombs. The other tanks drew away, and the infantry retreated with them. A second assault was also repelled.

Afterward, on the deserted road, we saw a little Balilla automobile coming toward us. Was it some sort of strategem? "Hold your fire until it gets close," came the order of Tomat, commanding us. "Then aim at the tires."

At fifty yards, the machine gunners sent rattling bursts into the tires. The car skidded, then stopped. A sergeant and two soldiers jumped out and signalled that they surrendered. Several hours of quiet followed. We ditched our trenches to drain out the water and prepared for more action as night fell.

A little before dawn next day, two trucks came into view on the road. I gave the alarm, and rifles pointed. "Hold your fire!" called Tomat and Rossetti. The trucks rolled closer.

"They were promised a ride to Madrid," laughed Faleschini beside me, "and they wish to enjoy the view."

Again we let the enemy approach to within fifty yards. Then I fired a burst at the tires. Others also fired. Both trucks skidded to a stop, barely ten yards away. Several men jumped out, staring in all directions. One of them returned to the wheel of the nearest truck, as though to try to drive on.

"Surrender!" shouted a dozen of us.

Most of them raised their hands. Several turned as though to run.

"Kill those sons of bitches!" shouted one of us.

"No, fire in the air!" ordered Malozzi, the political representative of our company. At the sound of new shots, all the Fascists surrendered.

Why had they blundered into us like this? It was a mistake,

one of the prisoners said. Brihuega, occupied by the Fascists, lay at the foot of the Tayna valley, and the road toward us lay through narrow, winding stretches. Ahead of our position, a secondary road led to the right and into the Fascist lines. These drivers had taken the wrong turn and had fallen into our hands.

The trucks held welcome loads of food and supplies. We happily ate canned meat and drank wine and smoked cigarettes. Between times, we read copies of "Popolo d'Italia" of March 8, 1937, which proudly praised Mussolini's contribution to the war against Republican Spain.

At noon, while we waited at the ready, two more trucks came slowly into view. They came to where the first two stood in the middle of the road. Men got out of them. One lighted a cigarette, while others fastened a chain to one of the empty trucks.

"Surrender!" Malozzi roared.

Some of the Fascists fell to the ground, others started to run but stopped as we fired. All held up their hands, begging for mercy. They had good reason to fear us. Only the day before, news had come that four of the Garibaldi Brigade had been captured and tortured to death.

Once more it was dark and rainy. We had been on the firing line for two days and two nights, with scarcely any food, sleep or quiet. Faleschini gruffly told me to get some rest, and I dragged myself under the canvas that draped my machine gun. Almost at once I was asleep. I woke to hear someone say that Comrade Gallo, commander of the International Brigade, had reached our front lines. Crawling from under the canvas, I found it covered with snow.

The dawn of March 13 broke with an icy wind that blew down from the north and swept across the plateau, raging among the trees. We squatted miserably in our trenches. The mud hardened, forming an uneven crust on the floor of our shelters. Shrapnel, fired without restraint, exploded above us, creating a shower of splinters. The enemy was using machine guns along with the artillery, even though we were some distance away. The whining of the howitzers was followed by the dull thud of the explosion against the hard ground in back of us. Several comrades assured me that a good number of projectiles had been sabotaged by the anti-Fascist workers in the factories of northern Italy.

Commissar Rossetti dashed over and threw himself down in my hole. "Watch out," he said. "They are attacking the zone of the fourth and fifth companies with small patrols. They wish to test our strength and then initiate the attack."

I ran out of the hole in a crouched position, and Rossetti jumped into another one. I continued firing in short sprays. The enemy showed no signs of activity. A half hour later, Rossetti returned with additional news: "We'll be in there soon. They are attacking the first company in order to break through our left and surround the battalion."

Communications were uncertain; the telephone line to the Command was continuously interrupted by the bombings, despite our efforts to repair it. The relay of messages was left to the couriers. Pietro Romazzini, a veteran of the battle of Irun mountain, and a courageous fighter of the "Gastone Sozzi," ran across the 500 yards which separated the first line from the Battalion Command every half hour, under continuous hammering from the enemy artillery.

The bombardment continued for the entire morning; then it slowed down in the afternoon, and finally ceased altogether. The machine gunners also fell silent. Then the enemy, thinking to have silenced us, attacked. Seven tanks suddenly appeared on the road. I watched them advance, and I looked at my watch. It was three o'clock. The entire second company was lined up in the trenches. When the tanks were a hundred yards away, our machine guns began firing. Then they stopped, and in the silence I heard the clear strains of the song "Red Flag." I looked around to the right, and I saw the men of the assault squad running ahead, singing as they went. The tanks opened fire with machine guns; the men threw themselves on the ground. They got up, ran ahead a few yards, and again fell prone.

With every forward movement, I heard the words of "Red Flag." The squad had now reached the first of the motor trucks; two of the enemy leaped down, their belts broken in the excitement, and started running around in a frenzy. Four ran away; one advanced, spraying bullets. Then he stopped firing and proceeded along the road. The men of the assault squad followed him and were about to jump him when someone shouted, "Let him pass. Surrender!"

The truck was rapidly moving along a few yards from me

and disappeared in the direction of our command post. Only later did we find that the driver had not given himself up; he had approached the Command post, firing; he had wounded two Garibaldini, and then escaped over a back road.

The enemy suspended the attack. None of us had been killed. This seemed incredible after half a day of continuous fire and tank assault. Rations finally arrived when darkness fell—some warm soup and a piece of bread. The night passed quietly. The next morning, we heard a tremendous fusillade of gun fire and automatic weapons. It sounded about a half a mile away. This meant that the fourth and fifth companies had started an assault upon the castle of Ibarra, which was occupied by a battalion called the "Wolves of Tuscany." The "Wolves" had attacked on our left the day before.

The castle of Ibarra, in the thick of a woods, was surrounded by rustic homes, storehouses, and barns, and was protected by a thick wall six feet high. The assault began at 11 A.M.; the two companies of Garibaldini, supported by the Franco-Belgian battalion of the Twelfth Brigade, attacked from the front and from the side. The fire of small arms and machine guns from five of our vehicles covered the men's advance. The Fascists abandoned their positions in the woods and withdrew the greater part of their forces to within the enclosure of the buildings. The Garibaldini, under the shelter of the surrounding walls, began a constant barrage of fire against the windows, doors, storehouses and barns.

The "Wolves" tried to break through the encirclement by bringing forward two small guns, but these were soon silenced. An attempted dash to the rear of the castle was thwarted by a group of Garibaldini. A little before three o'clock in the afternoon, the tower of the villa crashed down under the artillery fire. Wide breeches were opened in the wall, and the enemy responded to the firing with isolated shots from here and there.

Before beginning the final assault, Brignoli ordered the shooting suspended and shouted to the Fascists to surrender, assuring them that their lives would be spared. There was no response. A Spanish sapper approached the principal building with a load of TNT in his hands, lit the fuse, and ran back. Seconds later, a frightening explosion crumbled the walls, split the beams, and shattered the roof. The Belgian commander, Gelessen, led his troops from building to building. We saw the Fascists grouped together in a corner of the yard. Brignoli again ordered the Fascists to surrender.

A Fascist officer responded by yelling at him to put down his revolver. Just then, another Fascist officer threw a bomb, directly hitting Nunzio Guerrino, second in command of the company.

Our angry men were about to shoot for all they were worth, when Brignoli intervened, again warning the Fascists to surrender if they wanted to avoid a massacre. This time, the Fascists gave up their arms. The castle of Ibarra was ours; the enemy wedge at the rear of the Garibaldi battalion had been eliminated.

The enemy, continually replenished by the arrival of fresh divisions, moved in during the night. The offensive was broken when our positions held. We did not expect a new Fascist attack immediately, because they were waiting for replacements and new equipment. We received confirmation of this through interrogation of prisoners in the days following.

It was, therefore, a propitious moment for us to seize the offensive, to relieve the pressure on Guadalajara, to counteract the threat against Madrid, and to damage the enemy war machine.

Our impending offensive was discussed with greater frequency. Our battalion would initially have to keep the Fascist forces of the sector occupied. The break through the enemy lines, and the exploitation of this advantage, was to be undertaken by regular Spanish troops, supported by armed vehicles. The advance posts and communications lines of the Franco forces would be showered with a barrage of fire; shortly thereafter, our armed vehicles and infantry would be unleashed. The supporting troops of the International Brigade would mop up the pockets of resistance.

During the evening of March 17, we heard that the General Commissar of the International Brigade, Gallo (Luigi Longo), was in Madrid, meeting with the General Command to decide the final details for the attack. It was said that Gallo had already met with the commander of the fifth regiment, which was assigned to initiate the break-through. On March 18, we were warned to prepare ourselves. The morning passed calmly; half-armoured vehicles and Spanish troops continued to join us without incident. Once in a while a few planes soared overhead. At two o'clock, a salvo of grenades hissed over us, followed by a relentless din of thundering explosions. Sixty cannon continued their fire for forty minutes. When all was silent again, our planes passed over in successive waves. We saw them drop sticks of bombs on the enemy. At three o'clock, the armed vehicles came out of hiding from the woods; they overtook us, firing as they went, with the infantry directly at their rear. After a weak resistance, the Fascists withdrew.

The advance scouts told us that the enemy had broken their lines and had left the road. Our armed tanks could not follow them since they would have become stuck in the mud of the swamps.

The Spanish troops advanced rapidly, and we followed them. The advance forces penetrated the Fascist lines, threatening their flanks and rear.

We were assigned to take and occupy Brihuega, together with the Dombrowsky battalion, which was alongside us. As we moved forward, I heard somebody call my name. There was a miner from Grand Combe! We hardly had time to hug each other and exchange a few words when he had to rejoin his company. Before disappearing, he turned and waved goodbye. I never saw him again.

Cow dung, stone fences, and dead bodies were everywhere. The wounded were being carried to the first aid station. On the road, a group passed us; an old Garibaldino pointed out to me Luigi Longo, Giuliano Pajetta and Teresa Noce. I recognized Pacciardi among them.

The March 18 offensive ended that evening. We rounded up hundreds of frightened prisoners; many of them, with their hands raised, facing the leveled rifles, were crying like babies.

We descended from the heights; everything on the field of battle was in disorder. Wounded Fascists, some dying, lay collapsed in the ditches along the road; the fields were strewn with cadavers; guns, knapsacks and cases of ammunition lay scattered all round. While the medical orderlies stopped to gather the wounded, we continued our descent toward the town which now lay below us.

We encountered no resistance at Brihuega. The Fascists had fled; their commander, General Bergonzoli, had even abandoned his flag, which was still flying from the rooftop where he had been quartered.

## CHAPTER 5

# How Much Is a Gappista Worth?

In partisan warfare, objectives do not fall; they are destroyed. Enemy forces are not encircled; they are eliminated.

Early in 1944, the Germans did not think of Turin as a fighting zone, but we did. We were fighting troops in disguise, attacking the enemy's strongest points. We were glad not be be recognized as such. The enemy expected no blow at its most highly manned sector. Customary military tactics seek to concentrate a movement against the adversary's weakest point; in partisan warfare, it is the exact opposite, a blow where the enemy is most thickly concentrated.

The Germans had not yet learned this, despite their doleful experiences in Yugoslavia, the Soviet Union and France. They were well-drilled troops, fighting well under direction but without real success as individuals. And they knew nothing about us—who we were, how we moved, where we held our bases, what armament we had. Several of our people were captured, but they did not talk, even under torture.

We were few—a battalion of us could gather in a single room. We were always on the move, striking suddenly then fleeing from arrest. They felt us everywhere, all the time.

The Turin Railroad Station was busy with continuous movements of German troops and military vehicles. We planned an attack on a military train, to plant a bomb that would derail it. Spada, Riccardo and I would handle the details. It would be a simple feat if we could solve the practical problems.

The bomb must have a timing mechanism, to guarantee detonation at an opportune moment, at the same time giving us some margin of safety. Riccardo, who spoke excellent German, would plant the bomb aboard the train, and was not assigned to its manufacture. Lean, gaunt-faced Spada had some knowledge of explosives, but was perplexed until Ilio Barontini,[1] veteran leader of the *Francs Tireurs et Partisans*, gave him useful advice.

Get some sulphuric acid, a glass test-tube, and some thin, strong rubber, said Barontini. The acid would go into the tube, and over the tube's top the rubber would be spread, tight as the head of a drum. This device, turned upside down in contact with the explosive, would serve as a time fuse. When the acid ate through the rubber and came in contact with the explosive, the bomb would go off.

We obtained the sulphuric acid and the tubes, and conferred about what rubber to use. It must be thin and strong and of a certain delicacy. Again Barontini helped us. "Get contraceptives of good quality at the pharmacy," he advised expertly.

Such devices were rare in this stage of the war. Spada asked his wife Nucca to come with him to visit the pharmacist. Discreetly, Spada sought the counter and made his request in a timid voice. "And let them be pre-war," he murmured. "Products of poor quality offer no security."

"The price will be high, naturally," the pharmacist told him, "but it happens that I have a box full—a hundred—in stock. How many? A small packet?"

Spada knew that we were making six bombs, with more to be made in future. Experimentation would waste some material. He hesitated, and then Nucca spoke.

"Buy the full hundred," she told Spada.

The pharmacist's brows lifted, whether in disdain or admiration they did not know. But he gave Spada the whole box and Spada paid and brought it back.

Now we went to work. Carefully we poured acid from the bot-

---

1. Ilio Barontini, born in Cecina (Leghorn) in 1890, was commander of the Garibaldi Brigade in Spain, director and organizer of the "Francs Tireurs et Partisans" in France. He returned to Italy and became the leading spirit and organizer of the GAP. He died in an automobile accident in 1955.

tle into the bottom of a test tube. Holding it upright, we dragged a contraceptive over its top and pulled it so tight that when the rubber was touched it gave off a faint, shrill sound. Then Spada turned it upside down, holding it in his hand as rigidly as possible while I watched the clock to establish exactly how much time the acid would need to corrode the rubber and trickle through.

We made other experiments. What, we asked ourselves, if the rubber proved defective? What if the glass of the tube shattered by a jolt, pouring the acid out? Spada tried various ways of fashioning the detonator. Finally he stretched the elastic to its maximum, completely sheathing the tube with a tense area at the open top. We did our tests, scrupulously and minutely, until we convinced ourselves that these rubbers were of uniform resistance to the acid. The margin of security between placing the bomb in position and its explosion, as we ascertained after repeated trials, was ten minutes. If there were any error, the explosion would occur after this time and not before.

Satisfied with our efforts, we made three bombs. For each we used a big metal tube. In the bottom we set a test-tube, already provided with acid at the bottom and rubber stretched tightly upon it, with the bottom down. Around this we carefully packed high explosive, and over the top.

Meanwhile, Riccardo was dressing himself in a captured German uniform. He looked convincing, even dapper. We brought out a regulation German knapsack, and carefully lowered the three bombs into it, side by side. Around them we stowed a padding of rags. Once turned upside down, the acid would come in contact with the rubber and begin to eat its way through. With the utmost gingerly care, we set the knapsack on Riccardo's back and he drew the straps snug over his shoulders. Out he went, and I walked with him, like his civilian friend accompanying him to the station. It was morning.

Riccardo walked confidently, with a slight stoop under the weight of the knapsack. He was the sort who seemed to enjoy danger. I found myself troubled with hiding my anxiety. The most vividly imagined uncertainties about those homemade bombs came to mind. I had a tendency to lag behind, as though I would be safer there.

That assurance displayed by Riccardo showed his trust in the pyrotechnicians of our secret army. He had not assisted at the bomb-making. But I lacked his feeling of trust, and I know I turned pale when we turned a corner of the street and came face to face with two German soldiers, tramping along in the opposite direction.

Stepping aside to avoid bumping into them, Riccardo let the knapsack swing and brush the corner of the building. My heart seemed to stop. Away went Riccardo, and I quickened my pace to keep up with him.

"What the hell is the matter with you this morning?" he snapped at me, but I did not answer.

"You are silent, you seem preoccupied with something," he went on, his tone less angry and more easing. "You were scared to death of those two Germans."

That nettled me. I shrugged. "I was ready to shoot."

"So was I. Are you worried? Don't you remember the second of January at the cave on via Sacchi, with all the Germans there? What about January 23, when we made the SS command jump at the Genoa Hotel. You seemed on top of everything then."

"I don't feel well," I put him off.

Riccardo stopped smiling. We were in sight of the train that was our target. We saw German soldiers in the compartments, eating big sandwiches of ham and black bread. Just then, loud shouting rang behind us. My hand sought my revolver butt.

It was two women, shrieking as they ran to the train. Riccardo turned and shook hands, as with a friend who was bidding him goodbye.

"Remember," I muttered. "Turn the knapsack upside down, otherwise the bombs won't explode."

A German soldier hurried past us. He was going home, perhaps, thinking of his dear ones. Would he board that train only to die?

Riccardo followed him and sprang aboard. Standing at a distance, I saw him through the window of a compartment as he stepped aside to let a soldier pass. I moved away toward the waiting room, and watched from inside. Five minutes had passed when Riccardo came down from the car and sauntered toward an underpass and out of sight.

My assignment was to wait for the explosion. I waited in the station for an hour. The train rolled away. Nothing happened.

It seemed like failure, but later we heard that the bomb had exploded five hours later, after the train reached Milan. Soberly we discussed this surprising delay. The most plausible theory any of us could offer was that, after Riccardo had carefully set his knapsack upside down in the luggage-rack, a German soldier noticed it and helpfully reversed it. But the sulphuric acid had touched the rubber, and slowly ate its way through to come in contact with the explosive.

February was marked by several actions. On February 5, the Gappisti killed a Fascist sergeant who doubled as a spy for the Germans. In Borgo Crimea, several vehicles of the Todt organization were blown up as they rolled in column. On February 20, three Fascists were killed aboard a streetcar. Toward the end of the month, three Germans met their deaths during the blackout at Acqui. And Arturo Colombi, who had taken the battle name of Alfredo, visited me.

"On March 1 there will be a general strike here in Turin," he said. "The Gappisti must attack the enemy—set an example of daring to hearten the strikers."

People talked of the strike on streetcars and in bars. Pamphlets, clandestine newspapers and handbills were circulated, calling for participation. Some announcements were posted in plain view. Protest was loud in the air.

Three squads of us would go into action. Riccardo and Bravini would lead two of them, I would command the third, to disrupt streetcar traffic at Torino Rivoli. As we conferred, I felt less of the old lonely anxiety. The workers of Turin were shaking off their despair. As they worked side by side in the factories, they were an army.

Our objective was an assembly of streetcar switches in front of the car barn on the Via Biella. None of my team had ever used explosives, and I made the best of my own limited experience in directing them. I explained how to use the innocent-looking blocks of TNT, how to attach detonators, how to light a fuse. I conferred with Riccardo and Bravini, setting up a timetable for the concerted action of all our groups.

The hour when we would all strike was set for 4:30 A.M. on March 1. I woke long before sunrise in my lodgings on Via San Bernardino, where I kept two little rooms, with a closet, a couple of cots and a few chairs. Waking in the darkness like that always brought back memories of a more tranquil life, an early rising to go to dull, untroubled labor. I put on some shabby overalls, like a workman. My comrades met me outside. We mingled with the thousands of workers going to their jobs, the men with whom we would join in an uprising. Everyone, I thought, had his assigned post in combat. Not only we Gappisti, but the strikers, who would set down tools, sabotage machinery, demonstrate. Yesterday, the word went round, Di Nanni had killed a Fascist officer and had taken his weapons. Today we would repay the enemy, in the grimmest of currency, killing more of his creatures.

At 4:20 A.M. I reached the neighborhood of the car barns on Via Tirano, a bagful of bombs under my arm. The street was almost deserted. I saw one man, getting off his bicycle at a distance. He opened a little metal gate, walked through and closed it behind him.

I waited. It was ten minutes past the prearranged time, and Riccardo was nowhere in sight. Five streetcars had already crept into the building. Soon they would be leaving on their schedules. I could wait no longer if we were to succeed.

I lighted a cigarette. Reaching into my bag, I fetched out two cakes of TNT, each fitted with a detonator and length of fuse. The red coal of my cigarette was reflected on the glossy steel of the switch at my feet as I touched it to the fuse and watched the luminous speck begin to move slowly toward the detonator. Carefully I set the bomb at the switch, hurried to light another and set it on a second switch ten yards away, then straightened up. Even as I did so, I heard the heavy cadenced footsteps of a German patrol. Away I walked, as fast as I could without seeming hurried. As I reached a safe distance, a mighty thunderclap of sound shook the entire area. Glancing behind me, I saw flames start upward. Then I waited no more, but headed for safety.

At 8 o'clock, I encountered Bravin on the Corse Francia. He told me that all the switches on the track along Via Biella had been destroyed.

A little later, word came that the streetcar route through the main part of town had been blocked. A long strip of track had been bombed and destroyed.

We congratulated each other. It did not seem possible that everything had gone so well. But even as we gloated over our success, a streetcar came trundling past. We stared, and another street-car rolled in the opposite direction.

Our desperate bombing of the tracks and switches had come to naught. Working like demons, the repair crews had cleaned up the wreckage and got the lines in operation again.

Back to my lodgings on San Bernardino I stumbled, and threw myself on a cot. Discouragement flowed over me like cold water. Then at 9:30, someone entered softly. It was Spada, lean and grim-faced.

"Nucca told me that it went wrong," he said.

"We are too few," I groaned.

"No, that's not it. You forgot the feed-boxes that send power to the system. You'll never become an expert on trolley transportation unless you inform yourself of how a system runs."

"What's that?" I demanded, sitting up.

Quickly, authoritatively, he explained. If the feed-boxes were blown up, the streetcars would not run for days. They were at the Piazza Sabotino, supported on six close-set poles. I got up and rummaged for more TNT, more fuses, more detonators. Out we went together, Spada and I, without sparing a thought to how slim were our chances to succeed and come back whole.

By 10:15, the Piazza Sabotino was thronged with people. Nobody noticed as we lounged carelessly toward where the boxes were set on their poles. Both of us were smoking cigarettes as we went to work, Spada from the left, myself from the right. One after another, we set our cakes of TNT on the boxes and touched our cigarettes to the fuses. If anyone noticed us, he must have thought that we were technicians at work.

The fuses sputtered. "Run!" I bawled at the people around me. "Get away, get away!"

Spada, too, was shouting at the top of his voice. Those were times when a warning needed be given only once. The throng scattered like frightened birds. Spada and I ran, too, and as we ran the explosions shook the air. A streetcar jerked to a stop, and passengers rushed out of it. The system was paralyzed, would remain so for long hours.

Back home again, we heard from Riccardo. He was safe. During the night, a patrol of Nazi-Fascists had surrounded his house, a bomb-racked building on Via Luca della Robbia. They had opened fire as they burst in at the door.

Awake in an instant, Riccardo lost no time. The bombs he had taken to his room he now hurled out of his window. They exploded in the street, and in the confusion he dashed out. A shot had struck his foot, but he dragged himself away in the darkness and had knocked at a door. A woman opened it and let him in. They had not known each other, but bravely she hid him, at risk of her life.

That afternoon, I walked through the city. The strike was a success. Demonstrators stood grouped in front of the factories. Everywhere the appeal of the Piedmontese Liberation Committee was circulated. "The workers are resolutely entering the fight against the oppressors and the exploiters of our land. Through the general strike they pave the way toward the end of hunger and the achievement of liberty."

People talked boldly on the street. Newspapers carried the communique of Prefect Zerbino:[2] "This morning it has been verified that there is a partial absence from work in several establishments . . ." The Fascists threatened arrest, dismissal and deportation of the strikers, the closing of the factories.

The enemy placed the blame on us, and we were flattered. We had hoped the strike would fetch the faint-hearted in the Committee of National Liberation to face and accept risks. And we had wanted to win the trust of the masses, and gamely they had responded. I felt as if a crushing burden had fallen from my shoulders. The old feeling of isolation was gone. People thought with me, dared with me. This strike, the sharing of our profound desire for justice by the populace, finally justified our months of plotting, adventure, prowling.

The workers had openly condemned their oppressors, and it was our task to execute sentence. We could not march in uniformed ranks, terrorizing all Turin. Still we must move and strike with care. But behind our slim vanguard marched an army of roused comrades.

The workers defied retaliations and opposed tyranny in the

---

2. Translator's note: Paolo Zerbino was Minister of Interior in the Italian Social Republic (RSI) under Mussolini. He was later killed by the partisans at Dongo on April 28, 1945.

factories. Under the windows of Fascist officials appeared the scrawled words, THE GAPPISTI GREET YOU. The oppressors faltered, hesitating to visit their barbarous, indiscriminate terror on their victims.

At dawn of March 2, I met briefly with Giordano Pratolongo, a comrade who had fought Fascism in every corner of Europe. He told me that the Garibaldi command was happy with our success, but that the enemy prepared for reprisals. We must strike again, and hard, to show the workers that we supported and protected them. Colombi had sent word that we must meet and discuss new plans of action.

As usual, we met on the street, as though casually, but alert for any sign that either of us was followed. Swiftly, quietly, we entered into discussion.

The strike was flourishing. In reply to blustering threats, the Piedmont strike committee had published its Bulletin Number One: "If they do not give us more bread, more pasta, more salt, we shall not work." This declaration, backed by hosts of hard-faced, resolute workmen, gave the Fascists pause.

But we had not such strong support in the fields of streetcar and railroad transport. The damage we had wrought the day before was already being repaired. Operators and ticket takers aboard the trolley cars were under heavy guard. Uniformed police were stationed in the cars, and behind each operator was an armed Fascist, a machine gun at the ready in his hand. We had to stop the streetcar service, and not only for a single day.

Back to our planning we went, to organize a blow more complicated, more difficult and more dangerous than any we had yet attempted.

No more assaults on convenient stretches of track or feedboxes set in the open. We chose as our objective the important electric substation of the ATM[3] in Piazza Bertoia. It was underground, and in a way that was an advantage, for we could do our work away from curious crowds.

Three of us would be enough for the project. The resourceful Bravin readily joined me, and we chose another brave comrade, Mario. Columbi had sent me a helper, a woman named Lucia

---

3. Translator's note: Milan Transportation System.

who had been at Ventotene. She was invaluable, for she found a comrade among the streetcar workers and brought him to us. He agreed to mark our objective, and also furnished us with three uniform caps to make us look like regular workmen.

He told us that, in the floor of a certain underground station, was a manhole, closed with a metal cover. We must enter through that to reach our target. He would mark it with yellow chalk to guide us. We agreed on a time for action, and when it came we set out, wearing the caps and carrying innocent-seeming bags with explosives.

People stood or strolled in the station, and one or two watched, but without much interest, as Bravin inspected the metal cover of the manhole. It fitted snugly, and could be lifted only by way of a small aperture in its edge.

Bending over, Bravin pretended to tie his shoe. Stealthily he measured the small hole in the cover, then shoved into it a short rod of iron. It wedged snugly, and he pried out the cover, placing it in such a way as to hide the opening. Mario stood apart, watching somewhat nervously. I moved my bag of explosives close to the opening, while Bravin lowered himself into it with no more hesitation than he would show entering his own home. A few people watched us, only mildly curious.

"Pass me the bags and follow me down," said Bravin from below.

I did so, while Mario kept watch outside. In the dark beneath the floor we probed with our flashlight beams for the yellow mark our comrade had promised to make. We could find none. In vain we explored that long catacomb with the wires overhead.

"We'll have to do the best we can," I said. "We'll pick a spot among these cables that looks right. And take care you're not electrocuted."

A scurrying noise, and we started violently. It was only a sewer rat. We placed our bombs, lighted the fuses, and scrambled back to the opening and up. Bravin set the cover in place and we hurried up the steps. We heard the roar of the explosion as we went away through the Piazza. Dense columns of black smoke and blue flames rose behind us. Fifty percent of the trolley car system was paralyzed.

The workers were jubilant. The S. P. A. joined the strike.

Picket lines appeared at factory gates, defying guards and Republican militiamen. Exciting news travelled through the city, from mouth to happy mouth. The Turin-Barge train had been stopped by the Garibaldini, and the passengers had applauded as the Fascist guards were disarmed. In Cirie, a strong force of our friends captured Germans and Republican militia and seized power. Throughout Val di Lanzo, groups were proclaiming support of the strikers.

The enemy reacted furiously, arresting many leaders of the struggle. But we captured a written message from Consul General Spallone, and rejoiced over the uneasiness it expressed: "Situation grave in both city and the province: Turin virtually surrounded by well-armed rebel bands, organized for future general strike. I do not discount the possibility that rebel groups will create disturbances during the night and early tomorrow morning. I expect strong resistance and a violent general strike. I insist that adequate G. N. R. legionary reinforcements be sent."

That night I summoned every man I could count on. Tomorrow, I said, we would assault the Porta Nuova Station, turning back only if heavily resisted by enemy with guns.

At dawn we moved, loaded with explosives. From outside the city we followed a back road toward the station. Avoiding Fascists who might stop and search us, we arrived at the station platform and hid between cars on the track. From there we scouted.

A few hundred yards from the station itself, three locomotives stood side by side. Rapidly we stole toward them, planted TNT, lighted the fuse and turned to retreat.

Out of the station poured men in uniform, Germans and Fascists. The alarm had sounded, they were forming to cut us off. But just then, a deafening roar and a great flash of light, almost beside the station, as another locomotive blew up.

Another comrade, told to mine that locomotive, had nervously set off his bomb too quickly, without giving us time to get clear. But the charging enemy guards did not reach us. Our own three explosions boomed out, shaking the earth all through the railroad yard. Losing their heads, the Germans and Fascists whirled and scrambled back toward the station. We ran in another direction, to safety. We had made our day's contribution to the strike.

Signs went up at all Fiat factories and at many other factories: "The German and Italian authorities, having ascertained that the work in this factory has not been regularly resumed this morning, have decreed that this place shall be closed for an indefinite period, with consequences as outlined in the Communication of March First by the Chief of the Province."

Happily we heard other news throughout Piedmont. In Val di Susa, our partisans occupied the villages of Almese, Rubiana and La Torre. Railroad service between Turin and Modane was interrupted. At a factory at Venchi Unica, the Fascist union leader Giraud threatened women workers, who rose against him and forced the guards to open the gates for the workers to walk out on strike.

At home, I turned on the radio to hear the Voice of London. "The strike in northern Italy is a unique episode in the history of the war up to now," said the commentator.

And on March 4, came word that we would have a brief respite. The strike was in full force and would last until March 8, despite threats and reprisals.

❋   ❋   ❋   ❋   ❋

One thing was certain in my drowsy mind. The cold had wakened me, and it was completely dark. I groped for my clothes.

"Aren't you sleepy, comrade?" asked a voice. I was in a tent, a hand had opened the flap. Groggily I tried to understand. Had I dozed off in Turin and wakened in captivity? Then I remembered; I had come to this encampment of the Barge detachments, hidden in the country.

"How do you stand this climate?" I asked the sentinel outside.

"Come on outside," he said. "See how a Southern Italian sleeps with no more of a blanket than you have."

I pushed out into the open. From full thirty feet away came a rattling snore. In another tent lay a sleeper whom even a bomb couldn't wake. It was the military commander of the zone, "Barbato," Pompero Colajanni.[4] His gurgling somehow gave me a sense of peace.

---

4. Pompeo Colajanni, born in Caltanissetta in 1906, was a member of the P.C.I. since 1921. After September 8, he organized the partisan movement of Monferrato, under the name of "Barbato."

In the tent next to mine were Giolitti, a nephew of the old statesman,[5] and Comollo, warming themselves at a little brushwood fire. A pot hung over the flame, emitting the pleasant odor of coffee. Someone gave me a welcome cupful, and I heard two boys talking. Their home was a farm two miles away, and sometimes they would go to carry news to their parents. I wondered if such visits might not attract dangerous attention. But they seemed unworried. The war did not hang as heavily over them as it did over the tense dwellers in the city.

This countryside camp was like a dream to a fighter from the city. It was carefully protected, with regular sentries on post, and men slept in the tents as though in a regular army. Danger existed here, too, but not in the insidious form in which it lurked behind and around us on the street corners of Turin.

Somebody cracked a barracks joke, and I laughed more than it deserved. My anxiety lessened with each moment. I basked in the warm, confident atmosphere, in the feeling of belonging to an army. It seemed like paradise, I thought as I returned to my tent to sleep again.

Actually, that paradise had been a horrible inferno only a few months before, when the elite troops of Salò and German assault troops had carried out a mopping-up operation throughout the zone. But big guns, armored vehicles, machine guns and flame throwers had not wiped out the resistance. It had slipped away, and now it was back.

When Colajanni woke up, he assured me that arms and explosives for our operations in the city would be sent here, and that we would be assigned couriers. I decided to establish our chief supply and liaison base in the camp. Before I left, toasts were drunk, and we sang together.

Back at my city base on Piazza Campanella, near the Bessone, I gathered some news. The strike was over, and fear had settled on the streets again. People who had shouted defiance now whispered stealthily again. Pratolongo told me that the Nazi-Fascist reaction had been especially pronounced in the factories. Workers had been arrested, tortured and deported, and armed

---

5. Translator's note: Refers to Giovanni Giolitti (1842-1928), long-time Prime Minister of Italy (May 1892-Nov. 1893; Nov. 1903-March 1905; May 1906-Dec. 1909; March 1911-March 1914; June 1920-July 1921).

patrols stood guard in corridors and work rooms. Many were arrested on the flimsiest of pretexts, to be questioned and beaten. Such punishments were publicized in notices tacked up at factory entrances.

Our organizations warned the workers against isolated protests and resistance. We worked to reinforce our secret organization and to carry out sabotage against war production.

Some results of this endeavor began to show in the factories. Donations were made to increase the armed struggle, and signs of solidarity were seen everywhere. Where conditions made them possible, we staged mass protests against arrests and intimidation. Brave women were in the front lines of this battle. As soon as they learned that a comrade had been arrested, both men and women workers stopped work and remained immobile at their lathes and machines. Suspension of work often lasted for hours. Sometimes this silent protest succeeded in stopping the enemy's hand from striking.

But the situation was not rosy. In addition to the factories where there could be effective protest, there were also those where repression hit hard and where arrests had already created wide gaps in the organization. In these places, the terror was total.

The rule for partisans was firm, no matter what the circumstances: when one surrenders to fear, one is scratched by the enemy's claw. After having participated in mass action against the Germans, the workers would be victimized by terror if we abandoned them to retaliations. The progress made to date would be lost. It was obvious that the initiative was up to us. We were not numerous, but that meant that we could mobilize within an hour. Once again our moment came.

The German hostel on the Via Paleocapa was a good target. This was where the Germans got together for a little relaxation after performing their deeds of terror. Here the jailers of Via Asti mixed with SS members, who bragged to the Republican Fascists of their cruel success. Hardly were the black-out rules in effect, when the loud choruses of drunken soldiers and laughing female companions floated out into the night. But the sentinels were constantly on the alert. The hostel was surrounded by an uninterrupted line of marching soldiers.

Carefully we planned every detail. I visited the neighborhood of the hostel several times; I traced and retraced our future itinerary. The more I worked on the plan, the more it seemed to me that it was a one-way trip. The area was in the center of a nucleus of homes inhabited mainly by Fascist and German officers. Approach would not be easy, nor would retreat. One patrol was followed by another a few seconds later, forming a continuous circle capable of halting any attempts similar to those we had successfully carried out before.

In my room on the Via Pinetti, I drew a plan of the building, reconstructing with precision the immediate area of our next attack. As I studied my drawing, someone rapped at the door.

Instantly I turned off the light, snatched up my pistol, and peered through a crack in the door. A girl stood outside—Ines, the courier. I let her in, and she told me that more workers at the Fiat Mirafiori factory had been arrested and deported to Germany. She and another partisan would join us in our undertaking.

As she talked, I mechanically traced marks on the paper. Suddenly I realized that a line I drew ran to a corner of the building. That made me reflect that the old building had at least seven corners. Somewhere along the outside path of the patrols must come a brief break in their procession.

The hostel was surrounded by streets and houses, also multiangular and irregular. The vigil of the sentries was almost continuous, but not quite. One guard patrol could lose sight of the one ahead, if only for a few seconds. It was as though lines from outside broke up into segments an otherwise perfect circle. We might yet strike the hostel, and strike to the heart.

I conferred with Ines, another brave girl named Nuccia, and Mario. Too many of us might bring the operation to naught. Mario and I would go to a bombed-out house near the hostel, and Ines and Nuccia would join us with loads of bombs. Without telling these companions, I alerted two more Gappisti to arrive at the base just at the time for departure.[6]

At precisely 7:15 at night, Nuccia and Ines sauntered up to meet us. A chance observer might think it a tryst of lovers. They left the bundles of explosives and left again. Leaving Mario on

---

6. DiNenni and Bravin, who were in hiding in Berati's house, participated in this operation.

guard, I joined the two Gappisti in a makeshift underground shelter, and we watched Mario through a crack.

He was observing the movement of the patrols. I was restless. That circle of sentries moved smartly and continuously, in an almost unbroken line.

Mario struck a match—the signal for movement. I could not understand why he called us now, but we could not turn back. I hoped he had not committed a major blunder as I summoned my two companions and we all took up our loads of bombs.

The patrol moved along and out of sight around the corner. For a moment the line was broken. It was at least two hundred yards between our hiding and the hostel as we emerged. I examined my fuses—too long, I saw at once. We could not wait until the last moment before lighting them.

"We'll move separately toward the building," I whispered my orders. "Go to where that patrol disappeared, I'll go around and come from the other side to meet you."

Mario signalled that he was moving on. We others closed in on the hostel, lighting the fuses that sputtered as we carried the bombs. I heard excited chatter from inside the building, a snatch of song in a gutteral voice, the music of a small orchestra.

No sentries were in sight as I placed my bomb on a window sill, with the flaming fuse concealed on the inside. Slipping away, I saw sentinels again. Mario was running, and the other two had already disappeared.

As I ran to safety, a triple roar shook the silent darkness. A mighty rush of wind shattered panes, and a great pillar of flame shot upward from the hostel. Half-stunned, I kept moving. The sound of machine gun fire hastened me. I got home, and learned that the others, too, were safe.

On the following day, the Fascists announced the loss of "nine brave German comrades," and a reward of one million lire for capture of the conspirators. I began to calculate that I was worth several thousand dollars to the enemy.

## CHAPTER 6

# To the Assault in Turin

On the evening of March 31, news reached me that the Germans and Fascists had captured the entire Piedmont Regional Command of the C.Y.L. (Volunteers for Liberty): General Perotti, Eusabio Giambone, and all the others. The courier who had brought me the news did not know the particulars. "They were in Piazza San Giovanni Cathedral; nobody knows anything except that the Piazza was literally blocked on every side. The Fascists knew in advance and had set up the trap. And it worked."

Our actions as Gappisti had had their effect on the morale of the working classes and the partisan forces operating in the environs of the city. The entire underground movement was in full swing; plans which previously had been unimaginable, were being carried out; new moves, including perhaps a new strike, perhaps new demonstrations, were being considered. In every case, acts of sabotage in the factories and the recruitment of workers into partisan formations proceeded steadily and rapidly.

This roundup took us completely by surprise. In the last ten days, we had blown up a locomotive at Porta Susa and had shot down a high-ranking German officer[1] and an SS sergeant. And on the same morning that our Command had been captured, Bravin and I had eliminated one of the most ignoble figures of Fascist propaganda, Ather Cappelli, director of the *Gazzetta del Popolo*, the inciter of bloody reprisals.

---

1. A German command notice promised a 100,000 lire reward to whomever would assist in the capture of the "bandits."

This had been one of our most risky maneuvers. Cappelli was well guarded; in the morning when he left for the newspaper or for his seat in the Republican Federation, or at night when he returned home, he was always surrounded by an armed escort. It seemed impossible to surprise him. But after watching him carefully, we discovered the opening in the web of his precautions. Since he lived in downtown Via Largo Migliara, an area continually under the surveillance of Nazi-Fascist patrols, he felt secure in going to his home without escort at 1 P.M. every day for lunch.

He probably thought it impossible to be attacked in an area where a man could be seen three hundred yards away; the streets were wide and there were no arcades. Furthermore, Cappelli went home by car. For us, the use of bicycles was practically forbidden; we would be too easily noticed by the Nazi-Fascists.

We met with Bravin at dawn on Piazzale Susa. "Are you set to go for a walk?" I asked. It was a way to hide my tension. He, also, must have found himself at the limit of his nerves. For some time, neither of us stopped for a breathing spell. He did not yet know what it was that I wished to discuss with him. When I described the maneuver to him, he limited his curiosity to asking if the itinerary had been meticulously studied. I answered that I, myself, had supervised the preparations.

We arrived at our base. With the help of Ines, I had found a house with an unhinged front door, always open; the old iron gate had disappeared some time ago, along with the other iron fixtures which had been confiscated by the war-effort. It was close to Cappelli's house. Hidden inside, we waited for one o'clock to come. It seemed that the time would never pass. Fortunately, the area was not very busy. Most of the tenants had been forced to move away. But this did not lessen our anxiety.

We had spent the days and nights planning this move in a continuous state of alarm. We had been forced to watch every move, slipping closely along the walls at daybreak, and remaining inside the house when people were at work to avoid being seen by the patrols. If they had spotted us, they would have examined our documents too carefully. Finally, at the corner of Cappelli's house, we were embarking upon another of our nerve-racking waits.

"Let's go," I whispered to Bravin. It was a few minutes before one. I had observed that Cappelli was a person of utmost punctuality. We, also, were punctual as clocks.

We separated. I went to station myself at the far side of Via Largo Migliara. Bravin placed himself on the opposite side. About five hundred yards away, on my right, I saw Ines, exactly in her designated position.

At the strike of one, I took my place, trying to appear casual and natural. In that street, any man who did not wear a German or Fascist uniform could not tarry more than a minute without arousing suspicion. This locality was frequented by military vehicles, and the families of Fascist officials lived in many of the houses there.

Ines, pretending to read a leaflet, kept an eye on the direction from which the automobile was supposed to come. I saw her move to cross the street; it was the signal. I turned, perhaps a bit too precipitously, and walked in the direction of Bravin. According to my calculations, if everything proceeded normally, we would meet in front of the Fascist official's home at the right moment.

Bravin, also, came towards me with a carefree attitude, I could now distinguish clearly the taut face of this Gappista, one of my best men. He held a cigarette between his lips, and like me, had his hands in his pocket. I heard the sound of a car behind me. There was Cappelli! I cautioned myself to move calmly and casually. Running would give the alarm. Bravin also continued to walk in a carefree manner. We were now able to look each other in the eye; we were about fifty yards away from one another, and only thirty feet away from the entrance where Cappelli would stop. Bravin no longer looked at me. The roar of the motor subsided. Bravin looked around, pretending to be looking elsewhere. Now there were at most ten yards separating me from Bravin. We were just two men passing each other while walking along the sidewalk in a residential area.

At this moment, Cappelli's automobile passed me. We both continued with unbroken strides. My companion casually moved his hands into his pockets. He probably noticed the same movement on my part. Four yards separated us. I noted Cappelli gather certain papers, then open the door of the car, and alight.

Bravin and I fired at the same time. Seven shots hit him. The chauffeur, whom the command had suggested we save, was crying for help. "Keep quiet," I warned him, but he continued to shout. I silenced him with a shot in the leg. He lost his nerve there on the ground.

Now we had to get away. Ines was already safe. We had to hurry to a less deserted zone, where we could mix with the crowd.

Running in the open, with the risk of a Republican or German shooting us on sight, we held our guns leveled. All of a sudden, a Fascist officer and two soldiers appeared around the corner. They spotted us; I exchanged glances with Bravin. If there were only three, we would probably have the advantage over them. We continued along, our hearts in our mouths. If they were to plant themselves on the corner, we would be finished. But we could not turn back; the alarm would have been given by now, and we would end up in the arms of the enemy. Also, all entrances to the homes were closed. This quarter of the city had been built long ago, with robust bomb-proof entrances.

We were only about ten yards away from the Fascists. I gasped to Bravin, "As soon as I throw myself on the ground next to the wall, you do the same—but at a distance away from me; otherwise, they will be able to shoot at us together." Bravin answered with a nod. We ran a few yards closer. Now the shots from our revolvers would be effective. I was about to throw myself on the ground, when the unforeseen happened. The three Republicans ran away! They disappeared around the corner and down the street.

Finally we reached a crowded square. I boarded the first trolley that came; Bravin disappeared. We would find each other at a more opportune moment. Now we were safe for the time being. When I finally reached my room in Piazza Campanella, where I was a guest of the Bessone family, I flopped onto my bed. I had never had so close an escape.

At 7:30, I was brought an afternoon paper. It announced that a "reward is placed on the heads of the plotters of the assassination of our brave comrade, Cappelli." This was the eighth such reward for each of us. Later I was told the sad news of the capture of the C.V.L. Command.

The news arrived as though it had come from another world. They were putting Perotti and the Piedmont Military Command on trial. Somehow, some of us had to be present. But those of our men who had decided to go to the farce must conceal every feeling, the slightest reaction.

A representative of the C.N.L. (Committee for National Liberation) who had succeeded in courageously defending the accused in the courtroom described to me the way Perotti had attempted to assume total responsibility for the Command's actions. Another officer, Geuna, had in turn tried to save Perotti, by asking a death sentence for himself, a bachelor, in return for a life sentence for Perotti, who was married with three children. But the Fascist judges had already made up their minds.

Poor Mrs. Perotti was still begging for news of her husband after he had already been shot. Prefect Zerbino received her and asked her "not to make a scene" because there was a celebration being held in honor of the Minister of Internal Affairs, Buffarini-Guidi.[2] Then a non-commissioned Republican officer finally told her that "the so-called 'general'" had been condemned to death together with the others.

They had fallen, shouting "Viva free Italy." One of the condemned, Paolo Braccini, had been able to get a glimpse of his wife while he was being moved for the last time, and he had shouted to her affectionately "So long, darling." His wife, Marcella, had held back her tears and called back, "Courage, Paolo, I am thinking of the little baby." Giambone, old, dear Eusabio, whom I had known many years before, had refused the sacraments. He had, however, asked for the chance to thank the chaplin who had lent fraternal assistance to his comrade. When Father Carlo Masera had said "Ask the Lord to have mercy on you," he had answered, shaking the priest's hand, "I do not have to ask pardon of anyone, because I have always done my duty in my life."

Out of that trial had evolved the growing certainty that Italy was returning to unity. There remained only the task of eliminating the traitors and the foreigners outside the trialroom.

Our consternation, sadness and anger urged us to retaliate. We did not want to revoke the Risorgimento. We did not wish to fall into rhetoric. In his time, De Amicis had exalted the beauty of

---

2. Translator's note: Guido Buffarini-Guidi was appointed by Mussolini at the insistence of the German Government. He was subsequently dismissed, suspected by Mussolini of being an informer to the Germans. He was killed by partisans on April 28, 1945.

death for one's native land: "In front in a corn field a shot against the enemy." We had different thoughts. We loved life, but we also accepted death, without joy but with dignity and pride.

We had our inspiration. Our activity as Gappisti, always intense, now became frenetic. Men who were the living symbol of a reunited Italy had been killed. The enemy would be made aware of our anger.

After the execution of the Command, two Gappisti shot a Fascist major on via San Bernardino. Another patrol of Gappisti eliminated two SS officers who were indulging in a long walk after having tortured their prisoners. On April 21, a little over two weeks after the execution, two spies were found and killed. They had been condemned to death by the Committee of Liberation. We Gappisti executed the sentence. On April 26, in broad daylight in the center of Turin, we seriously wounded a Fascist sergeant and a German soldier.

We worked in groups of two or three. The enemy always maintained a battalion to face us. Every command was surrounded by barbed wire, every detachment had to mobilize sentinels. They searched everywhere, believing that there were hundreds of "bandits" still to be captured. Actually, there were only a handful. They sought us as though we were a multitude, whereas they should have been looking for us with a microscope. And so, their moves were indiscriminate and ineffective. They prohibited people from gathering in groups of more than four. This didn't inconvenience us in the least. They banned the use of bicycles. We joined the faceless crowd circulating on foot. They increased the price on our heads, thereby showing that they had learned their lesson from the recent trial. The enemy was composed of foreigners and servants; they could never understand that a new and different Italy was being born, one that had seemed impossible, even in our fondest dreams.

We worked at fever-pitch. Our acts of sabotage multiplied day and night. One of the rules of secret warfare was never to offer a fair target to the enemy. We never remained in one place. We changed bases of operations twice a day; this made it more difficult for the enemy to hunt us down.

A courier brought me news that deportations were being resumed at the Longotto factory; the Republicans were concentrating on this factory. The Germans, meanwhile, had completed massive reprisals in Val di Lanzo. In the evenings, we could make out the bright glare of fires outside Turin. Unable to stop the partisans, the Nazis burned various farms and shot many mountain people. The troops committing these deeds were then transferred to the city for "rest." We took revenge for this by shooting a junior officer on an open street.

Now action followed action. At Alessandria, in the old Benedictine convent, Germans and Fascists surprised one hundred young defectors. Among them were five partisans who hid their weapons, hoping to be saved with the others. They, too, were shot along with the hundred: five at a time. The last group to die stood by while the firing squad shot the other nineteen groups; they saw their comrades die and fall on the bodies of those already killed. The executions were taking place at the edge of a large pit.

This news reached our Command by means of a courier who, by pure chance, had escaped when the capture took place. Other horrifying particulars reached us. The Fascists and Germans had forced relatives to watch the shootings. "They are not worthy of burial," the Prefect of Alessandria had snickered to a priest.

Pratolongo related these facts, leaving to us the responsibility of finding and choosing our next objectives. Immediately, we set off several bombs outside the Republican military headquarters on the Via Po. With a burst from our Sten guns, we hit the Secretary of a Fascist group while he was walking with a spy, who was also seriously wounded. Then, on May 17, three powerful bombs exploded at Regent Park. The German Command was there, the same men who had directed the operations in Alessandria and who had ordered the massacre of the Benedictine convent. The bombs caused a veritable slaughter. Many German officers and soldiers were killed or wounded. We had not secured our revenge for everything, but these actions counted. The enemy knew that we were far from giving up.


Railroad traffic grew heavier. Germans and Fascists were constantly assembling search parties. Their operations were numerous, and the burden grew heavier for the partisans in the mountains. The Command ordered us to concentrate our efforts on sabotage of railway traffic.

Dawn had come. Bravin and I were lazy, cold, and tired; our fatigue could not be evaluated in terms of time. We felt a physical heaviness from which we could not free ourselves. We had passed the night behind a half-demolished wall. About thirty yards from us lay the switch cabin of Porta Susa Station. Since the previous evening, we had been studying the guards. Two German guards came and went with utter regularity on their course around the cabin. They met, passed each other and marched on in the opposite direction for about forty yards. When they reached a distance of eighty yards from each other, they turned sharply, as though they were going through a military exercise in their barracks, and resumed their march. Again they approached each other, met in front of the cabin, and separated again. It was hard to believe that they were not robots.

I felt a little worried; I would have preferred guards who were less zealous. "They are a little too rigid," whispered Bravin. It was true; they seemed overly preoccupied with their style of walking. We hoped this preoccupation would detract from their alertness. Later, however, we were somewhat comforted to see the two guards leave. There was a lull of several minutes before the arrival of their replacements. This was a weak spot in the impeccable mechanism of the Wehrmacht vigilance. At the end of their watch, the guards returned to the guard house, and were replaced. Their posts were left unguarded for almost ten minutes, long enough for our purposes. Bravin and I stood up.

"Now," I said, "Let's go and get a good sleep."

I returned to that place the following night. With me were Di Nanni and Valentino, and reliable Ines fetched the necessary explosives. At 11 o'clock I signalled for a cautious advance toward the cabin where the change of guard took place.

We had practised a special technique of walking in the dark. We were careful not to lift our feet too high, but almost skimmed the ground to make less noise if we struck any obstacles. As we drew near, we dropped to all fours and crept, wincing from the pain as our knees struck the hard ground. Fifteen yards away, we stopped and lay motionless.

Long minutes dragged past. Finally the two German sentries exchanged a few words and walked away in opposite directions. At once Di Nanni rose, walked swiftly to the cabin and entered. Five railroad workers were inside.

"Good evening," he said, and smiled disarmingly. One worker stood near a group of signal buttons. One might set off the alarm. But the whole five stood, frozen with dismay.

"Don't you know me?" Di Nanni asked one, who certainly had never seen him before. "I'm Luigi—we had a drink together the other night at the cafe."

Still they stood, motionless and speechless.

We others entered. Di Nanni swiftly disarmed the workers. Even had one been a Fascist, the chance to give an alarm was over. "Don't hurt us," one of them begged.

"Then help us," said Di Nanni authoritatively. "We are patriots. We must put the switch machinery out of commission."

A minute and a half were left. "Quickly!" barked Di Nanni.

The railroad workers led us out of the cabin. One of them, who had succeeded in recovering from the shock of the unexpected interruption, indicated the place not far away where the switch machinery was. Then another walked over and gave us a signal of camaraderie. They watched us assemble the fuses and ignite them.

"Run, run!" we shouted while we were finishing the job. They all dashed off in the same direction as we did. A few minutes later, the series of explosions began. A blue and white flash soared high in the sky, illuminating everything. But soon a curtain of smoke covered the station while the explosions continued. Our load exploded completely, punctually; our apparatus had worked well. We were able to escape easily; taken by surprise the garrison guarding the zone was disorganized and confused. The guards, far from the scene, began to fire blindly. The commander of the guard corps, hearing the shooting, thought that there had been a sudden attack, and answered with gun fire. But we were soon so far away, we couldn't even hear the shooting.

The operation had worked magnificently. Pratolongo and Conte did not overwhelm us with praise, but their satisfaction was obvious. Unfortunately, in this war, there were no leaves-of-absence granted for merit.

The next day, Ines brought me a new order. We were to sabotage the Germans' plan for transferring entire factories from Turin to Germany. Ines knew that in this operation, she would also have her own risky role, but she was not perturbed. Her calm was admirable. She was patient and industrious in our underground struggle. She transported her load of explosives with a tranquil air; her sturdy handbag was stuffed with cast-iron cylinders filled with TNT; she traveled the streets of Turin in broad daylight; crossed the block-post right on time. With her aid, we would attack the switch cabin at the Porta Nuova station.

This was a zone that we had already attacked effectively not long before. We would begin with an accurate inspection of the area that very afternoon. Di Nanni, the calmest and most courageous of all, would come with me.

As disguises, we wore two railroad employees' hats which had been lent us by the wife of a comrade. Along the way, I decided to complete the masquerade by buying a pair of badges of the Republican Fascist party which were on display in the window of a military uniform store. The salesgirl was a little bewildered. She did not often sell this type of merchandise. She probably thought me a most zealous Fascist. Di Nanni and I paused briefly in a passageway, and then walked out transformed into railroad workers with Republican badges.

The disguise worked. The Fascist guards quietly let us through the entrance to the shunting section of Porta Nuova station. Di Nanni had a tool box full of old iron under his arm. We entered with an air of experienced railroad maintenance men. We glanced at the cabin and walked toward a switch point. The mechanical operation of the switch was very easy to comprehend. It ran in a ditch specially made for it; if we were to block this, we would stop everything. We worked with two monkey-wrenches. Then, satisfied with our work, we left the area. On our way out, the soldiers asked us distractedly, "Is everything O.K., comrades?"

"Everything is fine," we answered. And Di Nanni raised the tool box in a salute, closing his fist over the handles. It was the salute of the International, and Di Nanni found his joke entertaining. So did I.

The following evening, Ines brought us the load of explosives in two suitcases. Di Nanni and I each took one. They weighed quite a bit.

"Ines is a robust girl," I laughed.

"You wouldn't believe it to look at her," answered Di Nanni, also loaded down by the weight of the bombs. "She seems so fragile." Meanwhile Ines was proceeding to her post. She was to wait near a telephone booth.

We left for the station. If anyone noticed us—and we hoped that no one did—he would think that we were two travelers about to take the train on a long trip. Our loads were heavy.

In the course of examining the area, we had discovered a small opening in the fence between the armed cement railings which encircled the station area and the cluster of tracks. After resting a bit, we managed to force open a space just wide enough to let one person through. Di Nanni slid through and I passed the explosive over the rail to him. "Good luck!"

"O.K., telephone exactly at 7 o'clock."

"O.K."

He disappeared.

I walked away to meet Ines. We entered a bar, keeping our eyes on the clock. The evening before, we had watched several railroad workers go to the cabin, stop a while inside, and then leave. It was possible that the cabin was now empty, since night traffic was lighter, but there was also a chance that, at the precise moment Di Nanni would be setting up the apparatus, some of the workers might be inside. We did not want any innocents to pay the price of sabotage. Therefore, one of us would have to telephone the station at 7 o'clock, the precise moment that Di Nanni would be lighting the fuse according to plan. Eight minutes remained to warn any railroad workers who might be there, and save them from death.

Gradually, with exasperating slowness, the hands of the clock approached seven. Ines and I felt ourselves gripped in a vise of anxiety. We must save the railroad workers, we agreed, but what if Di Nanni were late, for whatever reason, in lighting the fuse? Or if a guard were in the area, and Di Nanni was already at the objective? Our telephone call to the station master would give the alarm. If made prematurely, the enemy would thwart the operation and capture Di Nanni.

We had to reach a decision. It was only a few seconds before seven. I gave the signal to Ines, who had the telephone numbers of both the cabin and the stationmaster. I knew that Di Nanni was the type who could get himself out of any situation. If he were behind the established schedule, I thought to myself, he would leave the explosive somewhere and run off. At least, I hoped he would. The main worry was the possibility that there could be three or four railroad workers inside that cabin where Di Nanni would be placing the load of explosives, all fuses lit. The workers would be completely unaware that death lurked over their heads.

Ines started to dial the number. She was careful not to make a mistake; every second lost at this moment could cost human lives. "Busy," she whispered. I was very anxious.

"Telephone the stationmaster!" She had already begun to dial the number. She was now speaking with someone. She could not shout, because there were people in the bar all around us. But they did not understand what was going on. I signalled Ines to raise her voice. I turned around and took hold of one of the revolvers in my pocket. If anyone made a move, at least they wouldn't catch us by surprise. Now Ines was speaking slowly and clearly.

"Make the men get out of the cabin at Porta Susa. Make sure they get out quickly because, within a few minutes, everything will be flying in the air." Ines repeated her words two or three times. I hoped that anyone who heard her in the bar would think the whole thing was a joke.

Ines did not expect an answer. Sure enough, the person on the other end of the line briskly terminated the conversation.

"Did they understand?"

"I believe so," she answered faintly. "That was the stationmaster. At first he did not believe me, but then he became alarmed, I heard him start panting. . . ."

"Call the cabin again," I said. Ines dialed the number. This time it was not busy, but no one answered. I watched her face tighten and twist out of shape in the agony of waiting. I grabbed her hand, worried that she might faint.

"Aren't they responding?" I asked. "They don't answer." Her face began to relax. That unanswered ringing of the telephone was like music to her.

Enough time had now elapsed for us to be certain that the railroad workers had escaped. Now we began to leave. I was just about to walk out when Ines poked me with her elbow. "You have to pay the bill!"

"Right!" It would have been a terrible mistake if we had acted toward the waiter like Fascists in civilian clothes. He would come running after us, thinking us deadbeats. I paid and we left the bar.

We had hardly moved twenty steps, when a roar and a blinding flash of light startled us. The explosion was violent. Blue flashes lit the sky; electric cables were furiously burning. Another explosion followed only minutes later. I looked at my watch; Di Nanni must have waited before lighting the fuses. He had wanted to give the railroad workers one minute more than planned. Now he would be far away.

The shooting began. Bursts of machine gun shots were accompanied by hysterical shouts in German; they were mistakenly shooting at each other. It was the grand moment of confusion; the guards were crazy with fear and blindly shooting in all directions. The commandants were shooting at the guards, thinking that we were attacking in force. This was a good time for me to head for home.

❊   ❊   ❊   ❊   ❊

A Gappista could never think of going home; he had no home, only an address. In Spain, it had been different; there, when the battle grew furious and the cannons, the mortars and the machine guns shot at us from every point on the horizon, raining death all about us, when the incendiary bombs rained from the skies and there was no way to make ourselves invisible, when we could not find even a thought in which to take refuge; when one companion with whom I had barely spoken lay dead next to me, and a step away from him, another gasped with terror in his wide-open eyes, when the cold wing of death brushed our faces, and our moral resistance weakened. It was then that we dreamed absurd dreams of survival, in order to save ourselves from madness. The fighters who lived through those hours of interminable agony all showed one common desire: to get out of that nightmare at whatever cost and to return once again to a simple, uncomplicated every-day existence. We longed to live once again fully conscious of the steps, glances, words, sky and silences which were part of daily life.

I finally escaped from this inferno after the grand battle of Farlette, with several splinters still embedded in my spine. I was shifted from the first aid station, to the field hospital, to the grim and lamentable Red Cross train, to the hospital of Benicassin.[3]

I came out of the operation with a heavy head. The nurse, Carmen, was near me. I asked her how the operation had gone,

---

3. At Benicassin I found Marvin, Grassi, Falchieri, Suardi and Guia, and at Quintar of the Republic I found the Garibaldini Pegolo, Marvin, Boretti, Saccenti, Ferrer, Visentin and Captain Orlandino.

and Carmen nodded her head. I did not have to speak. I dozed off from time to time. After how many hours, how many days, I now seemed to be living a long, interminable day, ethereal and undifferentiated like the cots in the ward. An opaque sheet separated me from the world. I did not seem to be getting better, even though I succeeded in moving in bed, and attempted to walk with the aid of my companions.

Splinters! It was all the fault of those damned splinters that were lying passive and useless inside me and so many others! Had they taken them out? I asked Carmen the same question every morning. With great patience she helped me to adjust myself on the pillows, changed the bandages, and covered me with blankets, encouraging me all the while, with words and with her smile. She also came from France. She had left school to offer her life to Spain. We felt very close to one another. She spoke to me of herself and her loved ones and, at the end, revealed the truth about my operation. I still had the splinters inside me; it had been too dangerous to take them out. I was in a terrible state of fear, but Carmen was certain that I would heal. Little by little, I regained my ability to walk, and I went for long strolls with her in the hospital grounds.

Carmen died six months later in an aerial bombardment.

I returned to the Ebro, where the Garibaldi brigade was deeply involved. Several days later, the Command sent me to Albacete for the celebration festivities of the Garibaldi brigade. I knew the commandant, Vaia, who had fought at the Asturian front. At Albacete, I joined Quintinar of the Republic, and it was here that the Commandant gave me the sad news from home; my father had died.

I left the room of the Command that day, walking slowly, following the long corridor which led to the yard; I crossed the wide practice-area; I hid myself behind the little wall which ran along it. I sat on the ground, leaned against the wall, and for the first time in a long while, I broke into tears, thinking about myself, my youth, and of the man who had produced me, and who, in his own disorganized way, had taught me to distinguish between good and evil, between honesty and dishonesty.

My mother had remained in France with my brothers. They were still young boys, and needed my counsel and help. I knew that a short leave of absence would not afford me much time with them. At last, I was granted a two-week leave in January, 1938. On the tenth of that month, I boarded the train for Portbou on the Spanish side of the border; on the thirteenth, the local Command gave me a pass for Cerbera, on the French side.

I went from Portbou to Cerbera on foot, along a tunnel dug through the mountain. At the French border post, the French gendarmes threw me into jail. France, my second home, had spurned me. After a night spent under guard, I was conducted to the Commissioner of Police. He asked me when I had entered Spain, the number of my Brigade, the names of the Commandants and of the Commissioners; then, after having read the telegram which announced the death of my father, he assumed a paternal tone.

"If you will tell us all you know, we will let you go immediately, and within a few hours you will be able to hold your mother in your arms."

I remained silent. The Commissioner grew angry, shouted, cursed. I patiently repeated to him that I had gone voluntarily to Spain, that I had fought on several fronts and that I had been wounded. If he did not wish to let me go home, I told him, he could send me back. I was led back to my cell for the night, and at daybreak I found myself back at Portbou again. I recounted my adventure with the French to the Spanish Commandant. I insisted that I had to see my family.

It was decided that I would attempt to pass over a secret route with a guide who would be furnished me by the Commandant.

It was hardly sunset when we started off, and after a two-hour march, we stopped in front of a house. The guide knocked at the door. A woman opened the door, and my guide said a few words to her in an uncomprehensible dialect. Then, telling me goodbye, he went off. The woman's husband took over at that point, and escorted me to the border; he showed me the route into French territory.

It was dawn. I walked for several hours through the woods, until I came out from a thicket of evergreen shrubs, and saw a group of houses at the foot of a hill.

I had to decide whether to go directly over to the houses, or to go down the mountain through the woods and ravines. The second route was more secure; I would not run the risk of falling into a machine gun nest.

I was very tired; I had not slept for two nights; my shoes

were without soles; my hands were scratched, my pants torn, and my knees scraped from continuous falls. I had only a vague idea of where I was. I could not proceed without directions, without food, without a change of clothes.

Fortunately, I found a shepherd who understood where I was coming from and where I was going. He gave me something to eat and a pair of trousers. He was offended when I tried to pay him. Once in France, I had trouble only with the Commissioner of Cerbera! I reached the station of the nearest town and boarded the train for Perpignan, where the Red Cross, alerted in advance of my arrival, accompanied me to Nimes. At midnight, I knocked at the door of my house and flung myself into my mother's arms.

Nothing had changed at Grand Combe, but I had changed, I could not seem to regain the old bonds with my fellow workers. There was a division between us. I certainly could not blame them for not having volunteered for the war in Spain. They were, for the most part, immigrants on French soil. How could they have been expected to abandon their families in such destitute condition? They were all anti-Fascists; they all hated tyranny; and they had a profound faith in our ideals. Still, I felt that there was a rupture between them and myself. Perhaps I had been overwhelmed by my experiences, or perhaps I placed too much importance upon them.

When I left Grand Combe once again, this time for Paris, they were perplexed, and seemed to doubt my sincerity. They wondered how I could leave my mother and my brothers.

In Paris, I presented myself at the headquarters of the committee in charge of volunteers for Spain, in order to arrange for a visit to a doctor. I was given an appointment for two days later.

It was the first time I had ever been in such a large city, in a crowd so large and alien. The people were rushing along, meeting and greeting one another; not one person seemed to notice me. Everyone was minding his own business. I felt myself more and more alienated and disconcerted. My sense of isolation increased with each passerby that brushed past me. Even in the moments of greatest danger, I had never felt so lost. I had always had my companions or my gun close to me. I had felt the presence of time, the interminable length of the hours, the tufts of grass, the thunderous roar of the bombardment, my thirst, hunger, fatigue. I had been alive. I had known myself, fighting, suffering and hoping.

Here, I groped for answers to many questions. Why, I asked myself, were the people here alive and those who were there dead? People were dying defending the freedom and civilization of the French people, and France seemed not even to be aware of them. Or was I mistaken? Perhaps I was tired and depressed, and really deluded in my evaluations.

I had to get away from these grand boulevards, abandon these luminous and opulent streets and search for my companions, the workers, those who were suffering and hoping like me, and who were saving to send their sweaty francs to Madrid. I had to find the parents of Carmen and the brothers and wives of the men of the French Brigade who had fallen on the hill in front of Saragozza. I had to free myself from the fantasies of my sadness.

At the headquarters of the Committee I found a group of fifteen volunteers. We left together and climbed the Pyrenees on a rainy and sleety night of February, 1938.

## CHAPTER 7

# Death and Transfiguration

On Radio London, between piercing static and scratching sounds, Colonel Stevens' words came through unsteadily. They were often incomprehensible; now very faint, now a little stronger; they were always confusing in their waves of changing volume.

But, all of a sudden, that night in May, Colonel Stevens seemed close by; suddenly his voice issued forth clearly and uninterrupted to the people gathered in silence around the radio in the dark room. Instinctively, someone lowered the volume. And now, the sentences were perfectly comprehensible.

At that moment in Turin, four shadows were advancing along the right bank of the Stura. One hundred Germans were shooting at four men from the heights of a bridge on the road to Milan. Big reflector lights, maneuvered excitedly by members of the engineers corps, caught the figures and then lost them again. The shadows flitted toward the bridge, from which the only road to safety lay behind the engineers. A few yards from the barricade, the four opened fire. The sudden outburst disconcerted the Germans. A little gap opened and the four dashed through. But suddenly the blinding glare of the reflectors began to focus upon them from behind, and the shooting resumed with renewed vigor.

From the block post, an alarm was given to the German Command at Turin, which quickly sent reinforcements.

The uneven struggle seemed never to finish. Then, one of the four fell. He continued to shoot from the ground. The second one was hit, then the third, and finally the fourth.

We, listening to Radio London, with the voice suddenly coming through so clearly, knew nothing of all this. Many of us would not learn about it until years later.

That night shortly before the skirmish on the Stura, a rapid succession of tremendous explosions, three hundred yards from the bridge, had torn the radio station into pieces, hitting the grand antennae. These antennae had been the source of the piercing static and raucous croaking which for many months had kept the people from fully understanding Colonel Stevens' daily message of solidarity.

Everything had begun two weeks earlier, when I had kept my weekly appointment with the commanding officer of the Piedmont Garibaldi Brigade. As always, the meeting on the corner of a square seemed casual. We greeted each other, then walked together under the sun which already announced the presence of summer.

"The order is to knock over the radio station."

The military commandant could have just as casually have said, "Let's go for a walk."

"What radio station?"

"The one that interferes with Radio London. It's near the road to Milan, a few yards away from the river." We had walked along a bit further together so as to not create any suspicion; then we separated. I had had to cross the entire city on foot in order to get back home.

In reality, of course, it was not home. I slept there, but it did not belong to me. Other people came there from time to time; couriers with messages, comrades who were joining the Brigade. The locale served also as a storage place for arms and explosives.

I had no home, I had not had one since leaving for Perpignan eight years before. Nor had I had a home in Spain. I had slept in trenches, under the rain, and, more rarely, in the luxurious rooms of large hotels requisitioned by the Republican Army. Never had I possessed a bed which was my own. On the Madrid front, I had slept for many months under a tree without feeling discomfort.

The years spent in the coal mine shafts at Grand Combe had hardened me, had made me more alert.

"One becomes a man in half the time in the shafts," my father had said. "Send a little kid to the mines, and at thirteen he'll know everything there is to know.

"The mine is like war and famine," he had added. "He who experiences it learns quickly."

On the day that I had left Grand Combe, I had been sure that I had no more to learn. But in Spain, at Madrid and Guadalajara, I had to admit that I still had much to learn. When the Spanish Republic had fallen, and I was dragging myself toward the French frontier, I had been certain that I had experienced everything that a man could experience. At Turin, in 1944, I was learning anew. And now I had to learn quickly how to sabotage a radio station.

It would be a difficult undertaking, the most difficult that I had ever assumed.

I lay stretched out on the bed and began to look at the mildew-spots on the ceiling. As I stared up at them, they began to change. The large one in the corner became Casa Del Campo, as I had seen it the first time, beyond the big curve on the dusty road, with its buildings which looked dilapidated and empty from a distance. I soon learned that they had strong walls, like fortresses. And they were not empty. Inside were the snipers.

Another mildew mark, a long, contorted one, which cut the ceiling in two, looked like a street; the street of Jarama, teeming with Moroccans. I saw myself, almost alone, shooting with a machine gun; horses fell in clouds of dust. Moors with their red capes were shouting as they tumbled off their horses; the crazed horses were falling over the Moors, filling the streets. The survivors galloped off, and I continued shooting without even paying attention to the boiling of the water in the gun's jacket.

That ceiling made no sense: Jarama, Huesca and Madrid were certainly not Turin. Here everything was different; there were neither fronts, nor rear lines from which reinforcements could be sent. In Spain, one could move about and wait for a more appropriate moment if the attack failed. Here, even if the action were successful, there was no respite; it was necessary to plan in advance both the attack and withdrawal, to insure that one would be alive the next day. Then one began all over again, and continued in this fashion, wondering when, if ever, the days of peaceful work, of study, of leisurely walking would return.

These were the days of war; a war composed of audacious, unexpected attacks, of flights in the middle of squares, in front of barracks, in the waiting rooms of stations, in warehouses, along highways, and railroad lines. This time, we would concentrate upon destroying a radio station so that it would no longer jam the voice coming from another radio station beyond the English Channel.

The following day, I had still not decided anything; I had stopped looking at the marks on the ceiling and was no longer stretched out on my bed, but still I had not come to any decision.

I could still not think of a way to cover the withdrawal after the operation, both for myself and the others. I was trying to estimate the amount of time necessary for planting the explosive around the little structure containing the apparatus and the three gigantic antennae. The spot was isolated; its location helped not one bit.

We would have to cross the irregular flat terrain dragging packages of plastic, arms, and munitions. Then there was the guard who had to be taken care of before he could cry for help or fire a shot and waken the others from their sleep. For there would surely be others behind the little building. I knew that; but I did not know how many.

One cannot blow up a radio station while remaining seated in front of an open window, daydreaming.

I had not left the house for two days. I felt empty inside, and defenseless; the four walls of the room gave me some sense of protection.

Few noises carried from the narrow street to the second floor window; the people did not tarry for any length of time on the street; the danger of sudden police roundups hung over everyone.

In the silence, I fantasized that the war was a memory of long ago. I thought of a peaceful world in which people could speak, travel, and live without the anxiety of a sudden knock on the door, of a fatal encounter on the street. Without war, a man could work, study, marry, build something worthwhile. It was the same feeling I had had as a boy, when I would wake up in the mornings at Visone to get ready for school. I could smell the summer scents outside, and could see from my window the two grapevines extending up the hill.

But at that time, I would have liked to have been in another place, a place without schools and without teachers. When I used to enter the classroom, I was already thinking of the time ahead, after the questions in class, after school. I saw myself running toward home, the sturdy satchel bouncing on my shoulders, the notebooks inside knocking together in rhythm.

I would be shaken out of these daydreams when the teacher called my name, and I had to respond. It was the same thing now. Dreaming of the future would not do me any good; the reality of here and now had to be faced. And now I remembered that the radio station was still standing.

In every city and every country there was that fear of the here and now; it was for this reason that the people still spoke of freedom in hushed tones and within the confines of their homes. He who was not overcome with this fear was a "hero." But in reality, "heroism" had meaning in literature alone. It was a word used by people who probably never had any experience with it. In reality, people had only fear; fear of suffering, fear of death. Everyone wanted to survive this difficult period, to be alive afterward, when everything would be settled and there would be constructive things to do for the country, for the Party, for themselves.

I remembered feeling fear in the mines at the moment of the cave-in. While the beams were splitting, first with a quiet creaking, then with a loud crash, I had not been able to run away; I had watched the lumps of coal falling, the thick black cloud of dust nearly suffocating the little lamp. But I did not move; I could not move because I could not think. When the first aid squad had found me, and taken me out of the mine, someone had said that I had been saved because I had not moved; had I gone five steps away, I would have been crushed to death by ten tons of rock. The fact that I had been saved then was no reason to expect that I would always be so lucky.

In the Piazza della Republica, I had been saved because I had moved while I was wondering what to do. I still could see the two SS officers,[1] as I had fallen right in front of the little tables with their yellow tablecloths in the bar. I had still been holding the emp-

---

1. Following this operation the German command had ordered an 8 P.M. curfew and had promised a reward of 500,000 lire for capture of the Gappisti, and had ordered at the same time the arrest of fifty citizens.

tied pistols in my grip. I had run toward the street; I had heard the shots of the automatic pistol coming from a parked truck; instinct had urged me to flee, but reason had warned that they would capture me on the straight and open roadway. I had halted midway and had thrown myself onto the ground behind the corner of the building. I had reloaded my pistol. When the first panting German had appeared at the head of the street, I had shot him; then the second, and then at the third, who had fallen over, shrieking. This had been the right way: to think before acting and to act, thinking.

Three days later, I went out early in the morning for my meeting with Colombo. I stopped on the door step, and looked to my left and right to be sure. The street vendor stood over her large basket of vegetables. She greeted me and I responded with a smile.

Meeting a familiar face gave me pleasure. Walking along the street together with workers hurrying to the factories, made me forget my fear.

At a street corner, I met up with the first patrol; Italians in SS uniforms. They glanced at me and passed by wordlessly.

I walked along for half an hour. Then, following a complicated route, and looking back at every corner to make sure no one was following me, I reached my destination; I climbed two flights of stairs and knocked at the second door. Dante Di Nanni's mother answered the door, and told me that her son was still in bed.

Di Nanni quickly roused himself when his mother announced my arrival. He came into the kitchen, his bare feet leaving imprints on the cold tiles which were still damp from the wet rags with which his mother had just wiped the floor. Two long, thin arms hung from his short-sleeved sweater. He smiled while he fastened the belt of his pants.

"How are you? I haven't seen you for a week. Where have you been?" he asked me.

"Here and there."

"Away from Turin?"

"No, in Turin."

His mother understood that she had to leave us alone. To her mind, there was always something strange and unclear, when I came to look for her son. Afterwards, time after time, Dante would leave without any explanation, and often would not even return in the evening. Other times, he would go off with me, not saying anything, not even telling when he would return. And so with a heavy heart she left us alone to talk.

"I'm going down to the store," she said. She leaned the broom, still wrapped in the wet rags, against the corner of the sink. She took off the handkerchief wrapped around her head and walked out, her pocketbook over her arm.

Di Nanni went to the door and locked it.

"Everyone will be at the house this afternoon," I said.

I talked rapidly, coming directly to the point. "Well, then, is it difficult?" asked Di Nanni.

"Difficult."

Dante was not afraid. At 18, he had already lost his childhood fears. He knew no discretion, no hesitation. Although he felt no fear as such, each time we prepared for an operation he felt himself stiffen. He would gradually relax, but not until afterwards. He became tense as I told him all the details. He knew he had to evaluate the risks and had to plan how to avoid or reduce them.

Knowing what was wanted of him, he could then decide how to act. Then he would become his own master, feeling a genuine desire to accomplish all he could, and feeling a real capacity for action. But this inner confidence was not there in the beginning. At first, he felt as though he were trapped. And he did not like the feeling of being trapped; the weight which kept him silent in front of me was not pleasant to him.

"Then, you understand, toward evening at the 'house'," I repeated.

As always happened, Dante bluntly asked what had to be done; he asked in feigned indifference, realizing that this comrade whom the Party had placed in command of the Gappisti would feel uneasy in finding himself before a boy with so much inner anxiety.

He was hardly aware that I was leaving. He could not even remember if he had said goodbye. He returned to his bedroom and looked at himself in the mirror of his dresser. "Whatever has to be done," he mumbled, "will be done." To know something had to be done was not important. What counted was doing it. He looked at himself squarely, at his thin, long, angular face, his mouth which cut straight across, his thick dark hair; then he tried to imagine where he would be hit by a bullet.

"Exactly like the other time," he thought. He was thinking of the time when he had been anxiously awaiting the operation on Corso Francia.

Then it had seemed absurd to attack the militia command in broad daylight. At precisely 1:30 P.M., Bravin, Ivaldi, and he had bombed a German auto, a Wehrmacht major, a captain and some other soldiers.

Until evening, through all those hours, Dante felt the enormous emptiness in his stomach, like a pain, an anxiety that prevented him from doing the slightest thing, like eating, drinking or reading.

In the room, five people were seated around the table. As I spoke, I traced with my finger the map of the city. "We shall withdraw by going along the Stura. If we are discovered, it will only be because they were warned. It is a risk that we must take. I do not see any other escape route. If we went down along the river and retraced our steps, we would find the patrols right at our heels. The barracks of the Germans and Fascists are close by. We could try to cross the river and make our way eastward. But even if we could cross the river, we would then have no way of reentering the city, since the bridges, after the explosion, would be patrolled more heavily than ever, and we would then have to abandon our arms. By going toward the north and staying on the right bank, we shall be able to return to the city after dark, assuming that we are not discovered when we pass over the Milan Road bridge. No one would think that we would withdraw in that direction, which would seem to be the most dangerous route.

"Naturally," I concluded, "that's only the way I see it . . . there are five of us here, and someone might have a better idea."

"It sounds O.K. to me," said Valentino.

"If they discover us on the bridge?" asked Bravin.

"Then we'll have to open the route by shooting," I answered.

"How many will there be?"

"Perhaps fifty, one hundred, perhaps more."

"But we don't have enough guns and ammunition for a battle of this size!"

"We'll take as many guns as we can get from the radio station garrison."

Mario did not speak, but only nodded in agreement. He would not be participating in the conclusive part of the action; his job was to keep an eye on enemy movements and to tell us when to prepare for the attack.

It was like entering a deep, unlit cave with black walls; it was so dark, a dark curtain seemed to surround us. Only above could one see any light from the stars here and there in the sky.

We had left the street only a short while before. We suddenly found ourselves in difficulty because of the rugged and uneven terrain. We walked closely together, slowly, looking for a path. The arms and the packages of explosives prepared by Spada had been carried by Ines from Turin, several at a time and hidden in a prearranged location. There could be no allowance for any mistakes; deviating even a few steps in that pathless moor meant losing time in anxious wandering and the ruining of all our plans.

"Here is the first signal," I whispered at last. "Now we'll go a trifle to the right so as to avoid the hole which is a little ahead, and then we'll look for a broken gasoline can. Be sure you don't hit it; that would make a noise as loud as hell!" We found the gasoline can, but lost half an hour in a search for three stones; we retraced our steps to the can, and resumed our search once more from that point.

For a moment, I feared that during the day someone had moved the can to another spot. I worried that we would not be able to find the explosives that night. I decided to try once again; I started off slowly, and then, finally, I felt the bush under my outstretched hands; it was there, two steps ahead. I moved my foot and touched the stones. "Here we are!" I whispered, "it's right here."

I leaned over, pushing aside several small branches and clumps of grass, and drew forth the first package. It was heavy, and wrapped in strong paper.

"These are our arms."

From the bush I pulled out four more packages, which were heavier than the first one.

"This is the explosive. It isn't primed, but be careful; don't throw it in the air."

The wrapping paper was strong and rigid, and made a rustling noise in the silence as we unwrapped the packages.

On my knees, I worked slowly. We could barely see. My hands were groping; I found the knot of the cord and the longest side to unwrap. I removed the simple knot without difficulty; then I felt the outside edge of the wrapping which had to be held tightly while I worked. I found a pistol, then the Sten, and then the other pistols. After that, I reached for the package of explosive. Again that damned paper. Finally, I wadded all the pieces of paper together, made a big ball out of them, and threw it into the bush.

"I would never have believed that paper could make such a noise," whispered Bravin.

Di Nanni chuckled softly: "Just as if he were buying something in a shop."

I distributed the arms, a package of explosives to each man, the detonators—little cylindrical capsules, which, in the hand looked like containers for needles—and the fuses, with the firing material already attached at one end. Suddenly from over near the river we heard the sound of a truck motor which was quickly turned off, then started again in little spurts, like a cough.

"It's that synthetic gasoline of theirs. It doesn't burn," said Di Nanni.

"It works well only if the motor is warm."

"There is something moving on the bridge," said Valentino. "Watch out."

"They aren't sleeping," commented Di Nanni.

The motor stopped coughing and began to run smoothly and then accelerated. Finally, the truck moved off. We heard the shifting of gears. The two narrow beams of headlights briefly illuminated the street. It was going toward Turin; we could still hear the hum of the motor for several minutes as it faded away.

Throughout this whole time, no one moved, as though the motor were reason enough to make us hesitate, postpone our decision. Then we advanced slowly in the dark, weighed down with the explosives. We could not see the radio station, but we knew that it was at least three hundred yards ahead of us.

We crawled in the wet grass over the last fifty yards, and then we stopped, side by side. The dark outlines of the cabin appeared indistinctly in the night: my constant staring at it caused the illusion that either men or animals were moving in the shadows. I closed my eyes briefly; when I reopened them, the vision disappeared. But then it seemed to reappear. I again closed and reopened my eyes, and then I was sure that the figure was no mere illusion; it was right at the center of the building, just about where the door would probably be. The sudden flame of a match illuminated the area; the guard was lighting a cigarette. I could see his face for a second; then he moved the match away from his face, flicked it away, and it expired in the air.

At the same moment, the hand of a panic-stricken man grabbed my arm. I locked it in mine and held it tightly until my own began to hurt. When the trembling stopped, I knew that Valentino had overcome his crisis.

We remained on the ground, watching the lit end of the cigarette flickering up every few seconds. Then, the butt left a trace of sparks as it too was flicked away. In the shadowy outline of the hut, the door opened. The blue light from inside the opened door illuminated the grass. The guard entered and closed it behind him.

"Now," I whispered. And I ran ahead, followed by the others; I pushed hard against the door. To my amazement, it opened simultaneously.

Three carabinieri, who were seated around a table, stared at me in disbelief, without making a move. The guard was standing there with the barrel of his machine gun in his hand, the butt on the ground. He stuttered: "But no, but no. . . ." Valentino closed the door, and Di Nanni and Bravin took a position over the other guards who were sleeping in cots.

"On your feet, on your feet!" cried Bravin, motioning with his Sten.

＊　＊　＊　＊　＊

In the house on Via San Bernardino, I stood near the blood-stained bed. Di Nanni was lying down, his eyes open.

"Were Bravin and Valentino wounded?" he murmured faintly.

"Yes." I replied. "Both of them; they must have taken them by now."

"Yes, they must have taken them."

I moved away, limping slightly, took a seat at the window and turned toward the bed. I extended my leg and touched my calf, which was tightly wrapped in a knotted handkerchief.

"You, too, are wounded."

"Oh, it's nothing," I answered. "It doesn't hurt now; the doctor will be here in a few moments."

"It doesn't do me any good to talk," murmured Di Nanni, "it doesn't do one bit of good."

Di Nanni felt very bad. He had a premonition that they would injure him again, but he could not say how many times. He tried to move, but I forced him to stay down.

"Stay quiet, quiet. It's worse if you move."

I limped over to the boy and changed the bandages. I used towels and strips which I made by ripping a sheet; the blood and the shirt which Di Nanni was still wearing made it difficult to see the wounds. I tied several bandages all across his back and pressed pillows against them in order to keep the bandages from falling away.

"It hurts terribly," said Di Nanni, "and the doctor won't be able to do a damned thing, not a damned thing."

"The doctor is a comrade," I answered, "and he really is a good man. I told Barca to find him and to send him quickly. I am certain he is on his way, and he'll be able to do plenty; he'll clean out the splinters; he'll give you medicine and some injections to relieve the pain."

"It won't do a damned bit of good," said Di Nanni. "It's useless to have the doctor come here. And don't tell me that the wounds aren't serious."

I gathered up the blood-soaked bandages and went out to throw them into the bucket in the kitchen. When I returned, Di Nanni stared at me. "It went well for you. Perhaps you will be alive when it all ends." Di Nanni spoke slowly, without apparent effort. "I will be dead by then," he added.

"You should not think that way," I murmured.

"But I am thinking of them, I am thinking of them and I'm telling you. There will be a big celebration when everything is over. Everybody will be able to sleep and wake up without fear."

"That will be your reward," I said.

I was standing near the bed and spoke quietly, leaning forward.

"It will be everybody's reward," said he. "For those who are alive and for those who are dead, and it won't mean a damn thing for the dead to have some reward for all this." He leaned on one elbow, trying to raise himself. I had to force his arm to make him lie down. I sat down myself, holding him down firmly with my hands.

Above the rapid, irregular breathing of the boy, again lying on his side, his face hidden in the crook of his arm, one could hear distant sounds coming from the street.

"We should have killed them," he murmured, "we should have killed all of them. . . ."

Twelve hours earlier he had said the same thing when three of the captured carabinieri had run away while Bravin was bringing them out. We had advanced slowly because the dark hindered us again on the moor. But we had to hurry to pass across the bridge.

"We should have killed them." Di Nanni had come up quickly behind me and had spoken angrily, in a loud voice.

"Keep quiet. We aren't murderers, and furthermore, we weren't able to shoot. Did you feel like cutting the throats of nine helpless men with a knife?"

I had answered, barely moving my head, without stopping.

"We should have killed them, quickly," repeated Di Nanni.

"Perhaps they didn't run to give the alarm. Perhaps they only hid themselves on the moor, while we were mining the antennae."

"You know very well that's not the way it is," said Di Nanni, "you know very well that they are waiting for us."

At that moment, we could see the direct line of the bridge not far away on the road.

"We'll make it. Still fifty yards to go." I succeeded in completing the sentence. Then on the bridge, three reflectors suddenly flared up, one after the other, first with a red glow, and then bright white.

"Down! Down!" I shouted, throwing myself onto the grass. The three beams of light concentrated on the radio shack, illuminating it, and then turned in the opposite direction, searching the earth.

One flashed above the four of us lying flat on the ground. It passed beyond us and then returned. They fired the first round of shots. The bullets struck all around us, right in the circle of light.

While other reflector lights spotted us, the crash of the first explosion came from the radio station very loud; then the second, third, and fourth. After the sound of those explosions, the machine gun shots seemed like small but angry whistles.

"They have us," shouted Bravin.

"Out of here," I cried. I jumped to my feet and ran toward the left, then ahead. We got out of the blinding circle of the reflectors. Now the lights were moving in jerks, searching.

Machine guns were brought up with the other guns, perhaps two of them, and their violent bursts of fire dominated the dry, spasmodic shots of the rifles. Then I saw reddish tongues of fire from automatics in front of me in the clearing, and I knew that the troops had fanned out on the moor and were surrounding us.

"What'll we do?" cried Bravin.

"I don't know," I answered.

I loaded a pair of sub-machine guns on my shoulders. In turning around, I bumped into Valentino. I took advantage of the situation to rid myself of some of my anger. "Why the hell don't you get out of the way? It's useless to stay hidden here," I shouted. I fired a round, then two more rounds. I exposed myself in the open. I heard Di Nanni and the others shooting. I stopped to wait for Valentino.

"How do you feel?"

"O.K. Let's get out of here. Let's get out of here fast."

"Follow me and keep shooting."

My absurd irritation had restored my calm. It had always happened to me, even in Spain, after the battle had begun. The lucky one uses his head and survives. Now the four of us decided to go along and return blow for blow. The battle would be uneven, but the night would help us. "We should have killed all of them," whispered Di Nanni again. "And then cleared out of there!"

Bravin quieted him.

The Germans who had come down from the bridge were now shooting from behind mounds of earth hidden in the grass. It was difficult to get at them in that position. We could identify their weapons by the sound of the cartridge cases falling on the earth.

I leaned to one side, extracted a hand grenade from my pocket, searched for the clasps of the pin with my fingers, and straightened them out; then I placed my index finger on the seal, and ripped it away. I felt the pin slide out smoothly; I held the grenade and the little safety strip tightly in my hand. Then I flung it, and heard it whiz past my face. As the grenade went soaring through the air, I rose, and then turned and again threw myself in the grass.

As I pulled the pin of another grenade, I heard between shots the deafening explosion of the first, and saw the red flame. I hurled a second and then a third.

"This is the moment," I shouted, leaping up. I ran ahead until I stumbled over the body of a German; I rose again to find the others around him, thinking that I had been hit.

Now, after the long run, the shots sounded far off. We stopped.

"One minute," said Bravin, "only a minute in order to catch my breath."

"Well, we did it," said Valentino.

"Perhaps," responded Di Nanni.

We stood in silence, catching our breath. Then, there was a rustling in the grass, and again we saw quick flashes in front of us.

Di Nanni crawled on all fours to our left and fired a burst of bullets. He returned, still on his hands and knees. "Get away," he cried, "get away while they still think we're over there." We ran crouching, and found ourselves at the river.

"We're trapped!" gasped Bravin.

The shooting had stopped. The silence was more dangerous than the gunfire. We ran along for several yards. An isolated shot went off; someone shouted in an uncertain and forced voice; then a second shot was fired, and again all hell broke loose.

At that moment Valentino shouted. He had fallen a few steps behind. He was trying desperately to rise from his knees. Bravin ran toward him, vacillated for a fraction of a second, began to move his gun up to eye level, and then fell.

I ran back and threw myself on the earth alongside Bravin. Di Nanni covered me.

"It was my turn," gasped Bravin, "it is useless to think about it. Get out of here fast and leave me some cartridges. I can't feel my legs any more. They got me in the stomach—it's more than an inch inside. Get out of here."

"And Valentino . . . ?"

"Valentino will stay, too, he can't go anywhere now."

I touched Valentino; I shook him. It was like shaking a piece of rubber. I ran back to Di Nanni, who was still shooting from a squatting position. I could hear Bravin firing again. I pulled the pin out of the last grenade and rose to throw it; just then, a sharp blow on my leg knocked me to the ground. I threw the grenade as best I could. It exploded quickly, very close by. I felt the calf of my leg soaked with blood. I heard Di Nanni shouting something unintelligible. I took my handkerchief from my pocket, raised my trousers and felt for the wound in the midst of the blood. I found it quickly; it was a little hole, only a little hole. I tied the handkerchief over the wound and pulled myself upright with my hands. I tried to take a few steps, and the gunfire seemed to slacken.

I noticed that Di Nanni, too, had stopped shooting. I lifted him up on my shoulders and resumed the march.

✲    ✲    ✲    ✲    ✲

Moving along, I remembered an incident which had taken place during my days as a fighter in Spain, when I had become inert, alongside my machine gun; my legs had suddenly become paralyzed, and someone, a comrade, had saved my life. My brigade, the Garibaldi, which had been nearly decimated in the battle of Brunette, had been brought back to top efficiency with new supplies and political solidarity. The commander was now Carlo Penchienati, substituting for Pacciardi, who had gone back to France after a bitter dispute with the High Command. Pacciardi had wanted to send the Garibaldini off to France to recruit new soldiers from among the Italian emigrants. He had been sharply criticized, particularly by the Communists, who considered it sheer folly to remove men from battle at the most critical moment. The Garibaldi volunteers, conscious of the sacrifices which they were making, fought the enemy without respite. They were fighting in Spain against French, German and Italian Fascism. Unfortunately, Pacciardi's views had generated a certain atmosphere of distrust among the more politically naive troops.

When I had joined the brigade, the military and moral reorganization had been completed. Togliatti[2] was calm, sure of him-

2.   Translator's note: Palmiro Togliatti, before his death, was a longtime head of the Italian Communist Party. In Spain as head of the Communist International, he was attached to the Spanish Communist Party. With the collaboration of Luigi Longo, recently replaced head of the Party in Italy, and Edoardo D'Onofrio, he maintained contact with the International Brigade.

self, and persuasive. He arrived accompanied by Longo, Fedeli, and Barontini; his presence imparted a feeling of security and dispelled any remaining doubts.

Around the middle of August, the order came to leave for the Aragon front. On a rainy night, we climbed aboard trucks which lacked protective canvas tops.

We got soaked to the bone during that night, and the following day dried ourselves at the edge of a village which lay at the foot of a hill. At night we moved ahead on foot through scorched fields, constantly climbing and descending. At dawn, we found ourselves between rocky mountains, broken by deep crevices, and, except for some thorny bushes, devoid of vegetation. The heat now became more oppressive, and no one had one drop of water left in his canteen. Every once in a while, we stopped for a short rest, and then the march resumed under the blinding sun. Someone began to beg for water; someone else began to stagger under the weight of his knapsack and machine gun. The scouts of the advance patrols brought no word of any water ahead. We were given orders to halt at the top of a hill, to eat some food from our knapsacks. It was already afternoon, and no one had eaten yet.

We resumed our march on the burning earth. There was swearing along the long line; several of the men fell to the ground in a faint; others dragged themselves along with small staggering steps. Some younger men were not able to move along any further; the more experienced soldiers limped along silently.

Late in the afternoon, a mounted courier delivered an order to Commander Raimondi. Our next stop would be the top of the hill. We began to climb, sustained by the hope of finding water. Everything was lifeless on the summit; in the distance, on the plain, one could make out a farm. A village was situated atop a hill beyond.

I was ordered to go to the Command of the Brigade to ask that water be sent over to us. As I was leaving I saw a group of Garibaldini standing around a pool. Raimondi shouted, "Don't drink it; it's stagnant, dirty water. It might be poisoned. Don't you see those lifeless objects in there?"

While Raimondi was urging the men to go away, I threw myself on the ground and immersed my mouth in the mire, gulping down mud and water. I stopped for a second, caught my breath, and then went down again. The others were also lying around the hole drinking. Then Raimondi finally leaned over to drink.

Toward evening, the tank of water finally arrived. It had traveled a long time under the sun, and was tepid, but clean. Everyone drank to his heart's content and filled his canteen as well as a few bottles to carry in reserve. At night we camped at the foot of a low hill. We would secure the position at daybreak. It was still dark, and we did not notice anything around us.

Next morning, when the sun was up, we were startled by bursts of machine gun bullets and mortar. We were under the sights of some small enemy fortifications lying a short distance away. We could do nothing but throw ourselves on the sides of the hill for protection. Many cried out against the error which the Command had made in giving us an entrenchment right in the middle of enemy territory.

Our operation was to have been part of a vast maneuver against Zaragoza, which was occupied by the Franco forces. By inflicting pressure on Zaragoza, we could lessen the Fascist offensive. But we had come the wrong way, and now we were occupying a sector which never threatened Zaragoza.

In the middle of the morning, we heard the distant sound of a motor. The alarm was given.

Those assigned to the anti-aircraft machine guns placed their weapons in position. A flock of enemy planes appeared. Three planes came toward us, and their silver wings sparkled over our heads. The machine guns shot swift sprays of bullets, while the airplanes loosed their sticks of bombs. Explosions boomed all around us, and were terrifying. A bomb exploded a few yards away; I was thrown into the air, and fell on the dry, hard earth. The airplanes now returned to drop more bombs, and the machine guns fired again. Someone shouted, "He's hit, he's hit!"

One of the planes detached itself from the formation and fell like a rock. A parachute opened. The fuselage of the plane cut into the middle of the hill and exploded. The other two airplanes turned about, and their gunners inexplicably shot at the pilot, who was floating down under his large white parachute. We picked him up as he fell wounded; he was convinced that we would kill him.

"But it was one of his own who shot him!" exclaimed Malozzi.

The pilot was an Italian officer; he explained to us that he had enrolled voluntarily because they had promised him a promotion. We rushed him to the first aid wagon.

We waited until evening before moving along the valley. The surrounding mountains were occupied by Fascists, and we had to steal out of there silently in order to avoid being ambushed while in formation on some dark, narrow trail. During the entire night we traveled over paths which had been made previously. Just before dawn, a guide from the Command led us toward the position which we had been trying to reach for two days: some hilly strips of ridged plowed ground. The movement of soldiers and armed tanks was frenzied. We heard shooting in the distance. My detachment was now on the bare top of a hill, supporting a Franco-Belgian battalion and the "Rakosi" group. Before us stretched the rolling country-side, and ahead, we could see the outlines of houses with their lights blinking in the air above Zaragoza. We were completely out in the open.

We spent several hours digging trenches and machine gun positions, and then sought to establish telephone communications with the Command. We found ourselves right in the center of the vanguard; to the right we had the Franco-Belgians, to the left the Rakosi battalion. Before noon, enemy aircraft appeared and gunned us while their artillery opened a hellish fire. Once more, the airplanes flew close to the ground in groups of three. They were, ironically enough, Italian planes. The bomb explosions lacerated the hilltop, jolting the ground and filling the air with dust. After the first explosion, others followed, shattering our eardrums. The smoke made it difficult to determine whether or not the enemy infantry was advancing. The only thing we could do was to shoot blindly toward the plain, with the hope of containing or retarding the advance. The two battalions at our flank were also being subjected to an incessant bombardment. This could only mean an offensive against the entire sector. The telephone rang. The commander alerted us that our pursuit planes were arriving. "Hold on to that hill! Resist at all costs! Don't withdraw without orders!" he shouted at us.

Meanwhile, to our right, a violent battle broke out. Through my field glasses I saw the advancing enemy infantry, protected by tanks and supported by artillery, whose shooting was ever more intense. The airplanes continued to fire as they flew over. The situation was critical. Shrapnel exploded around our heads, spreading handfuls of iron on the trenches.

The wounded were being carried off by the medical corpsmen. The telephone line was broken. A courier whom I had sent to the Command had not returned. The sun was scorching; the men were covered with dust and sweat. I crawled under the hail of bombs to Cerbai and suggested that he move his machine gun to a spot where he could shoot more efficiently at the column of Fascists that advanced toward our hill, protected by tanks. I changed the position of another machine gun, relocating it in a hole to the left. The Fascists, now also crawling, were fifty yards away. I saw them clearly in my gunsight, and I fired; someone rolled down the slope. Others rose and ran for protection behind the tanks which were now firing their guns. The Fascists had seen us. It was impossible to move, and it would be impossible to resist for long. At every spot, on every yard of terrain, there was an explosion, and the air was full of the hisses of bullets. I sent another courier to the Command to ask for reinforcements; I saw him slip out of the trench and fall back dead.

We were cut off from all communications. We could only continue to resist as best we could.

Other Garibaldini were hit; many lay dead in the trenches; the wounded were groaning. I ran from one position to another, trying to encourage my companions; I ordered two Garibaldini to carry the wounded to shelter. This was a storm which upset and crumbled everything, reduced everything to shreds. A machine gun, squarely hit by a bomb, was left a twisted piece of metal; the bodies of the gun crew members were scattered by the explosion.

Several soldiers of the Franco-Belgian battalion, which was withdrawing, began to appear. Their formation had been broken by the enemy artillery. I had to remain with my detachment. That was the order. The remaining machine guns continued to fire, but they could not do much in the face of the armed tanks which were moving ahead.

A splinter killed a young Spanish machine gunner; another Garibaldino had his right arm cleanly cut off by a grenade. I would have taken time to stop the blood from his horrible wound, but I could not because I had to run to another machine gun which had ceased shooting; the machine gunner was bent over his gun with his belly torn to bits. I dragged him aside, and I continued the long sprays of machine gun fire. I then noticed that blood was coming out of my shirt; I touched my chest and felt a hole just under my shoulder. Now I heard the shouts of my dying companions amid the explosions. One called me, "Commander! Commander!" He extended his hand toward me; I grabbed it; I felt the pressure of his fingers increase, then relax. He was dead; a splinter had fractured his skull.

There remained only Cerbai's machine gun which was still firing. He, lying in the middle of the dead and the dust, continued to take aim scrupulously before shooting. I dragged myself again toward the machine gun, but a heavy blow hit me on the back; a spray of shrapnel had pierced me. I again tried to drag myself along; I thought I was advancing, but then realized that I was not moving an inch. "I am finished," I said to myself. I took my pistol out of its holster and considered killing myself, but decided to await the Fascists with a pistol in my hand. After a few seconds, I recovered my mental equilibrium. Cerbai was now leaning over me. "Almost everybody is dead," he was saying, "We must get out of here quickly." I tried to rise, but I couldn't move. I shouted that I could not use my legs, that he must leave by himself. "I order you!" I told him.

"You can still use your legs," shouted Cerbai. "All you have to do is make an effort."

I lifted myself with a great struggle. I succeeded in getting to my feet, but I could not move; perhaps the shrapnel had cut my spine, paralyzing my legs. I fell down again. Cerbai dragged me to a hole. From there, he pulled me along a few inches at a time, up toward the top of the hill.

There were only twenty yards to cross, but it took us about ten minutes, since we had to protect ourselves from the bomb fire. Now we were on the hill, and Cerbai made me roll down like a sack; when irregularities of the ground or a bush stopped me, Cerbai dragged me beyond the obstacle and made me roll on. He continued this until we reached the foot of the hill. When the Fascists arrived on the summit which we had just left, we Garibaldini, entrenched on the opposite hill, hit them with furious fire and forced them to retreat. We were saved.

✻   ✻   ✻   ✻   ✻

In the house on Via San Bernardino, I was looking out of the windows at the narrow street.

No one was at the front door, no one at the windows of the building opposite. It was a strange building, perhaps a convent; perhaps there were some monks inside. Perhaps it was a retreat, possibly even with an equipped infirmary—a place where the Fascists would never enter. I heard Di Nanni move, but did not turn; I continued to stare at the red brick building.

"Is the doctor coming?"

Di Nanni had spoken quietly, and I turned toward him. The boy was seated on the edge of his bed, his feet resting on the floor.

"Crazy, you're crazy, lie down." I helped him stretch out on the bed. "Now don't you move."

"I spoke out of anger, earlier," he said.

"You said what you felt. Do you feel bad?"

"I wouldn't say the same thing now. Now I wish the doctor would come and make me better; I wish he would get me back on my feet, because we still have many things to do. There is much to do isn't there?"

"Yes, much to do for all."

"At first," said Di Nanni, "I was not talking as a Communist should."

"A Communist is a man," I answered, "nothing more than a man, made of muscles, nerves and a brain, like everybody else."

"But I should never have felt so desperate, even if I am in such pain. You, too, are wounded, but you did not feel as though you were dead."

"It's different," I said.

"What's different?"

"It's different because one bullet is not like five or ten."

"Do you mean that they hit me ten times?"

"I'm not saying that, I want to say that they hit you more than once."

There was a pause. Then Di Nanni resumed, "It seems strange that you are speaking of these things, that you talk as you do, as though these matters were of no concern."

"These are things which do concern us," I said, "and we must speak of them."

"They are matters which concern the Party," said Di Nanni, "because we are part of the Party."

I sat down on the edge of his chair, leaning on the back rest, my wounded leg extended.

I took off my shoe, and rested the heel of my foot on the floor. There was a little less pain in that position. I looked at Di Nanni; the boy lay semi-prone; his face was very pale, but he seemed not to be suffering.

"Are you feeling very bad?" I asked.

"Not too bad. At first I felt like I was drunk, and I was saying strange things. I knew that I was saying them, but I couldn't keep silent."

"One feels like that very often," I offered.

"But one who makes war should not," said Di Nanni.

"Soldiers are also men."

"Bravin was a brave man. He didn't make speeches."

"Valentino was brave too," I said.

"Only we two remain."

"We aren't alone; there are all the others."

At that moment, there was a knock on the door.

I rose, gestured to Di Nanni to keep quiet, and took two submachine guns out of the cupboard. I gave one of them to the boy. Holding the other ready, I moved toward the door. I covered myself by standing to one side, my shoulders to the wall. I asked who was knocking.

"It is Giorgio," responded a low voice. "I have the medicine." I quickly opened the door, and the doctor entered.

"Where is he?" he asked.

"Over there."

I helped the doctor take off the boy's clothes.

"I have already put the water on to boil," I said. The doctor nodded, and I limped into the kitchen, lifted the pot off the weak flame of gas, carried it into the room and placed in on the seat near the bed. I brought over the basin and another sheet. The doctor ripped it into large square pieces and long strips. With two fingers, he took a piece by the corner and let it slowly dip into the water in the pot; then he took it out and placed it on the edge of the pot to cool a bit. He opened a case that he had brought with him, took out a syringe and a phial, and gave Di Nanni an injection. Placing some gauze on the chest of drawers, he laid the empty syringe on it. Then he began to clean the wounds with the wet piece of cloth. We could make out the bullet wounds, one after another. Little purple edges; one, two, three, four, five, six, seven little holes in his legs and in his stomach. Seven holes, seven bullets. The doctor examined his head, and discovered another wound. With a pair of scissors, he cut the hair around the head wound and cleaned the area. Di Nanni moaned every so often. When the doctor's fingers lingered over a wound, he would stifle a shriek of pain by burying his head in the pillow.

The doctor again took the syringe and gave him another injection. He waited a bit, and then, with the forceps, he delicately probed one of the small holes, then another. He took disinfectant out of his bag, soaked some pieces of cloth and placed them over the wounds. He bandaged the boy, but not too tightly. He gave him a third injection, replaced the instruments in his bag, and went toward the door, following me.

"You too, are wounded," he said.

I quickly shook my head. "It isn't anything, and there isn't time."

"Let me see."

"There isn't time. Tell me about the boy."

"Ugly wounds," said the doctor, "he must be operated on quickly. We must get him to a hospital."

"It's dangerous," I responded.

"If you leave him here, he'll die!"

I returned to the room. Di Nanni was lying on his stomach and seemed drowsy. He moved a bit when he heard the steps.

"What did he tell you?"

"That you must go to the hospital. They must operate on you to extract the bullets."

"In what hospital?"

"I don't know. He'll speak to the comrades about it. Within two hours, he will meet with someone from the Party. There is nothing we can do before then."

"And if they come and look for me in the hospital?"

"They will take you where there are comrades. They will say that it was an accident in the factory."

"If worst comes to worst, tell my family," said Di Nanni, "and look for Rossella in the house where I live. Tell her."

"Is she your girl friend?"

"No. She is only sixteen years old. We have an understanding that she will be my girl friend after everything is over.

"If something happens to me," Di Nanni added, "you must tell my family everything. You must wait and tell them afterward, however. After the war. My mother must not think that it is your fault. You came to me to take me home. You must say that you took me away, that you hid me in that farm, that you returned to get me and that you took me here."

"Why must I say all that?"

"Because it is true and that way they'll know that I was not abandoned by my comrades. Promise that you will say it."

"I promise you," I said.

No one spoke for a while. Then Di Nanni asked, "How are we going to get to the hospital?"

"Perhaps we shall be able to use an ambulance. In that way it will look like an accident."

"Will you come and visit me in the hospital?"

"Certainly, and I'll let you know about the new comrades who will be joining the Brigade."

"It will be difficult," murmured Di Nanni. "But sometimes I think that it will be still more difficult when everything is over. I would like to live to see it. Ours is a great Party."

"Yes, it is great because there are young people like you."

"The Party relies much upon the young people, doesn't it?" he asked.

"Much," I answered.

"Also, for the future," Di Nanni murmured, almost to himself. "Certainly for the future, when war will be over, and they will need so much strength to put everything back in order."

"Yes," I said, "for today and tomorrow."

"You know," said Di Nanni, "sometimes I think it will be even more difficult afterward. All we do now is shoot, and we know that it will be curtains for the Fascists in a short time. Afterwards, there will be a different fight, equally compelling, but longer, certainly more difficult."

"The Party," I answered, "will come out very strong from this battle. New cadres are being formed for the armed struggle, and tomorrow these men will be leaders and militants capable of fighting in other battles, perhaps less martial, but equally hard, equally difficult. They will need infinite amounts of energy to create a democratic country, new and different from any that we have known.

"It's strange," observed Di Nanni, "that we two, who don't

know if we'll still be alive tonight, are speaking of things concerning tomorrow, and so far in the future."

"It isn't so strange," I objected, "because we are not speaking only about ourselves; we are speaking also for the others. And there are so many others, all those who, like us, wish for a different kind of country, one in which everyone can be free."

"When we're finished with the Fascists and the Germans," said Di Nanni, "we shall truly be free."

"We shall be free to begin the struggle anew, the struggle for a true freedom, the struggle that every man has when he values himself in true terms."

"I understand," said Di Nanni, "and for this reason you say that what we are doing now is very important."

"It is important above all," I said, "because, if we don't do this today, there would not ever be a point tomorrow from which to begin truly to change things."

"I never could succeed in vocalizing all this," said Di Nanni, "however, I have felt it; what you say is not new to me, it is as though I had always known it."

He wanted to continue speaking, even though he was so weak, but I forced him to keep silent. He had to rest in order to make the trip.

When the boy seemed to be drowsing off, I arose from my chair and went into the kitchen. I took some alcohol, a pair of scissors and a strip of cloth. I sat on the floor, my back against the wall, and gently took hold of my left leg. I slowly pulled up the trouser-leg, I untied the bandage. The calf was swollen, but not too much. The area around the small hole hurt. I poured some alcohol on a piece of linen and pressed it on the wound. The burning sensation filled my eyes with tears. I removed the cloth, and the burning diminished. I repeated the operation several times, until the piece of cloth was drenched with blood. I took a clean piece of cloth, poured on more alcohol and placed it against the wound. Then, I bandaged the calf. I raised myself and threw the bloody pieces of cloth and bandages into a bucket, closed the bottle of alcohol, and came back into the room.

Di Nanni had not moved; he was still lying on his stomach and was breathing rapidly. I thought that he was sleeping and was surprised when I heard him ask, "Does it hurt you very much?"

I left Di Nanni alone in the house on Via San Bernardino. He was still lying on the bed, his arms bent, his hands pressed under the pillow, when I walked out. Di Nanni just had to talk when I returned after treating my wound in the kitchen. One has much to say, to explain, when one knows that one must die. A war like this left little time for conversation. One prepared for action and then executed it; when people met each other, every minute was taken up with practical, urgent questions. For the first time, we found ourselves facing one another, and we were able to speak —of ourselves, of the reason we were fighting, of tomorrow. Perhaps speaking of the future minimized the anxiety of the impending end. Or perhaps there were things that just had to be said, once and for all. Di Nanni was a mere boy, but he had so many things inside him, so many ideas, and a very firm conviction regarding our future. He reminded me of myself when I had left for Spain. The young people of today mature rapidly, I thought. I hugged him before leaving him to go look for an ambulance.

"I know what to do if they come," Di Nanni had said. He asked that the two sub-machine guns, the Sten and the bag of explosives, with fuses ready and inserted in the detonators, be placed beside the bed. Now he was lying motionless, waiting. Which would come first, the stretcher or the enemy? Just then a series of loud knocks shook the door. The others had arrived first.

He turned over slowly, leaned with his hands on the floor and slipped out of bed, hitting his knees on the cold tiles. He raised himself on his elbow. Folding his left leg under his body, he grabbed a sub-machine gun and shoved a magazine of forty rounds into place.

Before leaving, I had helped him to put on his pants so that he would be ready when the ambulance came. Now he slipped two hand grenades into his right pocket, and held another in his left hand. He dragged himself toward the door, clutching the sub-machine gun with his right hand.

"I'm coming," he shouted.

"Open!" cried someone from the stair landing.

Di Nanni flattened himself against the wall, put down the sub-machine gun, passed the hand grenade to his right hand and pulled away the pin, holding steady the flat lever. They were now trying to kick the door down from the outside, but it was a door made of good strong wood, and it resisted well.

"I'm opening it," shouted Di Nanni.

He leaned against the door post to the left, released the lever of the bomb, and counted. At the count of five, he pressed his thumb and moved the bar of the lock. The door, pushed from the outside, opened with a crash. Di Nanni let the bomb slide onto the top of the staircase and threw himself on his back, protected by the walls. After one second, he heard the crash, followed by the shrieks of the injured on the landing. One Fascist, hurled through the open door by the explosion, landed in the entrance hall. Di Nanni, lying prone, blocked his way with a short burst of gun fire, from a distance of three yards. The Fascist seemed paralyzed for a second. Then he let his sub-machine gun fall, and rolling from left to right on the floor, moved himself into the room, and lay flat on his face.

Crawling on his elbows, Di Nanni moved himself to the head of the stairs, which were blocked by the bodies of two Fascists. Leaning his forehead against the bannister, he was able to see others stumbling down the steps. He thrust the barrel of his sub-machine gun between the stair rails and fired; he heard them shriek and watched them fall like empty sacks.

He dragged himself back into the room and closed the door, which did not seem damaged.

The gun of the dead Fascist lay at the entrance to the room. Di Nanni threw it, barrel first, alongside the bed. He did not look at the body. He dragged himself further across the room, and he pushed the table from the kitchen against the entrance to the room; then he arranged a double barrier of chairs between the table and the wall; he used a stool to fill a last bit of empty space. The door was thus completely blocked, so that even if the invaders were able to break the lock, they would be stopped for awhile.

He could not do any more than this. Crawling under the table, he returned to the bed and climbed up. He lay on his stomach across the mattress in such a way as to face the top of the stairway. He was able to see a piece of railing, two windows of the house in front, and a little section of roof.

The body of the Fascist lodged behind the short wall, to the left, right in front of the window, where the bannister of the stair hooked onto the outside wall. He guessed the body to be in a sitting position, or partially on its back with knees bent; he could see the shoes extending from the corner of the wall.

A deep silence had fallen through the house. Perhaps nothing else would happen, he thought, perhaps I would return with the ambulance, and they would get him to the hospital. No suspicious noises came from the street, nothing that would indicate a new assault. Nothing would happen in that silence. However, Ivaldi would have to return quickly, because he was not able to hold out for long. He touched the bandages on his back. They were sticky. He looked at his hand. It was covered with blood. He had to remain calm, withstand the pain, and not lose his strength.

The shoes at the corner of the landing moved; they slipped forward. Di Nanni knew that the Fascist was dying.

Stories that he had heard of the other war came into his mind —wounded Italians and Austrians, isolated in a no man's land, had succeeded in understanding one another through gestures, exchanging cigarettes or a gulp of brandy, cursing in different languages with the same meaning, cursing both the war and those who had sent them down to die without their knowing why.

He gazed at those shoes which slipped forward in a pool of blood. His father had fought in a different war. Then, the soldiers had been in uniform, carrying rifles; and were given orders to shoot, but no reasons, no explanations. In this war, everyone made his own choice. Neither he nor anyone else had taken a gun without knowing why. He had chosen with full conscience the part he must play, and this, he supposed, was also true of the Fascist lying there on the landing. Everyone had to pay his debts, he mused.

Suddenly, from the street, came the sound of a motor, followed by several shots. Di Nanni knew that the moment had arrived. The ambulance would not be coming now, and he would not be going to the hospital, or anywhere else.

He heard the motor stop in front of the house, right at the foot of the staircase. Incomprehensible orders were being given. He heard many footsteps scurrying about, and a woman shouting with fear as she ran along the asphalt crying for help.

The second assault would be different. His best tactic now was to wait. This would be disconcerting to them. They were now anticipating a volley of gunshots and bombs and were probably hiding in some protected position. It would not make sense to shoot now; it was up to them to make the first move.

There was a long silence in the street. Then someone with a

strong German accent shouted, "Come on down. Surrender!" More time passed. He heard the sound of a second motor stopping in front of the door. A fire-engine ladder was now being moved toward the bannister of the stair landing. It wavered for a bit, as though in search of a point upon which to lean, and then stopped solidly. Then, it began to shake. Someone was climbing it.

The same German voice continued to shout, "Get him! Get him! He's crazy!" Di Nanni, face downward on his bed, pointed his sub-machine gun.

The helmet of a fireman appeared at the edge of the landing, followed by the face of an old man. He seemed to hesitate; he glanced perplexedly at the body of the Fascist and scrutinized the room. He did not see Di Nanni, and resumed climbing slowly, cautiously. He leaned over to say something to someone who was following him up the ladder, someone whom Di Nanni did not yet see; then, he jumped over the bannister, glancing at the dead Fascist, without approaching him. Then he saw the gun pointed at him. The other one who had followed him remained astride the bannister.

"Get out of here," said Di Nanni in a calm, low voice. "I'm not crazy. I'm a partisan."

The firemen were startled; this boy with the machine gun lying on the bed was no one to trifle with. The dead Fascist had taught them a lesson. To advance was one thing; to die, another.

"He isn't mad!" he shouted down to the second fireman who was still astride the bannister. "He isn't crazy!"

Angry words came from the street. "Go and get him!"

"Get out of here," repeated Di Nanni, "I don't have anything against you."

The fireman retreated two steps and was back again on the landing.

"And what about this one?" he asked, indicating the dead Fascist.

"Take him with you," answered Di Nanni.

The fireman lifted the body over the bannister to the other; the old man then made a gesture toward Di Nanni, as though he wanted to say something as he was climbing down.

Now he had to move; he rolled off the bed and crept to the landing. They were not able to see him from below in this prone position. They had not yet thought of sending someone onto the roof of the house in front or onto the bell tower nearby. Di Nanni looked to the right and saw that the narrow street was being blocked by a group of Germans, barring access to a small crowd. To the left, also, the street was blocked by Fascists. There were townspeople there, too; mostly women. Underneath, where he could not see, he was aware of large groups of Germans and Fascist soldiers.

He carefully observed the windows and facades of the convent opposite. Everything was closed and barred. He released the safety of a hand grenade, and placed it on the floor. He then repeated the process with a second grenade and threw them, one after the other, between the barriers of the bannister. He heard the explosions and the shouts. He turned to the left. The women were running away, leaving the Fascists, who were leaning against the wall, to themselves. He fired a small and then a larger burst of bullets. Three Fascists fell. He fired in the direction of the others who were running for shelter. He hit one right on the corner of the street.

He crawled back and remained prone at the threshold of the bedroom door. Here, he could keep watch over both the roof in front and the bell tower. A few minutes passed and, then, slowly, a helmet appeared above the corner of the roof, and then a red face. While he was taking aim, he saw another German appear in the belfry of the bell tower. He tried to set his aim on the enemy on the roof, but the gun against his left shoulder was not firm. He leaned his right elbow on the wall and took aim anew. He fired a few rounds. The German's face disappeared. Di Nanni quickly aimed at the bell tower. The second German showed himself for a fraction of a second, then lowered his head. He reappeared then lowered his head again. He looked like a mechanical toy. Di Nanni watched him lower his head a third time, waited an instant, and then shot inside the empty opening; at that same second, the German raised himself and fell away shrieking. The bells, hit by the spray of bullets, started ringing as though for a joyous holiday. He dragged himself far from the wall. It was now their turn. He had to wait for them to act, so that they would think they had him cornered.

He hid himself behind the corner to the left of the window and waited. First came single shots; then machine gun fire. They kept on shooting for a long time. Panes of glass from the window broke away with a dull clatter. Shots from down below, perhaps from the front entrance, ended up in the ceiling, knocking away the plaster.

Then the firing diminished; the volleys became shorter, then stopped. Di Nanni waited until he heard the first knocks on the door. Then he dragged himself toward it. They continued to knock. Di Nanni aimed his gun just over the table. He squeezed the trigger as he slowly moved his aim from right to left, and then back to the right. He heard shouts and moans. He pointed downward this time, and fired his last volleys of bullets.

He stopped to listen. It sounded as though they had surrounded the house in full force. They were shouting orders in German and in Italian; but the voices were now coming from farther away, from beyond the head of the street. They were playing it safe, and taking cover. They fired again; single shots and huge volleys. Perhaps they thought they could block his movements, or perhaps they hoped to hit him with a lucky bullet. It certainly could not continue this way for long. They had to do something decisive; the entire quarter was now alerted, and hundreds of Germans and Fascists had been fighting for two hours, incurring heavy losses, against one single partisan.

He knew they would have to do something new, quickly. Just then, there was the growl of a large motor. Di Nanni crawled onto the landing; meanwhile, they began to fire from the more distant roofs. He looked between the bars to the left. An armored car was slowly approaching in the center of the narrow street. Ten or twelve Germans and Fascists were following it in a crouched position. Suddenly, the barrel of the machine gun which projected from the tower began to jerk. Di Nanni turned himself on his side and rolled into the room. The shots ripped off the edges of the landing and bounced off the iron bannister.

Di Nanni extracted five chunks of TNT from a package and tied them together with a strip of cloth; in the middle, he inserted a detonator with a short fuse and the ignitor set in position to be ripped off. He returned to the balcony. The machine gun was now silent; the rhythm of the idling motor sounded as though it was at the foot of the stairway. He unscrewed the top of the ignitor and pulled the cord. It sounded like the snap of a match against a brick.

He counted five seconds; he threw the TNT over the bannister. The explosion came immediately; it was tremendous; the whole house trembled. The motor of the armored car was silent. Someone who remained was trying to get it started again. Di Nanni returned to the foot of the bed, prepared two more bundles of TNT, and dropped them from the landing, not stopping to count, since there would be no one below who would be able to put out the fuses.

After the explosions, there was silence; the Germans and Fascists must have been broken up. They must have retreated to their shelters. The armored car was immobilized and the dead were strewn around; perhaps the enemy had begun to doubt that they were fighting a lone partisan.

Di Nanni returned again to the bed, prepared other packets out of all the remaining explosives, set the detonators and lay flat. He heard an amplified but distorted voice over a loudspeaker coming from the street. "Surrender. We guarantee that your life will be spared. Surrender and you will be saved." Then something incomprehensible followed.

The metallic rumble of chains announced the arrival of a tank. It was advancing slowly, revolving its gun turret, with its little machine gun slits open. Di Nanni waited until it came directly underneath, so that the view of his landing would be lost to the men in the tank. Then he lit the fuses. He grabbed the string with his right hand, lifted the first packet of explosives over his head and threw it over the railing onto the street in front of the tank. Then he flung the second, and the third.

The driver must have seen the packets fly toward the ground but when he tried to stop, it was too late; one of them exploded less than a foot from the right tread and ripped it apart. The other two explosions completed the job. The tank began to spin around, pushed on by the remaining chain, and crashed into the wall of the house opposite.

The motor stopped, and the men cautiously climbed out of the hatches and ran away. Di Nanni could see them no more.

Now everything was quiet. There was a second's truce: peace, just before the impending end. His explosives and hand grenades were all gone. There were only six shots remaining in the magazine. Di Nanni extracted one of the bullets and put it in his pocket.

He dragged himself back to the landing, placed his finger on the second trigger of the sub-machine gun, the one for single shots, and looked out on the street. Three Germans were advancing from the left, moving in a crouched position along the wall. They were not carrying guns, but were carrying grenades in their hands. Their plan was to throw them from this position, through the French window over the landing. Di Nanni took aim behind the barriers and shot at the first Nazi. He fell forward. His second shot missed the man behind him, but the third hit him. He aimed at the last one as he started to run away. The Nazi fell, then got back to his feet and limped off. He managed to save himself by flinging himself around the corner of the street. At that moment, a rapid, violent burst of shots came from the roof opposite. The German sniper was supported against the tiles of the roof top; he was not trying to hide. His volley should have been decisive, but it passed over Di Nanni's head who, in turn, struck him with his last bullet.

He saw that the enemy forces had assembled on the street, in the bell tower and in the more distant houses. They were all around him; there was no means of escape. Di Nanni took the last cartridge from his pocket, set it in the breech and locked it in place. The way to finish was to lean the barrel under his chin, and pull the trigger with his finger. But this seemed a ridiculous way to end it all. Meanwhile, the firing continued all around him. He again rolled over on his stomach, pointed the gun at the bell tower and waited, safely protected from the shots. When the appropriate moment arrived, he aimed carefully. The Fascist fell.

There was now really nothing more he could do; and so he grabbed the bars of the enclosure, and with a desperate effort, lifted himself to his feet to await the gunfire. Instead, the shots ceased and the Fascists and Germans came out of hiding on the roof, in the street, and windows of the houses. They looked at this Gappista who had killed so many of them and had sent them into flight. Uncertain, disconcerted, they stared at this boy, covered with blood, who had fought them. They did not shoot.

At this moment, Di Nanni leaned forward, pressing his stomach against the railing, and saluted them with raised fist. Then he threw himself with open arms onto the narrow silent street.

"The years and the decades pass; the hard and sublime days in which we live today will soon appear distant, but entire generations of young sons of Italy will have been educated in a love of their country, in a love of freedom, in the spirit of unlimited devotion to the cause of human redemption, as exemplified by the admirable Garibaldini who today, with their red blood, are writing the most beautiful pages of Italian history."[3]

---

3. From the clandestine booklet published in Turin, June 4, 1944, "To the Glory of the national hero, Dante Di Nanni."

## CHAPTER 8
# *Goodbye to Turin*

The days became nightmares. "You think too much, you give too much weight to impressions," I scolded myself angrily. A guerrilla fighter in the city is alone, living behind invisible bars to escape the solid bars of a prison cell. Each day I planned my movements, planned the hours when I would leave the house or remain inside. I did my sleeping during the day. When strangers appeared on the street outside or in nearby houses, my women neighbors warned me. The night was less secure. The Fascist police or the SS might appear without warning and I would be trapped in my room. I felt more confident when I was occupied with some sabotage action at night, despite the curfew. It seemed paradoxical that obvious danger could be preferable to the unknown, the unexpected.

"Will they be coming tonight?" I would ask myself, picking up a gun or grenade. I preferred the risks brought on by action; I preferred fighting to waiting in seclusion, in what might be a trap. But just now a search for a new base of operations was not advisable. People knew me in this quarter of the town. They were trustworthy, they were workers and allies. Without ever having been told, I felt that people helped me keep watch—the family next door, the one on the floor below. But the lingering hours of night were daunting. I was continually on the alert. I knew when the deafening roar of the factory machinery would start, before daybreak; the hour that a certain train would rumble into the station; what time an enemy patrol would march along the nearby street.

I began to hate the little room where I stayed locked up all day. I went out only at dusk, losing myself in a crowd of homeward-bound workers. I knew I was being hunted, and I purposely broke contact with my comrades, because the enemy would not be content with my capture alone. The Gestapo and the U. P. I.[1] would hope that I would lead them to my fellow partisans. Therefore I imprisoned myself by choice, and did not see or speak with any of the other Gappisti. I gave myself only an hour each evening to walk in the open, with no goal in view. I tried to feel myself as one of the throng of people on the street, to rid myself of that loneliness that can lead to madness.

"At least prisoners are only in jail," I mused. "I am in a prison with unseen bars that cannot prevent the enemy from seizing me, putting me in a prison of stone and steel, then taking me out again to stand me before a firing squad." These were black thoughts. I felt tensions like none I had known in the past.

We partisans had known a period of triumph, had suffered losses ourselves. Now we were passing through a difficult time of lull. Our struggle with the enemy was not fought with bombs, pistols or machine guns alone. It had become a battle of nerves, a battle which one must win within himself first of all. The enemy had scored against us, but still feared us. A mere half-dozen Gappisti had forced the enemy headquarters, stations and barracks to protect themselves behind barbed wire and ramparts of sandbags, to double their guard details. The corps guards of the Fascists went at a nervous alert, fingers on their triggers, ready for a surprise attack at any moment, in any place, from any quarter. Though Di Nanni had died, though others were captured, the enemy feared us in force. Nobody on the Fascist side believed we were a mere handful.

"Why are we so few?" Di Nanni had often asked me. And what could I have answered? That in this city, our city, it was a new kind of battle? That there would be new replacements selected from the forces in the mountains? Now the few survivors, although temporarily inactive, and Dante Di Nanni, although forever at rest, were continuing to keep the unsuspecting enemy unaware of what was going on. The enemy was alarmed by this pause, which they attributed to preparations for one of our large-scale

---

1. Unione Popolare Italiana.

offensives. The Fascists and the Germans were reinforcing their defenses. And so I was not alone in feeling like a prisoner, I mused. Those Fascists and the Germans, behind the barbed wire, sandbags, and guards, were also prisoners, in their barracks and inside their commands. I felt less oppressed, almost relieved, with this realization.

As I lay in my bed one night, I heard a noise at the door. Still half asleep, I held my breath in order to hear better. Someone knocked. I cautiously rose from the bed, without making any noise, and approached the door. I could not see anything by looking through the hidden peep hole. They were still knocking. I finally saw two men, and succeeded in making out their faces. It was Dante Conti, with a comrade. I opened the door, Conti introduced me to "Augusto," who also had fought in Spain. He was an inspector attached to the command of the Garibaldini Brigade.

If Conti and Augusto were coming to see me at this time, there must be something important in the air. "The comrade will talk to you," said Conti, "I must go off." We said goodbye to one another. I already knew what Augusto was about to tell me.

"Do I have to leave the city?" I asked.

"Yes, and quickly. The Fascist police aren't playing blind man's buff any more. They are going through the adjoining zone with a sieve.

One time or another it had to happen. The Minister of Interior had intimidated the Prefect of Turin.

"They know that your battle name is Ivaldi," Augusto added. "It is better that you don't use it any more."

"Very well." Changing a name called for continuous control of conditioned reflexes. I had already had the experience. If someone had called me by my true name, I would not even have turned around. But how would I have reacted to a familiar voice?

"How long must I be away from Turin?"

"You won't have to be far away from Turin. You are to move to Milan to reorganize the Gappisti. Rosetta[2] will accompany you to the station. At Milan, you will go the Piazza Firenze where, at 11:30, a comrade whom you know will lead you to your base in Milan.

---

2. Wife of Gavaldo Negarville, whom I had known at Ventotene.

"So long and good luck." The door closed. Through the half-closed blind, I watched him walk away with quick confident steps. I was stunned. I could not think. I could only make the preparations necessary for my departure. Rosetta would carry my suitcase, packed with clothes, to the station for me.

"There isn't much to prepare for a Gappista's departure," I thought to myself. If I wanted to make the first train, I had to rush. Everything was ready. I left my room and knocked on the door of the Bossone family. I told them the news. They understood, but were sad that I had to go. I could not hide my own emotions. They were people who would have had to share my fate if the Fascists had ever found me.

"We shall see each other when Italy is free," I told them.

"We'll see you soon, then," they answered me.

Once again, I was riding in a war train. When I had boarded the train at Acqui to go to Turin, I had not yet experienced the sensation of being pursued. At the end of September 1943, I did not know that my nocturnal flight from my relatives' house, from the too-orderly city, from the vigilant eye of the police, was the beginning of an interminable course. At Acqui, for a short while, I had escaped being captured in a most casual fashion, when several agents of the police had informed the Republicans and the Germans of my actions. Whatever they had been, the police were not evil, but only weak cowards. I wondered whether it was right to attack them. These were times when all men lived in fear, when a foreigner, some unknown person, decided a man's fate.

Certainly, I thought, not all the police in the service of the Republicans were evil. But what difference did it make whether their character was good or bad, if they eventually became enemy spies? A man's conduct demonstrated the goodness of his soul after all.

In the compartment, facing me, sat several older people, two women, and a young boy. The train had begun its journey to Milan. I remembered the times when one could travel on speedy express or local trains in Spain. But the aerial bombardments, the mined bridges and the necessities of war had eliminated every distinction; all became local trains. I wondered what the train on which I was now traveling had been originally. Now, before coming to a curve or a bridge, it would stop. The old ladies, wrapped in shawls, would prepare to descend, but there would be no station. Many minutes would pass, and it was sometimes more than a half hour before the train would start up again.

It occurred to me that the police guards at the station were also fundamentally good men. They had remained in service, at the orders of the "Command." If they had been on their own, they would not have hurt anybody and would not have touched anything which did not belong to them. They wrote home to their mothers in the south through Red Cross channels. I pondered the strange things that happen in war. We were attacking Republican radio stations. The Fascists were not aware of this, but the carabinieri were on the watch. The carabinieri were not Fascists, and we wanted to save them, as we did the railroad workers. Instead, they gave the alarm. Yet they were not Fascists; they were good men. War certainly upset everything.

The train puffed along. Slowly, it was taking me away from the long months of struggle, away from Bravin, Di Nanni and others whom I had abandoned in some unknown cemetery—away from the people who loved me and who had risked their lives for me. They were people who, in normal times, would not have to feel inferior to anyone; good people who had nothing to gain from me, but everything to lose. Yet they had risked their lives to give me room and board, to hide the dynamite, the guns, the hand grenades, the fuses. This was something more than goodness. It was goodness full of justice in the most significant sense, a justice which compelled them to aid those who were defending their own destiny. In these factories, the destiny of two or three generations of workers was tied together. A son learned from his father what it meant to be a worker. He learned it without words. It was something that one could read in the faces of members of the same family, of the same block of houses. These thoughts confused me now. Fatigue and the pulsating rhythms of the train gradually lulled me to sleep. When I awoke a quarter of an hour later, we were in Milan.

Once again I looked at the ugly station from which I had departed for Ventotene, handcuffed along with other anti-Fascists. The city seemed to be full of shattered glass and looked sickly. The people bore an expression of those who, after a hurricane, were preparing themselves for something worse. They were carrying all their possessions with them, as if from one moment to the other they might lose everything. Many had already lost their homes and their families.

I arrived at Piazza Firenze. Since I was a quarter of an hour early for my appointment, I ordered a drink in a bar. Then, completely relaxed, I walked over toward a large sign which read, "Enlist in the X Mas."[3] I waited for the comrade whom I should recognize.

He arrived on a bicycle, and gave me the key word. I followed him, searching my memory for something to help me remember him. "You are Ghini," I said to him at last.

"Have you finally recognized me?" he asked.

"But which one of the twins are you?"

"What difference does it make?" he answered expressionlessly. "We are both fighters."

It was not an enthusiastic response, but this was not the time or the place for explanations. Ghini looked a little older than he had when they had handcuffed us together; he already had grey hair at that time. I had been very young when they took us to Ventotene, that remote forsaken island, where I would find something that existed nowhere else.

Our guards had dragged us down there, an isolated group. We had met; up to then unknown to one another, we soon had become firm friends.

It had been terrible to have no news of our loved ones, to be isolated from life, to end up in a forgotten and rocky island of the Mediterranean, even though it could be considered a sort of oasis. Those who had hoped for the "forgiveness of the Duce," had been isolated or had disappeared. The others stayed with us. I had dreamed of a Utopia, absolute equality, fraternity. I had found it there. It had been necessary to pay a high price, but that was true of everything worthwhile. We had been recluses, but men. Only a word, a little letter begging forgiveness, had been necessary to

---

3. Translator's note: X Mas (Decima Flottiglia Motoscafi Anti-Sommergibile: Tenth Torpedo-boat Flotilla) was a Republican contingent consisting originally of several hundred marines, under the command of Junio Valerio Borghese, a dashing young officer dedicated to the alliance with the Germans. It was later converted to a commando land unit with its headquarters in Milan.

gain a Saturday morning on the mainland. Since there was a space
of only several square yards in the tombs, everyone of us who remained on the island begged for conditional liberty on the mainland. When a package arrived, each of us divided it with our comrades, divided it with joy, because the happiness of our comrades
had been the most precious thing for us all. It was difficult for me
to vocalize, even to understand what one had left during the tremendous suffering of internment. We had all been of clear conscience, and brothers, too.

* * * * *

The memory of Ventotene was inextricably bound to memories
of the last days of the anti-Fascist resistance in Spain. In July 1938,
our resistance on the Ebro prevented Franco's forces from advancing for several months. Although they had encountered light skirmishes with patrols between April and June along the broad Spanish river, there was no reason why the Franco forces would not
have tried to cross it. They were well-armed, well-equipped and
their divisions well-trained. As for us, after several weeks of con-
structing defenses and training the Brigades, we were ready to hold
back the enemy offensive. We were very sure that some day soon
the Franco forces would show themselves beyond the river. The
appearance of the assault troops would not have surprised us.

What did surprise us, however, was our Command's amass-
ment of boats, cannon, mortars, machine guns, and heavy weapons.
The policy seemed to be "We shall not await the enemy; we shall
attack." The Spanish Lister Division, waiting in the woods, was
ready to unleash an offensive on the Ebro. The Garibaldi Brigade
would enter the battle as soon as it began. Advance patrols were
increased and advance posts were set up beyond the river to capture prisoners and reconnoiter the positions of the enemy troops.
Big developments were looming ahead; the first sign was the amazing speed with which our engineers threw the footbridge across
the river.

It was fifteen minutes past midnight July 25, 1938; the first
Republican soldiers had crossed the footbridge and made contact
with the enemy. Boats followed, carrying more soldiers across.
There were other bridges which supported and flanked the first
bridgehead; thousands of Republican soldiers were soon on enemy
ground. It was already daybreak when our artillery opened fire.

The surprise element was the key to our action. Perhaps for the first time in the history of modern warfare, a grand offensive had not been preceded by a barrage of artillery fire. Here, on the Ebro, in the largest battle of the entire Civil War, the infantry had advanced with no such support. The first detachment had pushed the advance elements of the enemy from their entrenchments. Our artillery was hitting distant targets. We had already penetrated several miles into enemy territory. The enemy guns were beginning to slow down their counterfire. The Garibaldi Brigade awaited orders, to join in this offensive phase in which it had not participated.

The battle increased considerably when the Fascists ascertained that the Ebro had been crossed, not by the usual patrols, but by troops in force. Even after having been spotted, these troops continued to advance decisively. We of the Garibaldi Brigade witnessed the aerial encounters taking place on the other side of the river. New Republican divisions were constantly moving in front of us; they crossed the river in boats and moved ahead.

The wounded who were coming back across the river told us of the outcome of the encounter. The first day, the Republican offensive concluded with the consolidation of conquered positions. The Fascists held all the hydroelectric plants of the zone, including the reservoirs and the dams of the Ebro tributaries, Ciurana, Nughera-Pallaresa, Noguero-Ribagozzana and Segre; they could increase the flow of the Ebro current from eight-tenths of a meter to six meters a second, or they could raise the water level. They opened the dams of the reservoirs in the surrounding area of Zaragoza, making the level of the Ebro tributaries rise a meter and a half. This increased the impetus of the current, and our bridges were swept away.

The second day of the offensive passed, and then the third, without the participation of our Brigade. The wounded and the couriers brought news of the bitterness of the battles, the hand-to-hand fighting, the villages conquered house-by-house, heights taken, lost, and then regained by assault. We still remained inactive.

Strange rumors started to circulate. Some said that the International Brigade would be demobilized and would have to abandon the struggle. The attempt of the Republican government to deactivate the foreign troops carried the implication of a counteraction. With our exclusion from the fighting, the war would be decided only by the Spaniards. An order to pack our knapsacks and fall back to a position behind the lines seemed to confirm this rumor.

We began our retreat at dawn. After fifteen miles, we stopped near a wood, pitched our tents, and awaited mess call. We were disheartened; our fight in Spain was finished; we would have to consign our arms to the Spanish authorities and leave.

Toward evening, the order came to return to the front lines immediately. Finally!

On September 5, 1938,[4] the battle grew more and more bitter. There was fighting on the ground and in the sky. The field fortifications were inadequate; they were being continuously bombarded by Franco's bombs and shells. Low-flying planes machinegunned them. The artillery hammered at our positions incessantly. We went to the attack five times in ten hours; after advancing yard by yard we reached the top of a hill and held it for an hour. Then the Franco forces attacked by the thousands, and we had to engage in hand-to-hand fighting in order to drive them back.

The next day, we remained among the twisted trunks of the olive trees. Desolation reigned in this arid, barren land. The Franco forces occupied hill 416, which dominated the countryside from Mora d'Ebro to Gandena. The battle grew more furious, and formations were disrupted. I found myself near several Garibaldini of the second battalion who, for some reason, were fighting in the sector of the fifth. The commandant shouted the order to attack for the fifth time, and again we leaped from our holes and rushed together, both fifth and second battalions, against the barricade of fire. The Commandant, Rubini, wounded during the attack, had fallen, and was urging his men to go ahead. A flood of news came through. The fourth battalion had conquered hills 362 and 363; the Garibaldini had had to abandon hill 413; the commander of the third battalion Mario Berti, was dead; the commissars of the Macarion company, Lopez and Fecchini, had fallen; so had the aide of the first battalion, Mario Perez Rasina. Mario Rulgenzi, vice com-

---

4. The Garibaldi Brigade was commanded on the Ebro front first by Alessandro Vaia, then by Luis Rivas, with Emilio Suardi as political commissioner.

missar of the brigade, who had come to Spain from Argentina, was dead. It could be said that the Garibaldi Brigade was his creation.

When the Franco forces attacked the next day, we succeeded in repulsing them. Their artillery fired incessantly. We abandoned hills 409, 421, and 455. Reinforcements arrived and we went to the attack again, led by Commandant Vacchini, who shouted over and over, "Long live the Republic!" There was an explosion of grenades, and a Garibaldino fell a few yards from me, shouting, "I am hit! I am hit!" But in that inferno, no one could answer his cry. Too many wounded fell, too many cries for help were drowned out by the explosions. The fourth battalion succeeded in conquering hill 368. An avalanche of armed vehicles stopped us. We counter-attacked again. The Franco forces withdrew. Their artillery resumed firing.

On September 8, I again joined the offensive, bayonet extended. During a Franco attack we left the trenches and met the enemy face-to-face. I closed my eyes at the precise moment when I saw the bayonet of a Franco soldier pointed at my chest. I charged him, holding my weapon in front of me. I felt the impact of my bayonet as it drove into an obstacle. Reopening my eyes, I saw him kneeling, with my bayonet transfixing his neck. He was staring at me with his mouth wide open uttering not a sound.

The assault continued. Faleschini, a commandant, succeeded in setting up a machine gun which held back the second wave of Fascists, permitting us to advance and reach hill 467. Faleschini was hit as he was urging on his men. The Fascists fired incessantly upon hill 467 and returned to the assault. We fought for hours on end against the waves of infantry. Hill 467 was lost.[5] Violent encounters took place around hill 356, which was held by our fourth battalion. We resisted one attack after another without yielding one yard of ground to the Fascists. They shot at everything that moved, including the orderlies, and even the stretcher-bearers.

Hill 356 was still ours that evening. Orders arrived for the first battalion of the Garibaldini and a battalion of the Fourteenth Brigade to recapture hill 467; the assault groups of the two formations crept along in the darkness to within a few yards of the Franco trenches. Then they leaped ahead, throwing grenades. They were

---

5.   While he was directing the fire of his machine gunners at hill 467, Joseph Boretti, a student from Milan, died.

followed by the main forces of the two battalions. The Fascists abandoned the field; hill 467 was again in our hands.

At dawn the next day, we still had not slept. The Fascists had resumed their artillery fire. The ground was broken up with craters. The battalions fought together; even the sappers and scouts held guns in their hands. We heard a shout, "Reinforcements are arriving!" At the base of the hill a group of Garibaldini attempted the climb. It was detected by the enemy and hammered with bombs. The battered group reached the summit of the hill. The Fascists fought back fiercely on hill 471; our men defended it for hours on end, but we received neither reinforcements nor replacements, and were forced to abandon it. One-half hour later, we received the order to recapture the hill.

During the night of September 10, there was the sudden illumination of gun fire. Only one of us, overtaken by fatigue, succeeded in catching a few winks of sleep. At dawn, we attacked hill 471 for the umpteenth time. Our weakened formations bogged down on the slope. The battle continued without respite for two days. Guido Bernini, political commissar of the second battalion, was killed. Giovanni Baesi, one of the first Italians in Spain to fight the Franco forces, was also dead. Condemned by a Fascist tribunal, he had been sent from one prison to another; in exile, he had gone wandering in France, Belgium and Luxemburg. Could one say that he found his peace in Spain?

We attacked hill 471 again the next day. It was littered with the dead and wounded. During a period of calm on September 12, we buried the dead, who were putrifying under the sun. Our patrols had reported new concentrations of enemy troops. From one moment to the next, we expected a major offensive.

The next day, the enemy broke loose all along the front, using both artillery and aviation. We fought in a cloud of black smoke. It seemed impossible that men could survive in the heat of this inferno. Enemy infantry ran to the assault. But there was always some one with a machine gun firing against the advancing tide. Even the wounded, those who still could use their arms and legs, joined the fighting. The survivors in the second and third companies of the second battalion, and those in the assault groups of Lieutenant Emilio Rodriguez, had resisted for three consecutive hours an enemy that was twenty times as strong. Guns, airplanes, machine guns, armed vehicles—all were thrown into the assault against hills 440 and 450, which were being held by the second battalion, now reduced to one company. An enemy force had infiltrated the valley, going along the Fattarella road, in an attempt to capture hills 480 and 496; the third company of the third battalion did not wait for them, but moved up to face them and chased them back. That day was the turn of the first company of the second battalion, commanded by Lieutenant Carlo Pegolo; the Garibaldini had held hill 435 for a day and a night, under the concentrated fire of the enemy artillery. We had repulsed the constant assaults without the help of any other formation of the Brigade. When night fell, hill 435 was still resisting; the Garibaldini were defending it without cartridges, without bombs. After the Fascists' last bayonet assault, six surviving Garibaldini went forward with bayonets extended against the enemy, who was moving ahead in the night. The others were all dead.

The next morning, even before the sun was high in the sky; the enemy artillery had already resumed firing. Their airplanes reappeared and rained their bombs. In the distance, we saw a man under a shower of shots from an anti-tank gun running toward us. He fell, rose again, and resumed running. It was one of our couriers. He was worn out and exhausted, but not wounded. He brought orders to evacuate. Just then, a grenade explosion threw me to earth. I was suffocating. I could barely draw a breath. Near me lay a dead man; the grenade had killed the courier. That night, I found myself in an infirmary overflowing with wounded men. I met Menegazzo, commissioner of company of the second battalion, who had lain for two days in no man's land until his own Garibaldini were able to rescue him, still under fire. Now they were standing around his bed excusing themselves for not having been able to rescue him earlier.

Twenty-four hours later, they transported me to the old hospital in the city of Barcelona. Terrible news reached me here. After one week of furious attacks, the Fascists had broken through the Ebro front at several points. In spite of the fact that they were encircled, the Garibaldini, with their bayonets, repulsed the Fascist forces wherever they had infiltrated.[6] But the following day,

---

6. Amongst the fighters of the battle of the Ebro, I remember Ferraresi, Zanella, Carini, Nicoletto Sacenti, Gruni, Spadelini, Poma, Rossi, Zazzetto,

September 22, the President of the Council, Negrin, speaking at Geneva, asked for the withdrawal of all foreign volunteer troops.

As it turned out, only the International Brigade would be withdrawn. This plan of Negrin was of no advantage to the Republic. On the contrary, it hastened the end. I left the hospital several days later in time to participate in the big withdrawal of the Brigades from Barcelona. It was the last moving salute to Spain. Then the Fascists advanced on Barcelona, and the city was evacuated in an atmosphere of chaos, in the middle of the night, in the darkened streets, midst the outcries and screams of women and babies. Groups of soldiers, worn out and exhausted by tension, and left behind by the rear guard, organized a precarious line of defense while the Fascists airplanes bombed the city at random.

On the morning of January 26, we were assembled in the square of a small town. Giuliano Pajetta and Luigi Longo arrived. They had seen Franco's soldiers massacre civilians in flight. Longo asked us to resume fighting again to protect the civilians. Shooting echoed on the square.

From here began our fight up to the border. For two days, the Garibaldini and other Republican forces lent all their troops to the counterattack in order to prevent the Fascists from slaughtering the unarmed multitudes in their flight. The French finally opened the frontier to the refugees; the civilians passed through first, followed by us soldiers, after we had fired our last shots against the enemy. Civilians and soldiers then found themselves thrown together in the French concentration camps. But fortunately, I succeeded in escaping and jumped aboard a train. I traveled for the entire day, avoiding inspectors, and, finally in the evening arrived at Grand Combe. I was home again, but was imbued with a deep feeling of humiliation.

Hundreds of thousands of lives had been sacrificed. If the great democracies had not stood by silently watching while the generals and traitors, aided by Hitler and Mussolini, were massacring the Spanish people, the Fascists would not have been able

---

Talari, Boretti, Ferrer, Cerio, Allari, Zucchella, Ronzano, Vacchieri, Ponza, Montamari, Vergari, Bellucci, Manini, Fachini, Vincenzo Sposito, Antonio Gruden, Galli, Mario Romei, Bianchi, Benatti, Umberto Negri. I remember Mehmet Shehu, the actual President of the Council of the Popular Republic of Albania.

to move on toward the conquest of all of Europe. Now everything seemed finished.

At Grand Combe, I looked for a job to provide some income and to help my mother and brothers. While the dictators were delivering their last blows, I lived from day to day. I found a small job, but I quickly lost it through the intervention of the Commissioner of Police. My French identity card expired, and I could not get it renewed. I had to report to the Commissioner every day. When World War II broke out, my situation got worse. There was a security prison in France for the Communists. I secretly crossed over one more frontier and reached Turin. For some months I succeeded in covering my tracks from the Fascist police. They arrested me on March 23, 1940. After long questioning, they transported me to Alessandria. Italy. On June 10, while I was stretched out on my cot reading, I was told that Mussolini had declared war on France. Six months later, I was taken from prison and interned on the island of Ventotene. There, the company was good, for I found Terracini, Soccimarro, Secchia, Roveda, Frausin, Camilla Ravera, Spinelli, Ernesto Rossi, LiCausi, Pertini, Bauer, Curiel, Ghini, and others. Eventually, Longo, DiVittorio, Bardini, Alberganti, Carni, and many others arrived from the French concentration camps. For me, a new education was beginning.

✿   ✿   ✿   ✿   ✿

All these memories came back to me, as I was placing Ghini's face. "What will happen afterward?" I asked myself, now thinking about the present war. It might turn out as it had at Ventotene—one for all, all for one—or it might end, as it had in the Risorgimento, with the Garibaldino, Crispi,[7] ordering bloody repressions in Sicily; or with the Garibaldino, Bixio,[8] who drowned on a ship with a load of slaves; or with the Garibaldino exiled on Caprera,[9] or the many Garibaldini disarmed, condemned, vilified.

---

7. Translator's note: Francesco Crispi (1819-1901), Sicilian, member of Garibaldi's "Expedition of the Thousand" (Laspedizione dei Mille), which invaded Sicily in 1860 during the Risorgimento, and led to the unification of present-day Italy. He later became Prime Minister (Aug. 1887-Feb.1891) (Dec. 1893-Mar.1896).

8. Translator's note: Nino Bixio (1821-1873). Garibaldi second-in-command with the Expedition of the Thousand (see note 7 above).

9. Translator's note: Giuseppe Garibaldi, himself.

"Where are we going?" I asked Ghini.

"We still have ten minutes to wait for the others," was his answer.

"He doesn't trust me," I thought. "Was Ventotene in another world?"

## CHAPTER 9
# Milan

Ghini's manner was cold, detached, impersonal. He seemed to have forgotten all about our captivity together at Ventotene. His face was stern and rigid, like that of a soldier on duty. What little he said seemed unpleasantly cold. It was as though he reminded me that the war was too brutal for any possibility of sympathy between men of the opposing forces.

The laws of underground warfare were iron-clad; any relaxation of vigilance brought danger that could be fatal. But one bit of news warmed my heart. The first group of Gappisti in Milan had covered themselves with glory.[1] They had killed a Militia graduate on November 7, 1943, at the beginning of the guerrilla war. They had attacked a Wehrmacht rest home and had disposed of three spies—Gerolamo Crivelli, industrialist of Monza, the clerk Primiero Lamperti, and Piero de Angeli, the ill-fated informer in the Caproni organization. All had been responsible for many arrests and executions.

Their operations in Milan had culminated in the execution of

1. The first GAP Brigade was commanded by Rubini, Commissioner Bardini, head of the Roda General Staff; also in the Brigade were DiSella, Oreste Ghirotti, Arturo Capettini, Eugene DeRosa, Antonio Gentili, Vito Antonio, Lafrata, Aline Zanta, Giuseppe Sapda, Vincenze Zantu, Panariello, Amos, Sergio Bani, Cesare Bescape, Alfonso Galasi, Carlo and Delio Milanesi, Licinio Piccardi, Giovanni Valtolini, Zerbini, Ruggero Brambilla, Mendel, Bruno Clapir, Gianni, Dino Manfredi, Pozze, Angelo Giacometti, Alfonso Cuffaro, Paole Cappelletti, Alde Mirotti, Angelo Valagussa, Giuseppe Clerici, Pompeo Recchia, Barbireni, Luigi Seresini, Remo Terri, Antonio Zacchetti, Luigi Zontini, Giulie Abbiati, and Arnaldo Zanca.

the Fascist party official, Rasegna, on December 18, 1943. Then
bloody retaliatory measures had begun. Rasegna's death had been
avenged by the shooting of nine patriots held at San Vittori. Care-
less, overconfident behavior had made the Gappisti pay dearly
for their deeds. Rubini[2] was arrested. The Fascists knew him as
a veteran of the fighting in Spain, commander of a Maquis formation in France and recruiter of young Milanese patriots into the
GAP forces. They tortured him mercilessly. They pulled out his
fingernails, tore away his hair by handfuls, and used a red-hot
iron to reopen, one by one, the scars of wounds he had suffered in
Spain. When he fainted, they left him in his cell, then returned to
inflict more tortures. But it was too late. He had revived and, sum-
moning his feeble strength, had torn his sheet into strips and tied
the strips into a long cord. Tying this to the bars of his cell, he
had hanged himself.

All this Ghini told me, bleakly and bluntly, in ten minutes.
The conclusions were clear; we must set up a new organization.
At last Ghini pointed to a radio equipment store.

"Giorgio is waiting for you there," he said, and strode away.

I entered the store. My blood ran cold as ten big, reckless
boys came out of the back room and one said loudly, "Are you the
new commander of the GAP? Are you the one who led the Gappisti in Turin?"

In horror I looked behind me at the door. Anyone else entering from the street would have been amazed at that strange, loud
assemblage. But these were not times when customers besieged a
radio equipment store; even bars were seldom frequented.

Roughly, I pushed the boys back into the rear room and followed them through the door and closed it.

"Give me the telephone number," I said curtly. "Who is my
contact?"

"Diego," they said, and gave his last name, too, too loudly for
my taste. Undoubtedly, they were brave and loyal, but the way
they threw caution to the winds made me tremble.

"Wait for a telephone call," I said, going out again.

"We'll see you soon. Good luck."

One followed me to the threshold, and I paused to admonish

---

2. Egidio Rubino, born in Molinella, November 1, 1906.

him. "You fellows are crazy," I said. "Use some caution if you don't want to fall right into the hands of the enemy."

I went away, using every trick to avoid being followed. My heart sank as I thought how easily the enemy could introduce spies into the ranks of that young pack. Perhaps a spy had already joined them. I spent two quiet days finding an apartment as my new base. I toured the city, comparing it to Turin. Germans and Fascists were there in plenty, but they circulated boldly, even carelessly, as though they felt secure.

I telephoned Diego, giving him my new battle name, Visone, and made an appointment several days ahead, saying I would confirm it only at the last moment. I also asked to meet Secchia on the Via Nino Bixio, and went to await him.

Secchia approached, carrying a leather bag and walking casually like a man on some business errand. He peered at me through his spectacles as I told him of my disapproval of the situation at the radio shop.

"It's something to worry about," he agreed, and I felt relieved at that. "But you see, dear Visone, it is for just this reason that we called you to Milan. Finding and mobilizing men is as dangerous as handling dynamite. You'll have to use all your experience and all possible discretion."

I must start, then, from the beginning. But we could not leave Milan undisturbed in enemy hands. I went to meet Diego, and asked him if I could count on him and his men for active service.

"I can guarantee it," he replied. "All my boys are ready."

"Do you know them well?"

"Of course," and he laughed heartily. "We are all friends. We live on the same block or in the same neighborhood, and we have known each other since childhood." I had hoped that this would be the case, but it also had its negative aspects. All friends, all neighbors: and so, the capture of one could bring the Fascists directly upon the entire group. I would have to put them to the test. I asked Diego to have his group perform certain tasks which were not excessively complicated. We agreed to meet again in a few days.

The choice of the meeting place was preceded by a thorough examination of the possibilities of escape in case of ambush. Again, I verified that Diego was not being followed by police or suspicious looking persons. We shook hands and sat at a small table in a bar. "The boys are happy that you trust them. As a matter of fact, they have enlisted others already."

"But have you had any experience up to now?" I interrupted him. It was evident from his reddened face that "his boys" had not executed anything together. Actually, I had known this when I had seen him coming with his cordial manner and smile. No one smiled like that after having engaged in a serious action.

I had to make a radical decision. I felt that these people represented a danger to themselves as well as to others. It would take several months and many tragic experiences before they were properly trained for underground warfare. I faced him with this.

"Diego, you don't have to answer. I know very well that you have not worked together on anything. You all are undoubtedly anti-Fascists, but you have not yet grasped the difference between a partisan formation and a band of idealistic young boys. You believe that the Germans are like the neighboring team with whom you trade punches. But war is not a joke, and this war is the most serious of all."

I had sized him up well. He was inexperienced, a bit of a braggart, but not a fool. He accepted my proposition—to go "get some practice" with the partisans. He took his friends to an area on the other side of the Po, near Pavia, where they were soon organized into a formation. They distinguished themselves in several encounters. In one of these, while protecting the withdrawal of their own groups in a skirmish with the Germans, Diego fell, fighting gallantly.

After that meeting, I had to make contact with groups of patriots who could start acting immediately in the city. It was a difficult and heavy task, but a fruitful one.

Not far from Milan, at Mazzo, a little town near Rho, I experienced one of the most pleasant surprises that a guerrilla organizer could hope for. I discovered a group of young men who had already done military service and had a keen knowledge of arms and explosives. They were commanded by a courageous and decisive junior officer, Balzarotti. They had not, thus far, been pursued during their activities.

When I joined them, I found them all together on a large farm, and I realized that they had a guard system. I did not succeed in seeing where the guards were placed, but I presumed that they were in the trees.

These young men were a heartening discovery. They inspired trust from the first moment. I spoke to them about the necessity of getting an operation underway immediately, and then I listened to what they had to say. We did not brag to one another. Balzarotti spoke like a responsible person; he had already fought, had seen death at close hand and did not talk nonsense. He was, however, perplexed by the concept of a Gappist action. It was a type of combat that was completely new to him and his men. Others of the group, which was made up of about a dozen people, spoke. They were all lively, intelligent types, but they had been trained in a very different kind of warfare. They had set up their combat force, and they were ready. They possessed arms and explosives, and they knew how to use them. When would they go into action? They were awaiting the opportune moment to exploit their particular organization and their enthusiasm. This moment would be at the time of a general insurrection. I knew the political atmosphere of the Valle Olona. I knew that was the source of their attitude, and that their combative spirit must impel them to action without hesitation. But these boys' attitude of waiting was hardly helpful. They wanted to act, but they did not know how to get moving.

"But who will initiate the insurrection?" I asked. "Who will set the example? And what good is an army which lies in wait while the enemy oppresses, hangs, and destroys people?"

I did not wait for an answer; the question answered itself. The political climate of the zone, the influence and prestige of the believers in the "wait and see" attitude had paralyzed action. It was necessary to minimize this influence. Then the results would come.

I suggested they they go to Milan. I thought they would prefer this kind of solution. They would be operating far from their own territory and away from the inevitable supervision which the enemy imposed over such a little settlement; they would have greater freedom of movement, and probably less anxiety. Several of them consented to follow me. Several days later, we found ourselves in the city.

The results were disastrous. They were ill-at-ease in the large city; they did not know how to find their way. When I returned with them to Mazzo, I realized that their familiarity with their own environment could be a useful factor in confronting the enemy. They knew all the paths, little roadways, and hiding places; they confidently followed dried-up ditches and paths across the fields. They seemed to possess a special compass, so strong and precise was their sense of orientation in the countryside.

The problem was to set them an example. After participating in some operation, these boys would have need for only a little direction. I began the second phase in my relations with this group: emphasizing the necessity of scrupulous vigilance and accurate organization. First it was necessary to divide the formation into squads, for more agility.

After each meeting with these young men, I would return to Milan feeling quite comforted. Their number was increasing, but the enrollments were the result of selection. The young men of Mazzo now constituted three squads, and they subdivided their areas of operation. This preparatory work had brought on discussions, talks and political debates in which all the young men had taken eager part.

Now I had to show them that the tactic of "wait and see" had little value from a military point of view, and, above all, to demonstrate that action was always possible. It was difficult to convey this idea. Drilled for combat, these young men did not understand guerrilla warfare.

During my persuasive attempts, I found an ally, a young sapper. He was splendidly trained in the exigencies of guerrilla warfare, especially from the psychological, rather than technical, point of view.

Almost all the boys were peasants; their origins made them particularly adapted to partisan warfare. In his relations with the administrator of land, the peasant lived in inferior conditions just as he did when faced with living in the city. Subjected to the demands of the boss, restricted to work which required no education or instruction, he soon acquired the habit of stealth. For centuries he had existed outside the conventional order. This reflection, which seemed presumptuous, had its counterpart in reality; the rapidity with which these boys adapted themselves to underground warfare was due in no small measure to their peasant origins. "We won't have to wait too long to see the results," I said to myself.

And so the moment came to get down to essentials. Their innate secretiveness and their familiarity with the area would be put to good use when combined with a real desire to fight. Now was the time to bring to them the reality of combat, to move into action, something so different from that which they had known.

The operation to be undertaken was to explode two grids of electric energy. This involved the problem of handling the explosives and determining the appropriate nerve centers of the electric system. A shack which was being used to store agricultural tools was selected as the rendezvous.

When I would depart from one of my bases for that shack, I would tell no one its location. Not one of the men, even if tortured, would be able to reveal that address, which served as a stopping-off place and refuge for comrades. In secret warfare, one always has to anticipate the worst possible situations. The young men of Mazzo seemed to share my attitude. Unlike city boys, they never asked any questions other than those of a political or tactical nature. They never asked me where I had slept or eaten. They avoided questions which would have necessitated an elusive answer.

Realizing that secret warfare was not made up of military action alone, I talked with the boys one by one, in order to instill this awareness in them. There were those who had come from farms, who had a solid compact strength. The training for war seemed a mere preparation for a force which could last forever. There were students, the sons of clerks and well-off peasants, who were animated by a feverish anxiety, by a fervent hope. The farm boys fell naturally into underground warfare, through a sort of political gravitation. Perhaps this was because the peasant had nothing but his family and his work; he felt free and at ease on the land; it was the only thing in the world that did not deceive him. The boys who had gone to higher grades in school had a different feeling about the fight against Fascism. For them, the fight was against the "bad African business" and the imperial influence. This contact between students and peasants seemed to me extraordinarily promising, but I did not want to lose sight of the military objectives.

Several of the young men were not cautious enough around the shack; they raised their voices, they allowed their Sten guns to glisten in the sun. There was a restless air of nocturnal movements. I hastened to point out that guerrilla warfare had its own discipline, its own style, and that from the earliest moment it was necessary to use every possible precaution to avoid surprises.

It was up to Balzarotti to lead us toward the objective. The boys were silent. Balzarotti moved with ease; he gave a low whistle and the young men lined up; he nodded to one of the boys, and he ran to call two other boys. All three marched ahead, like an exploring patrol. We followed the dried-up bed of a ditch, walking rapidly in silence. When I stumbled, I always found a strong hand ready to support me. The boys moved like cats in the ditch, which was full of pebbles and holes. The group stopped; Balzarotti gestured silent orders. We left the ditch and went toward open ground. Two of the boys crawled on the ground toward some bushes, then signalled us to follow. The entire group moved ahead on the open ground, following an almost invisible path.

These young men really impressed me. They were on their way to execute an extremely risky mission; their manner was that of crack soldiers. It was pitch black; the path had disappeared from view. We passed through a hedge and found ourselves in the middle of a low wooded area. We had arrived at our destination. Balzarotti sent out the guards, checked on those assigned to protect the withdrawal, and on the two boys who would execute the action.

The electric energy grids stood out in the field. Now a little nervousness circulated among the boys. This was their first operation. Two boys seemed to hesitate; the others looked at them anxiously. Balzarotti intervened with calm, normal tones, repeating the directions which they had already known for some time. This familiarity relieved their minds. They started off.

A little afterwards, we saw two reddish flames. The pylons had been mined. Balzarotti ordered the withdrawal. The group moved expertly into the night. I shook Balzarotti's hand. Now it was my turn. I had to join Grassi for the operation on the tracks, disrupt enemy communications.

Balzarotti turned me over to a young man who would be my guide. He was about to jump out of the ditch, to walk out into the open ground, when I quickly grabbed him, holding him back at the edge. Several seconds passed, then two violent explosions lit up the night and made the air vibrate. We quickly started on our way, following unimaginable paths as short cuts.

While the enemy was pursuing the group, I went in the opposite direction toward the tracks. I arrived at the rendezvous, a water trough at the foot of a huge tree. Grassi, an imposing and massive man, joined me. The sky was very clear; every sound could be heard from afar in the deep silence. At the tracks, a shadow approached. I raised my gun, but Grassi caught my arm. It was a soldier, a Czech, who had deserted the Wehrmacht and whom Grassi had encountered earlier. The Czech was supposed to have been far away from there, but not having understood all of Grassi's gestures, he had not succeeded in finding the farm where he was to have been hidden. He followed us.

Grassi carried two cases of explosives. At the road bed, we laid them across the track, attaching the detonator with mercury. I looked at my watch; we still had ten minutes to wait. After a last minute inspection, a last minute test, we sped away. We could hear the ever more distinct whistle of the train coming from Milan. The explosions went off punctually; an unbelievable noise accompanied the flashes of the explosion. We quickened our step.

The enemy, as we had expected, was on the alert from the earlier assault. They shouted and fired; we heard the barking of dogs. Grassi led me and the Czech. To our right, an intermittent light indicated the way. It was the signal marking a safe course, set up by Balzarotti. That man was born for our sort of warfare, I thought, as we hurried along. He and his people had united in an age-old vocation. The cunning of the peasant, his natural resourcefulness against the tyranny of those in power, were now set in action. Balzarotti, born and living in a rural environment, knew all the tricks of conspiracy. He had arranged the withdrawal at the most opportune moment. A signal from a distant window indicated a safe route. We split up. Our first action had been a success. Now we must plan and execute others.

Some days later, facing the reality of the situation, I disregarded guerrilla tactics and consented to a meeting with Balzarotti's boys. We all met in the stable of a large farm house.

After a few words, Balzarotti deferred to me. First I praised their courage and decisiveness. "If you want me to be frank with you," I said, "I expected the courage, astuteness, decision and acceptance of risk that you showed. I congratulate you for the way you came through." They were happy. They were grateful for my having watched every step they had made, minute by minute, while waiting, on the march, in action, and in withdrawal. It was then that they realized how close we actually were. They opened their hearts, besieging me with questions. They wanted to know everything. They sought information with desperate intensity—what the prospects for the future would be after the defeat of the Germans and Fascists—what would happen tomorrow. They wanted to understand clearly, not only whom they fought, but why they fought him.

Their questions were at first cautious, and rather naive. Then they became more explicit. What was the final objective of the struggle? What ideals had inspired the first fighters in the War of Liberation? What had been their inner thoughts?

Before answering them, I asked myself who these boys were. I looked at them one by one; every face reflected a specific situation, a family environment, a definite experience. The students had at one time accepted the Fascist doctrine, won over by the concept of imperial greatness. The glitter had worn off; they had rediscovered the wisdom of their fathers, whereby one fought valiantly against an enemy who made oppression his credo. However, the students did not wish to risk their lives against aggression of a different nature.

It was true here, as it had been in Spain, that one does not fight without faith, without an ideal. I had to answer.

It was a difficult answer to give, because every one of us thought of our country's future in a different way. I had to present a simple concept that would unite them for the threatening struggle at hand.

"We are like a family faced by a fire which is threatening to destroy our home," I said. "Before thinking of how to cultivate the garden, we must put out the fire." But this was not enough. I had to find a language which would convey proof of loyalty. What did they want, what did they fear? I did not know, and I could not find out now. Their eyes were fixed upon me; they were the clear eyes of honest and courageous people, of Italians who were fighting with the same simplicity with which they worked in the fields or factories. I could have been talking to my companions of long ago in Spain, to the "muchachitos," or to my dear brothers in the mines of Grand Combe. These were the same people that one always found on the front lines of strikes, and in any struggle for liberty.

Suddenly I felt that the truth had suddenly exploded within me. "This war began for many reasons," I said. "It is a war that the government did not declare at the outset, because the government disappeared. Every Italian who has lined up with us and is in agreement with us has declared war. There are those who have declared war against the Germans because they have seen our brothers locked in cattle cars; there are those who have declared war on the Fascists because they are servants of the Germans; there are those who hated the Germans from the other war; there are those who hate them now. There are those who are fighting this war because they are sick and tired of the arrogance of the Fascist Party and want to think for themselves; there are those who cannot stand being pushed around by the people in power, and who see themselves deprived of dignity and freedom. But to fight against all this means to fight to create something different; an Italy without Germans and without Fascists, an Italy where the people can think in their own way and not be forced to give the Roman salute before the Republican guards. We want another Italy, without Black Shirts, without cudgels. We want an Italy whose citizens' opinions are respected, no matter what they are. We are fighting Fascism and all the lies which it represents so that they will disappear forever. The principal problem is to be united in combat in order to create this new Italy."

A thin, pale boy spoke up. "I am Catholic, and I would like to explain my situation," he said.

"What is it?" I asked.

"The situation is that I am Catholic."

I sensed the implied question. "Does it seem to you," I asked, "that Catholicism is respected today with the gallows of the Black Brigades on the squares, or would not the tenets of your religion be better carried out tomorrow, in freedom and peace?"

"But you, you Communists, what will you do?" It was the question which was in everyone's mind; the question which was asked in every family, the question upon which the enemy speculated.

"Today, we are fighting murderers, we are fighting so that the slaughter of the innocent will end. We are fighting because man has dignity, and the dignity of one man is not dissimilar to that of another. We are fighting against arrogance, against lying, against the oppression by Fascist leaders, who are the incarnations of the tryants of yesterday. I am not Catholic, but I respect you and those who think like you because you care about the simple people, freedom for the poor, dignity for the downtrodden. What more eloquent or convincing words can I give you than these which I speak today on behalf of every one of my party comrades?"

I wondered afterwards where I had found the inspiration for these concepts. Perhaps in Romain Rolland, or perhaps in the discovery that the world of these boys was, in spite of its dissimilarities, the same as that of the French mines and the Spanish trenches.

The Milan-Turin turnpike was, at that time, filled with long columns of German and Fascist military vehicles. Whenever the flow of trucks increased, large mopping-up operations took place in the Piedmont valleys. The highway served as a route for the men of the SS, and of the X Mas, to move to the fighting zone. They were the ones who built the gallows in the mopped-up areas. If we could interrupt and hinder traffic on this turnpike, we would decrease enemy pressure on our mountain formations and hinder the Nazi-Fascists' projects.

There were already some signs that our first effort had had its effect. A curfew had been imposed for 8 o'clock. The stores had to close at six, this had an important effect upon the city, and was useful to us.

We had an advantage over the enemy: the choice of time and place.

The squad commanded by Balzarotti and Political Commissar Cremascoli was lying in ambush along the highway. When an enemy machine passed by, two of their boys, dressed in the uniform of the "Muti"[3] rotated their flashlight, as though at a road block.

---

3. Translator's note: The Muti were a group of crack Fascist police, named after Ettore Muti, former Fascist Party Secretary and Fascist resistance leader after Mussolini's fall from power on July 25, 1943. Muti was mysteriously shot to death on August 24, 1943, at Fregene. After his death, he became a Fascist legend of heroism and martyrdom.

Three other partisans were hidden on the ground, in the open, with guns pointed.

The wait was not long. The hum of the motor, followed by the faint gleam of the dimmed headlights, announced the approach of a German military car. Cremascoli waved his flashlight for a halt. The car approached, then braked to a halt. The driver leaned out, brusquely demanding an explanation.

Even as he spoke, it was too late for him to understand. A spray of machine-gun bullets struck him. With his foot off the brake, the car rolled into a field and turned over. The German officers riding in it were killed. The booty consisted of four Stens, five pistols and a quantity of explosives.

The fighting boys of Mazzo were eager for action. A second attack was made on the Milan-Varese highway, on August 2. This was less frequented than the Turin road, and served the Germans as a route to the front lines in the Varesotto. The partisans blocked another military car in a perfectly executed action—first the burst of machine-gun fire by a partisan, who promptly vanished. The trapped, stalled enemy fired into the darkness, until a rain of fire from both sides of the road did its work. One German officer and several Fascist officers were killed. The partisans captured three sub-machine guns, four pistols and precious enemy dispatches.

That same evening, another of Balzarotti's patrols exploded a powerful mine on the railroad tracks at the Certosa station, blocking the Milan-Varese line. Several days later, at another point on the same line, they blew up a trainload of reinforcements for the Wehrmacht. On August 13, a group of partisans waylaid a patrol of Muti escorting a group of young prisoners, called "deserters" and destined for prison in Germany. The partisans shot down two of the guard, the others threw down their arms and fled. The "deserters" joyfully sought their freedom again.

## CHAPTER 10

# The Battle of the Tracks

Greco was a small settlement on the edge of the Milan suburbs, isolated from the city by clusters of railroad tracks that cut through the center. It was not an attractive place; locomotive smoke blackened the houses and the bridge. The narrow road over the bridge led toward Prato, Centenaro and beyond toward the farms and big estates of the affluent. War had brought an aura of sadness to the place. A sense of desolation weighed on everything. The rich estates had been abandoned by their proprietors, who had moved to safer places, far from the bombings.

For more than twenty years, the Communal Center had ignored the democratic discussions of the Council. At one time, the mayor, after work, used to play a game of cards at the inn or exchanged a few words at the pharmacy or in the cafes. But the memory of these times had faded. The people were different now.

Many who had lived in this little suburb of Milan had gone far away and perhaps would never see their homes again. They were young men whom the war had carried off to unknown territories where they had never imagined they would go, much less as Axis soldiers. Other people had arrived at Greco—trained, hard, hostile men of the Feldgendarmerie, of the Wehrmacht-SS Railroad Engineering Corps—cautious, suspicious of every one, including the Fascists. They were responsible for the administration and supervision of the large railroad repair shops.

When they were on the job, many of the railroad workers could not walk any distance without being followed by a guard, as though they were in a concentration camp; they talked in low tones and quickly fell silent when a collaborator approached.

Long columns of freight cars were lined up along the tracks. Pleas for help would come day and night from the bolted and sealed cattle cars. Desperately-needed bank notes were thrown by those inside, in hopes of a sip of water or a crust of bread. Whenever possible, cars were pried open, and the engineer would slow down on a curve more than was necessary. Some prisoners could jump down in time from the train which was headed toward the concentration and extermination camps. A railroad worker from Greco, opening a vent, sometimes could slip a water flask or a piece of bread into the freight cars.

The men of the Feldgendarmerie detachment did not trust the railroad workers; they trusted no one; they lived in fearful isolation. The population lived in anxiety and hunger, hammered by air raids, trapped in the round-ups of the Black Brigades, threatened by the nightmare of deportation or execution. But their tenuous thread of hope grew stronger as the Nazi situation on all fronts grew more desperate.

The Wehrmacht was undergoing severe setbacks on the Eastern front. The forewarning of catastrophe was Stalingrad. The partisans all over Europe had taken the offensive, striking at the enemy relentlessly. The pressure of the Anglo-Americans on the the Western front was increasing.

The "battle of the tracks" began in Italy. The military of the C.V.L.[1] set up the objectives of this sabotage activity, which was directed toward hampering German troop displacement on the fronts threatened by the Soviet or Anglo-American attacks. Greco was now an operation zone, an important target; the railroad lines leading to the Swiss mountain passes, and the annular lines which circled Milan and veered off in every direction; all passed through Greco. But the importance of Greco was augmented by the presence of the repair shops which were crowded with bombed or sabotaged locomotives.

Every day, the Greco railroad administration received ever more pressing telegraphic demands from various divisions and territorial heads of Hitler's Railroad Engineering Corps. Railroad traffic moved mostly at night in order to escape Allied bombings; it could not, however, avoid partisan attacks. The war equipment which was damaged by raids or by sabotage often could not be

---

1. C.V.L. (Corps of Volunteers for Liberty).

moved or repaired. Nevertheless, the damaged locomotives continued to arrive at Greco. The communications system of the Wehrmacht had to be broken up.

On the first of June, the Regional Command of the Garibaldi formations ordered one of the most important sabotage actions of the Resistance, entrusting it to the Third GAP Brigade, the "Rubini."

This group had suffered heavy losses, and many of the fighters had been forced to leave the city for the mountains to avoid being captured. The enemy had found out too many of our bases of operation; too many patriots had been shot. The men feared that they were being singled out easily by the Fascists and the Gestapo. By June of 1944, the Rubini Brigade had lost so many men that it had to be reorganized and reconstituted with fresh forces.

I succeeded in recruiting four railroad men from Greco: Guerra, Ottoboni, Conti and Bottuni.

During this period, two young girls were making trips between Milan and Rho. The roads leading outside the city were always crowded. The hope of finding a little more flour to supplement the insufficient ration card allotments caused many housewives to make trips into the countryside, to the farmhouses and to the homes of the peasants. It was, therefore, not strange for these two young girls, Sandra and Narva, to ride down to the terminus of the old trolley line, the now-defunct "Wooden Leg," to Rho, carrying empty bags. Some time afterward, they would ride back to Milan, their bags fully laden. But the train trip was not always possible because of raids, bombings, machine-gun fire, and long delays. At those times, Sandra and Narva rode their bicycles to Rho, pedaling vigorously. These two slight girls with their youthful appearance, dressed in the style of the times, with high heels made of cork, went smilingly on their way. The soldiers began to recognize them due to their frequent bicycle trips and responded to their smiles, not even taking time to go through their bags. They hardly ever gave them a second thought. Sometimes, some gallant policeman would carry the girls' loads of explosives for them. Some years afterward, they were given the nickname, "the TNT girls."

That year, Sandra and Narva were among the most active Gappisti scouts. Explosives were running short in the Rubini Brigade, and it was necessary to take them from the secret storage place at Rho to Milan. About two hundred pounds were needed for the operations at Greco. Because of the caution required to elude the Nazi-Fascist vigilance and to avoid accidents in transferring this dangerous material, Sandra and Narva were chosen for the job.

The explosives were moved in small quantities successfully. In Milan, the technicians quickly set themselves to work, and after several days, they communicated that everything was ready.

I gave the word to Guerra, who was the head of the operation. I examined every detail with him, and we carefully set up our plans. Guerra was a quiet, good-humored young man. As the time for the operation neared, he showed surprising calm.

He was no novice. He was popular in Greco and was known to be a good worker. He had many friends among his fellow workers in the shops and was also liked by the people in the old farm house where he had rented a room on the ground floor from an old lady. From his window, Guerra could see the coming and going of the German policemen as they entered and left the command post. The main building of the farm, which was connected to the house where he lived, had been requisitioned by the Kommandantur and assigned to the Feldgendarmerie. They were the same men whom Guerra met in the railroad shop where they often peered at him suspiciously. The head of the railroad Gappisti of Greco was always only a few yards away from the policemen. A guard stood over him at work; at home, the guard corps of the Command was just beyond the window.

The bombs were consigned to Guerra, who then hastened to find a secure hiding-place. Outside, the heavy steps of the military police echoed on the pavement in the yard and blended with the laughter of the soldiers at their meal.

Sandra was responsible for bringing the bombs to the prearranged place.

The trains passing through Greco seemed to have a furtive air. The railway buildings and the cement water tanks had been retouched and painted. Yellow, green and olive intermingled with dark colors. The effect of camouflage was disconcerting.

From above, it was supposed to seem like an inocuous farm, cultivated with corn and medicinal grass. Laborious projects were undertaken, experts employed. The camouflage hindered Guerra, Ottoboni, Conti and Bottuni not at all. The locomotives were as familiar to the four Gappisti railroad-men as the anvil was to the blacksmith. The locomotives were lined up, easily identifiable along the camouflaged railway network, on the tracks which led to the various sections of Greco's "railway hospital." The German guards who walked back and forth in front of the shops at night and who jumped at the first unusual sound also formed part of the scene.

This was the enemy; he was called Fritz or Rudolf or Heinz. Sometimes he greeted them and smiled. The railroad men of Greco responded to his greeting; they sensed that Rudolf had a girlfriend who awaited him in his hometown, that Fritz, who was older and fatter, had at least a couple of children and a small shop; and that the dark-faced Heinz had more than one thing on his mind. But there were also the Hauptmannkommandant, the shop managers in Greco, the Hitler and Mussolini squad members, the sealed cattle cars loaded with men and women, old and young, en route to the North and, eventually, to Germany. At this point, what was really important? The memory of the competitive exams given to the railway personnel? The pedantic questions of the examiners? One's fondness for the large, black machines? Now all the skill and experience accumulated over many years of work were being used for an act of sabotage.

I was aware of all this while discussing details of our plans, during a meeting on the eve of the big event.

Guerra and the others were workers who knew the locomotive piece by piece. They also knew every corner of the shops. They were preparing to set the packages of explosives, with twenty-minute fuses, in the fire-boxes of the steam engines. They would destroy the engine apparatus and the driving gear of the locomotives and the movable bridge which ran along a ditch connecting the large railway shops of Greco. Thus, the arrival of damaged equipment to Greco as well as the outflow of newly-repaired locomotives would be substantially slowed down.

The hours of waiting were interminable. The four understood the necessity of watching not only the Germans, but also the Republicans who directed the shops, and all their co-workers whom they did not know.

This was no time to be day-dreaming. The memories which persisted now had to be cast aside. Thoughts of the serene days of long ago, memories of simple people, pleasure trips with friends, a family party of years past, the face of a loved one—all had to be pushed away.

It was night, a night of war. The four men with their deadly loads were lying on the bank of a stream, and were sizing up the dark outlines of the surrounding area and the water tanks that stood out clearly in the starry night. A train had passed and had stopped briefly at the station; the yardman on the tracks left what he had been doing; he was probably talking to the German inspectors riding on the train.

An order was shouted, and the response came from the locomotive cab, "Jawohl, jawohl."

The train moved on. Every so often one could hear the regular step of the guard in front of the deserted shops. A stone fell on the metal rail, ringing loudly. A continuous, deafening hum came from the Pirelli factory in the distance, where work went on all night. The wind changed direction and carried with it echoes from another place. Silence returned.

The moment had arrived. Guerra had already jumped to his feet; Ottoboni, Conti and Bottuni followed him. The two German guards were now changing posts at the railroad station. The four partisans moved toward the assembly yard from the opposite side. They followed a short path, crouching as they moved over a patch of grass which ended at the tracks.

"God damn it! Maybe we should have tied rags around our shoes!"

The curse was provoked by the crunch of the gravel in the forbidden zone.

Now came the moment to separate, to remember one's own instructions as well as the others', so that one would not mistake one's comrades for Germans.

The guard would soon begin the patrol. The four men hurried over the last hundred steps to the silent locomotives which were lined up awaiting inspection. Every inch of the way was familiar to the four railroad Gappisti. A heavy step was heard approaching. They wondered whether they should hide. Bushes grew thickly along the walls of the shop and at the foot of the wall enclosure.

The four spread out on the ground. They held their breath. They remained there motionless, feeling their tumultuous heartbeats. Guerra squinted, trying to pierce the gloom. A sound made him put his head down. Ottoboni gnashed his teeth and pressed his chest hard against the earth. They heard the steps coming closer, and then the guard's outline appeared at the corner of the building. They checked their revolvers.

Ottoboni and Conti were numb. Guerra felt a cold shiver in his back. He grasped the revolver tightly. If the German came too close, it would be easy to hit him. But the shot would alert everybody.

The guard walked off, methodically examining the locomotives and tracks with his flashlight. Still, they could not go into action. They had to wait until he made his rounds three or four times, to make sure of his itinerary. The four lay in wait, spread out along the enclosure wall. The locomotive pit lay open at their side; the wall ahead ran to the shop building; to their rear was a wide passage between the wall and the second shop. A watchful guard could leap forward from there.

At last they heard the soldier's steps again. The short boots had the slow cadence of a man who was not very young.

He appeared at the same corner of the shop and continued along the same route. He did not seem to be the type that would surprise them. Rather, the pace of his coming and going afforded them a minute more than had been originally calculated. It was a minute earned. The sound of the steps faded. Guerra gave the signal. "First, the locomotives; and remember that the fuses are set for twenty minutes' duration."

They tiptoed along the tracks. In the distance, a tiny flame appeared, then went out; the guard had lit a cigarette.

The iron ladder of the locomotive had a dozen rungs, usually scaled with one leap. At night, with a load of TNT on one's shoulders, it was easy to stumble. One of the four hit his knee against the metal; he bit his lips to hold back a curse.

The fire burned in one locomotive. Guerra had to climb down quickly from the cab, rush inside one of the shops, and climb aboard an electric locomotive. He still had to prime all the charges.

He thought he noticed a little red flame. One of the others had already primed a fuse. The tick-tock of his watch had an anxious beat. The passage-way of the electric locomotive resembled a narrow intestine; at least it allowed the use of a concealed lantern.

Opening the motor room door, he finally lit his fuse. He had some difficulty keeping his hand from shaking. Was he anxious? Or was he out of breath from running to get to the shop? Twenty minutes time. How many minutes had passed? Four, five? At the most, six. Here was another locomotive. The metal was cold; the fire-box was cold. A leap without difficulty. His practised hands opened the fire-box door; he set the load in the middle of it. The fire-box had now become a powerful chamber of explosives.

His anxiety began to fade. He was well on his way to setting up the explosion, and he estimated that he would finish earlier than he had anticipated. Five locomotives had to be mined. Guerra still had two loads of explosives to set up. The others, he thought, had probably already finished. He calculated that they were now beginning to depart. In actuality, this was not the case; the others were walking circumspectly; one detached himself from the group and climbed aboard a locomotive; a flame lit and was suddenly snuffed out. There was the sound of steps. How many minutes had gone by since the priming of the first load? Ten, fifteen? Whoever had lit the last fuse had to stand by, motionless, to watch as it burned, and had to hide the faint light with his hands. Inch by inch, the little reddish ember moved. Boots also advanced on the track; they approached the mined locomotives. Guerra still had to set up a load in the engine of the "ferry," as the railroad men called the apparatus which shunted locomotives from one track to the other.

The man who was crossing the tracks suddenly shouted something in German. Guerra stood, paralyzed. The voice was approaching. Guerra did not move a hand, did not touch his guns; he hoped the German had not seen him. There was the chance that he would notice any slight movement or gesture. Guerra remained motionless, wondering if the others would hold themselves back. Everyone asked himself the same question. All remained immobile.

They could not understand what the guard was shouting. From the other side of the loading platform a voice answered him. A man crossed the tracks. Then, he stopped. He stood there with one foot on the gravel path and the other on a cross bar. Something gleamed from the right eye, perhaps a monocle. The man raised his foot and crossed the tracks, going toward the station. Now there was no more time for caution. The fuses had almost burned to the end. Guerra was near a locomotive with its fire-box burning. He primed the fuse and set it between the axles of the machine. There remained only one more thing—the explosion, itself. "Boys, let's get out of here!" he cried.

On his way, Bottuni spied a shadow moving in the darkness, and this suddenly reminded him of something. He stopped as if in a stupor. While the group ran off, Bottuni retraced his steps back toward the locomotive he had just left.

Earlier, a railroad worker had opened the door of the locomotive to find himself a quiet place for a nap. But that locomotive was about to blow up! Bottuni climbed aboard, grabbed the explosive and lighted fuse assembly in his hand, and rushed with it toward another locomotive.

The time interval between one deflagration and another didn't appear to be so important when one first thought about it, but the first explosion immediately revealed how significant it was. Fourteen explosives went off, one after another, sounding like a low-flying air bombardment. The Germans did not fire. They did not even rush to block the roads around the freight yards. The four partisans had plenty of time to get away before the Nazis realized that there was no roar of planes overhead.

After the explosions, the oil tanks broke into flame. Now the "maschinengewehr" (machine pistols), and even the four-barreled sub-machine guns started crackling; the bullets' tracks shot across the clear sky. But the four men were silently heading toward home.

Guerra's bed was right next to the Feldgendarmerie guard corps. Near the farmhouse where he lived, he noticed an old lady descending into a hole which was being used as an emergency air-raid shelter. This hole, which was about two feet deep, had been used originally for wine storage. Now, in this hole dimly-lit by a candle Guerra encountered an unpredictable adversary: his landlady.

"I know that you are the one who is responsible for the explosions!" The woman, overcome by fear, was shouting. Guerra tried to calm her down. He was impressed by her intuition.

"I know that it was you who caused all the disturbance. What's going to happen now?"

She had the sweet face of a grandmother, void of any trace of evil. But she was shouting too loudly; someone could easily have heard her. The Feldgendarmerie guards were only a few yards away.

Guerra reflected for a moment. Then he grabbed her and started to embrace her—a calculated move, mixed with his own feelings for this dear, sweet old grandmother.

Silence returned to this small refuge dug in the yard. Guerra and the old lady looked at one another in silence. The sound of shooting died down outside, but there was still shouting. Guerra eventually prepared for bed. But through his window, he noticed the last available man of the Feldgendarmerie, the cook, running to participate in an emergency search.

The railroad men's work schedule in the shops of Greco was often interrupted by inspection and questioning by the Feldgendarmerie. After the raid, this happened more frequently. One day, the workers were surprised by the arrival of a high German officer with his staff of uniformed soldiers, accompanied by the director of the works, a friend of Mussolini's from the Romagna. The workers instinctively stood at attention when this procession entered, but the Fascists and the director ordered them to resume their work. The rigid skeleton-like German general surveyed the shop, staring at the men as though they were stuffed animals on display in a museum; anger boiled under their icy masks. The German general had a superior, Kesselring. Kesselring had reproached him about the communique from Radio London telling of the recent partisan action. The feeling of contempt for an inferior race was written on the face of the German general, but the workers' suppressed rage was even more apparent.

The message making the rounds of the shops was to watch out for spies. The news on the "phantom radio" was not good. Not all Fascists in the Greco freight yards wore black shirts. One could not differentiate between real and imagined spies, but, at least, one could recognize one's friends. There would be no liaison with the Gestapo, nor with the U.P.I. (Office of Republican Investigations) nor with the Muti Brigade.

The spies were faced by an impenetrable barrier of silence. No one talked. During working hours, almost all the railroad workers were present in the shop, with the exception of those who were on an irregular schedule or were absent because of sickness. Forty reported for work every day.

At the end of 1944, the workers arrived at the shop as usual, but were arrested by the Germans. They were led to the "Sicherheitsdienst," to the Gestapo and to the U.P.I., where the attempt was made to force confessions out of them. But the power of the Wehrmacht broke down against the determination of these poor devils. They cried in jail or shrieked with torture, but no one talked.

On July 16, twenty days after the explosions, a prison van arrived at Greco. It was nine o'clock in the morning. Around the farmhouses of Greco, bright red poppies dotted the wheat fields awaiting mowing. The night had passed without alarm, without the bright flares which announced death from the sky.

Colombi, Mariani and Mazzelli were three anti-Fascist railroad men. The Germans now said that they had found leaflets on them. Although this was not really so, it was true that the three were anti-Fascists.

At first, they were filled with fear in prison, but they soon adapted themselves to life behind bars, among so many other people.

They slept on the large table in their cell. The German "camerati" (fellow Fascists) let them sleep. At dawn, they moved them into the van, which took them directly to the shops of Greco, where work was about to begin.

Who could say whether or not formalities ceased at the moment of death? Perhaps it was better to be made to sign something, whether it was the release of one's life, or some document filled with official stamps. There was no judgment "guilty." One had committed a crime, and the executioners did not have to worry about citing the articles of war. A sentence without appeal needed no legal jargon. In this case, however, the Fascists were killing three innocent men. The fact that they were not even tortured was proof that they were not, in the least, suspected of being the instigators of the bombing. But the butchers said that this was the law of warfare.

Admittedly, the German law of warfare was barbarous; even that, however, was not applicable in this case. No, this was the law of the uniformed bureaucracy. Fieldmarshal Kesselring, commander of all German forces in Italy, had strongly chastised the commander of the military forces in the Milan sector. The latter had subsequently passed on this rebuke to the detachment at Greco, which had been doing everything possible to single out those responsible, but unsuccessfully. Fieldmarshal Kesselring had not been content with vague reassurances. He wanted the guilty punished. And so the commander of the Milan sector, in accordance with a plan arranged with the commander of the Greco detachment, was given three anti-Fascists chosen at random. Any three served the purpose, as long as they were railroad men, and Italians. The bureaucracy was satisfied. Colombi, Mariani and Mazzelli stood facing the rifles, facing also their comrades who had been forced to witness the execution. The German officer read a document. One could understand only that Mariani, Colombi and Mazzelli had refused to give the names of those responsible for the explosions. A volley rang out, and the three fell over on their faces.

✿ ✿ ✿ ✿ ✿

The planes that supported the Nazi-Fascist search maneuvers in Piedmont and Lombardy took off from the Cinisello airfield. One day, Tullio (Bonciani) and I set out on the Zara road. Bonciani was a partisan who had organized the "Francs Tireurs" in France and who today had come to reinforce our thinned-out Brigade. We were on our way to get our first look at Cinisello. Leaving the road, we took a path which wound between trees and shrubs. Proceeding slowly under the scorching sun, we observed the scene from a thicket. The automobiles were darting quickly along the Zara road; in a nearby field, a peasant was busily cutting grass. He looked at us, stopped his work, and filled his pipe.

Later, I sketched the area and plotted the reference points of the airfield on a sheet of paper. That evening, we met with others of the Gappisti "Walter Perotti" group of Niguarda, to discuss the plan of action. At the end, we came to an agreement to operate during the day. The field was enclosed by barbed wire; it could be scaled easily. After we lit the fuse, we would have all the time in the world to get away.

Tullio and Impeduglia prepared the explosive. Four of us dressed as peasants, equipped with sickles and bags, walked along the path between the fields.

"Follow me step by step," Conti directed. "If I fall to the ground, you fall too." Conti walked with extraordinary speed, cutting directly across the fields, taking advantage of every tree and of every bush for camouflage. Conti had a firm sense of orientation; he remembered having come here as a child to play with other children. Every once in a while, behind him, one of our group stopped and cut a tuft of grass with a scythe; another picked it up and put it in his bag. Conti suddenly halted; he crouched on the ground and remained motionless. We did the same. After a few seconds of waiting, our hearts beating rapidly, we heard the sound of voices in the distance. Two peasants appeared on the path. "They are on their way to mow the grass," Antonio whispered.

We went on for another hundred yards across the fields until we arrived at the place I had marked off in the sketch. Conti whispered to Giuseppe, "Get ready. Tell the others." "We are ready," Giuseppe answered. Narrowing his eyes, Conti could distinguish two human forms stretched out on the grass of the field, under the wings of a four-motor plane. "Take it easy," he warned, "don't move. We'll see if they're really asleep."

We remained immobile. "It's impossible to set up the bombs," Enrico concluded. "The only thing to do is to come back another time." Conti decided, instead, to act. He crawled ahead, followed by the rest of us. The two Germans slept on, their heads resting on a pile of straw. Conti placed the first bomb under the airplane; Antonio and Romeo set the second bomb alongside the propeller of the other one.

Suddenly a camouflaged plane appeared from God-knows-where, stopped a hundred yards away. We moved away from there fast, sickles and bags of grass on shoulders. Ten minutes later, a roar shook the air. A flame and a column of smoke were all that remained of the two four-motor planes.

✻ ✻ ✻ ✻ ✻

At 4:30 P.M., July 12, 1944, I was walking with my companions toward a particular manhole on the Corso Vercelli. We were carrying work tools, a ladder, and tool chests; the last of the group tagged along behind, his hands in his pockets.

The manhole was appropriately in front of house number 27. We stopped. Corso Vercelli was not as crowded now as it was in the mornings. The flow of pedestrians was, as usual, interrupted by the trolleys jerking along between the bicycles and vans.

We pulled our shoulder straps loose and set our tool chests down.

A tall young woman came along with a baby girl in her arms. She stopped on the sidewalk near the trolley-car stop, only ten steps away from us. The little girl, under her golden cloud of curls, eyed us curiously, and then smiled.

"Mamma, mamma," she shouted, "look at the workers from the Todt group."

We "workers," embarrassed, took our time; we ambled toward the little girl who was responsible for our delay.

She twisted herself out of her mother's arms and started to run to us. The mother deterred her.

"Stay here. You know you have to wait for grandmother."

"Then can we take the trolleycar with her?"

"Yes, my dear."

"But won't that blessed grandmother ever arrive?" I asked myself, worried. We "workers" had to go down the manhole, set up the explosives, light the fuse, climb back up to the street, and disappear—all in a few minutes' time. It was important that nothing delay us. It was dangerous to wait. I came to a decision. I approached the young lady.

"Excuse me," I murmured, "but I could not help overhearing that you are awaiting the child's grandmother. If I am not mistaken, she went off a little while ago. I saw an old lady waiting here for at least a quarter of an hour. She asked me if I had seen an attractive woman with a small blonde girl, and then she left."

"Grandmother has already come and gone," exclaimed the disappointed little girl. "Let's try to catch up with her."

She waved goodbye to us from the trolley car window. At last we could begin! One of us lifted the manhole cover with a lever and set it aside. It was now a question of only half a minute more, but, meanwhile, two German soldiers, armed with sub-machine guns, descended from a trolley car. They seemed particularly menacing. If their attention was in any way drawn to us, our operation would be ruined. Stepping onto the curb, they passed right by the man in work clothes, making a slight gesture of greeting and proceeded on their way.

Now one "worker" climbed down the ladder into the manhole while another prepared to follow. Time was of the essence. While one "worker" passed the tool chest to another whose face barely emerged from the manhole, a bicycle suddenly stopped alongside. The rider called, "Giovanni, Giovanni!"

"What do you want?" asked the worker.

"That fellow who went down the manhole is Giovanni, a friend of mine whom I haven't seen for three years!"

"Giovanni?" exclaimed the perplexed and alarmed worker.

"Do you mean to tell me that I don't recognize him? We were in the service together for three years!"

All that we needed now was the reemergence of Giovanni and an ensuing effusive greeting!

I intervened hurriedly, "Oh yes, Giovanni, he is Raffaele's brother. That's him over there in the Piazza Baracca. If you hurry, you'll catch up with him."

The bicyclist looked dubious, but finally left. It seemed, however, that a worker standing around was an irresistible attraction.

"Excuse me, you seem to know your way around here. Can you tell us where the Rest Home for Musicians is?"

An elderly, pleasant, but bothersome couple stood there awaiting an answer.

"They told us that it's somewhere around here," the old man insisted.

"Oh yes, the Piazzale Piemonte, that's where it is. Go to the right and you'll find the rest home right there. But you had better hurry, because they'll be closing in a quarter hour."

"Let's hurry, Carlo. Thanks, thanks, very much. I told him we should have started out earlier. I hope we get there in time."

They'll arrive in time, I smiled to myself. A few minutes later, while two elderly and annoyed people were recrossing Corso Vercelli toward the Giuseppe Verdi Rest Home, a deafening explosion stopped them on the sidewalk.

"Carlo, let's get out of here! There must be an air-raid shelter close by!"

❖   ❖   ❖   ❖   ❖

At the officers' mess in Turin, the colonel-in-charge was holding a meeting. The general was expected any moment from Milan.

"The general," the colonel announced, "will review with his officers the situation on the southern front, with particular attention to the system of communications. You officers know the importance of this, from both a tactical and a strategic point of view. One must always remember that *liaison is as important as arms or military units.* Our arms and our units may be efficient on every terrain, but our communications network in Italy is hardly so. The reasons for this are known. In recent months, communications have become so bad that we cannot hold to one primary offensive. It is of utmost importance that communications improve, that every obstacle be pin-pointed and eliminated." The Colonel interrupted himself to look at his watch. The proverbial punctuality of the general caused him to stare at the door, ready to order everyone to attention. Instead, a radio-message was brought by a junior officer.

"Telephonic communications between Milan and Piedmont interrupted by an attack stop meeting with officers postponed to tomorrow evening same hour stop intensify vigilance stop hold fast."

"The General," proclaimed the colonel, "has had to stay in Milan to put into effect emergency measures due to the interruption of telephone lines. The General will hold a meeting with his officers tomorrow at the same time. The gravity of this problem can not be overly stressed!"

＊　＊　＊　＊　＊

At our next meeting, I listed the recent operations completed by the Third GAP Brigade.

In the first days of July, the group from Niguarda had waylaid a truck on a Como street, killing two Germans. One comrade, Erminio, was wounded.

On July 9, a Gestapo agent, Domenico Davarelli, was killed.

On July 11, a big bomb destroyed a work-truck in front of the Gallia Hotel; two Germans were seriously injured.

On July 14, two Gappisti seriously wounded Odilla Bertolotti, a Fascist spy, and that same evening, two Gappisti destroyed a large German truck on Viale Tunisia. A German officer who attempted to intervene was killed. Between July 20 and August 8, eight large trucks and two German staff cars were destroyed. Three large trucks were set on fire with Molotov cocktails. On Via Leopardi, a German tank was set afire. Two officers were killed.

On August 2, another German tank was set on fire. Two SS officers and a member of the Black Brigade were killed.

## CHAPTER 11

# Spies, Hangmen and Executioners

At the last moment, Conti had not shot him. The spy, unaware and undisturbed, had boarded the trolley car on the way to his office. He had already sent out seventy reports against patriots to the authorities. These reports had been followed by as many arrests. For as long as the spy remained in circulation he would continue to be harmful to us.

I had gone three times to our area of operation, accompanied by Conti, Giuseppe and Antonio; we had passed along the street both during the day and night, hidden among the crowds and protected by the shadows; the store windows had become familiar to us, as had the entrances, the manholes, the purple lights, the automobiles, the bicycles, and, above all, the crowd made up of workers, housewives, errand boys and police.

The spy had left his house at seven-thirty in the morning. He had gone one hundred yards away from his door when Sandra had spotted him and had signaled Conti. But at the last moment, Conti had not shot him.

The other two Gappisti, who had gone with Sandra to participate in the action had returned to their bases, perplexed and furious.

That evening we gathered at a secluded inn in Niguarda which offered good protection from ambush. The aged, very expert Conti, who could relate a long history of brave deeds, was now forced to justify his inaction.

It was a long, confused and trying discussion. The boys wanted facts, but there weren't any facts. It had happened to me; it had happened to so many others—at the moment of pulling the trigger, one remained as though paralyzed, incapable of making the slightest gesture. Was it fear? Yes, and so many other things with it. We wanted a Gappista to be superhuman, but after all, he was only a man, with a man's weaknesses and failings.

How could Conti explain something to which he himself did not know the answer? He was furious both with himself as well as with the others who were scolding him. For once, I had to make peace between my companions, to calm them, to provide Conti again the opportunity to make good. We would repeat the action the following day, and Conti would again have the chief responsibility.

✻ ✻ ✻ ✻ ✻

I arrived at the Piazza del Duomo and descended from the trolley car. I had an appointment in the arcade of La Scala with Sandra. Sandra was punctual. We walked together; in the Piazza Cavour, we saw three militiamen carrying sub-machine guns; and in Piazzale Fiume, the cadenced steps of a German patrol on its way to the Command HQ made us apprehensive; on Viale Tunisia, we darted between trucks crammed with soldiers. We walked arm-in-arm slowly, like two lovers with so many things to say to one another.

At the head of Via San Gregorio, we saw a couple of soldiers. Our rendezvous was at the trolley stop on the corner of this street and Corso Buenos Aires, where the two Gappisti were awaiting us and also watching the house of the Fascist.

A policeman was waiting at the stop but he boarded the first trolley. Conti, dressed in workman's clothes, leaned his bicycle against the wall, bent over and grabbed the pump, pretending to inflate a tire. Sandra approached him. Both kept looking in a shop window which reflected everything that was going on behind them. It was Sandra who saw the spy leave his home.

"Be calm," she whispered, "we're all set."

The Fascist walked several steps along the street; he looked around as if to make sure that he was not in danger. Then he walked more rapidly toward the trolley stop. Conti, with the two Gappisti behind him, followed and emptied his pistol without hesitation. The Fascist fell over with a hoarse cry.

People ran in all directions to take refuge under the arcade. Several cars stopped. The Gappisti jumped on their bicycles and rode off toward Piazza Loreto. Everything seemed to have come off well. I had just passed my pistol to Sandra, who stowed it in her pocket book as she went off, when a patrol of militia on bicycles appeared from a side street and rode in pursuit of the Gappisti, shooting wildly. This was the error that the Fascists always committed; scared, they tried to conceal their fear by shooting. Our people did not lose their heads. They sped along toward Via Morgagni, jumped to the ground, and began sniping at the patrol. Two Fascists fell; two more ran off without waiting for the others.

The way was now clear. We met at the base that evening. Everyone shook hands with Conti. Peace had returned to our establishment.

❊  ❊  ❊  ❊  ❊

I left the house; it was one of those inexorable August days, laden with electricity and heavy with humidity. I knew that I should not let myself be noticed, nor should I cross paths with anyone who had seen me previously, even if only for a few moments.

In spite of every precaution none of us had been able to avoid leaving some trace. The door-keeper of a building where a Fascist official had been hit could furnish some particulars to the police, even though the excitement had probably prevented her from "photographing" our faces; but many particulars could make up a portrait. The Gappista had to be an anonymous fighter. He lived shut up in his house; he passed long hours alone for days, and even weeks. He felt the wings of fear fluttering around him; a thousand faces loomed in his mind; he was ever on his guard, always taut with nerves. Although Republicans and Fascists seemed to be ignorant of our actions' timing, they were obviously fearful of their frequency. Our guards reported signs of tension. Mussolini's and Kesselring's men, victims of their own nervousness, had become suspicious of anyone who lingered about in the vicinity of the barracks. The guard watch was intensified. The anxiety of the enemy was growing. But after our operation, the situation was reversed; we were the ones who were overcome with anxiety and nervousness.

Tension took hold of me even though I had long experience in underground warfare; even though I had not forgotten any of the necessary precautions, I reflected. It made no difference whether or not I had closed the shutters of my door, pretending to be away from home, or that I never opened them without first making sure that the people on the stairs were tenants of the building. I was restless; there were too many people whose suspicions were quickly aroused. A Gappista with a minimum of experience, and with possibility of choice, would select a base in "friendly" territory. But there was always someone who, overcome with fear, could be forced to speak. I knew that I was attentive; no particular escaped me; in the evening, I would review my behavior as a tenant, looking for any revealing statements I had possibly made. I could not ever relieve myself of my isolation. I could not confide in anyone. I could not speak.

I pondered all this that morning of August 10, while taking my daily walk outside the house. There was a dearth of the "official" news usually furnished to me from time to time by the Command couriers. The shadow cast by the trees protecting Viale Romagna from the sun drew me to the newsstand there. I held a newspaper in my hands, and my eyes focused on a report of the killing on the Piazzale Loreto. Fifteen hostages had been shot. Feverishly running down the list, I found the name of Tremolo, the head of the Pirelli cell. He had been one of the best and most courageous of us all. Now he too had fallen.

From the Viale Romagna, I walked in a narrow straight line along Via Porpora and then turned to the left. There were cordons of Republicans everywhere, militia after militia, always denser, always more dismal. An upset and frightened crowd was huddled in the Piazzale Loreto. I could still smell the pungent odor of gunpowder. The massacred bodies were almost unrecognizable. The black-uniformed gunmen, pallid and nervous, were twisting their light-machine guns; they were talking loudly, in a state of excitement after having shot their entire load of ammunition. Fierce-looking young toughs, lined up with the criminals of the old guard and accustomed to the flow of blood at such a massacre, had an air of menace and challenge as they turned their backs to the victims and their sneering faces to the crowd. Suddenly, a platoon of Republicans was stirred into action. It spread outward, guns poised, and lined up right near the fallen bodies.

"Get out of here. Get out of here! Disperse!", the soldier cried.

Spontaneously, the people hastened toward their dead. Now the crowd was pushed back and was caught between the cordons of Germans and Fascists. I heard women shouting, shrieking and cursing.

"You'll pay for this!"

The Republicans pointed their weapons at the crowd. From the corner of the square, I could see the Fascist formation near our dead. I could easily have begun to shoot if the Fascists opened fire. At that moment, a woman broke through the crowd. She advanced slowly and calmly, holding aloft a bunch of flowers. She reached the front lines and walked right up to the cordon of Republicans as though oblivious to their livid and dismayed faces. I watched this incredible scene from afar. This woman with her lovely, soft face, crowned with white hair, slowly advanced the few remaining steps, untied the bunch of flowers, and spread them out in front of the wavering barrels of the machine guns. The Fascists were thunderstruck by this unarmed challenge and the sudden silence of the masses. The woman leaned over, set out the flowers on the street, then quickly vanished in the crowd. And so a silent procession began, as though born from a sudden tacit agreement. Other women arrived with flowers, passed before the militiamen, and placed them before the fallen ones. Those who carried nothing stopped for a moment in front of the martyred dead. For every bunch of flowers, a hundred people stopped to pay their respects.

The muffled sounds of these footsteps were distinctly audible in spite of the murmuring of the crowd. Next to me someone whispered: "Do you see that one over there, to the left? He tried to get away. He jumped off a moving truck and ran toward a side street. We thought he would make it because he was already far away. But, the soldiers saw that he was limping; he had been hit in the leg. They captured him, threw him in with the others who were already rounded up and waiting. . . ."

The last face I saw leaving the square was that of a Republican, laughing hysterically. That laughter was an indication of the infinite distance which separated us. These were people from a different planet. We were fighting a hard war in which death was an ever-present possibility for all. But when we killed, it was with sadness and anxiety; we killed through the necessity of doing what had to be done. There was nothing in us remotely similar to that look, to that mockery in the face of death. These soldiers were smiling. They had just killed fifteen men, and they were jubilant. We were fighting, I realized, against that obscene laughter. It clearly separated the world; on one side, there was barbarism; on the other civilization. The Republican lines, it seemed, were always this way. At every "passage," at every check point, I had met with their insolence, their arrogant meanness—their sub-machine guns prominently displayed, hand grenades hanging on belts, evil faces, dismal black shirts.

Encountering the merciless cruelty of the young Nazi-Fascists, I recognized the two worlds, the two opposite paths of life, just as I had in Spain. We wanted to live as free men. They wanted to kill and to oppress. They forced us in our turn to accept warfare, to kill and to be killed. We were forced to fight without uniform, to go into hiding, to engage in surprise attacks. We would have preferred to fight with our flags unfurled, with knowledge of real names of the comrades fighting at our sides. The choice of guerrilla warfare was not our own, but that of the enemy, who displayed the bodies of our dead and "made an example" of the assassination. The beast, now pursued from every side, defended himself with terror.

I took refuge in my house; I was overwrought. A courier came to me in the afternoon. The Republicans had shot over the heads of the crowd marching past the fallen bodies, to scare them away.

The following day, the workers left their jobs in protest, at Vanzetti, Graziosi, Trafilerio, Motomeccanica, O.M., and other factories; at Pirelli, the workers assembled in silence. It was now our turn. That same night, we prepared eight highly powerful bombs. The technician, used to a regular work schedule at his job, expressed his anxiety at being missed, but adjusted himself to the unusual circumstances. The next day, Narva, Sandra and I went to the church on Via Copernico to receive delivery of the explosives. The priest, preparing to perform the mass, advanced quietly from the rectory. Utter silence reigned in the empty church; there was an incredible feeling of peace. The technician arrived with the bags. The priest, standing immobile between the altar boys, was present at the exchange. Had he understood what was going on? I did not know. There could be nothing strange in these times.

We left and I accompanied the girls to their appointment with Conti and Giuseppe for the last transfer of the bags.

"I'll protect you from behind," I told them. "Be calm, and play it cool. There won't be any surprises."

The two Gappisti needed no words of encouragement. They had the self-confidence of professionals as they prepared the bombs; with a quick wave they disappeared down a narrow street. Then, one, two, three explosions shook the air; windows crashed to the ground. The Command post lounge for German officers was as devastated as a battle field. We had set up the bomb loads in such a way that the explosives would strike first at the windows and then at the exit of the club.[1]

The next day, Fieldmarshal Kesselring sent out contingent forces to round up the saboteurs for hanging in the public squares. The Commander of the Milan forces was anticipating a blackout at 10 P.M. The enemy realized that the weapon of terror would ricochet against him. We had to press on.

Azzini and Gianni attacked the Republican Command where Italian workers were rounded up to be sent to Germany.

On the morning of August 14, a high ranking German official and two subalterns were having a discussion in an office of the Palazzo, when Azzini crouched at the window, detached the safety of a grenade and threw it inside. The officer threw himself on the floor; the others were wounded. In the corridors, Germans and Fascists ran in panic. The curfew did not stop us. On August 16, Azzini and Gianni killed another Fascist. Two days later, another squad hit an SS officer at Porta Volta. "They shall pay" was the slogan of the day for the people and for the Gappisti. The month of August was a full one for the Milan Gappisti.

On August 3, two Molotov cocktails hit several trucks in the yard of the Command in Via Mascheroni.

On August 9, in Piazzale Tonolli, a captain of the railroad militia was cut down. This was followed by a battle between the Gappisti and a group of Fascists.

On August 18, a hand grenade was thrown into a group of soldiers from the Porta Volta district. The following day, a German officer was hit in broad daylight. That same evening, a squad of Gappisti sabotaged a section of track on the Milan-Novara railroad line. On August 28, while Conti was about to be arrested, he killed two Fascists, and succeeded in escaping.

---

1. The attack against the German Command took place on the corner of Via Guarnico and Via Mondello.

On August 30, a locomotive was derailed on the Milan-Certosa-Rho railway line. Another group exploded a metallic grid and some high-tension cables. The broken cables fell, entangled, onto the street. The wheels of a German truck passing by at just that moment were caught in the cables, and the truck was soon ablaze. Two Germans were burned to a crisp.

* * * * *

No one was more dangerous than a Fascist spy who was acquainted with the patriots, especially if the spy had been an agent of the OVRA (Opera Volantaria per la Repressione dell'Antifascismo) until 1943, and had become familiar with the anti-Fascists who had been arrested at that time. Toward the middle of August, 1944, Franco informed me of the existence of a spy. No one knew his or her name, face or address. This spy represented a great anonymous threat to a large number of anti-Fascists and was a significant hindrance to the Liberation Front.

Two weeks later, we had absolute proof that the spy was a certain lawyer named De Martino, who was director of the political office of Milan police headquarters. A prudent criminal, he left his house on Via Telesio always with escort, jus to go to police headquarters and return. Via Telesio was a "militarized" zone, seat of Fascist and German Command posts, protected by maximum security. It was an elegant upper-class district which bordered the park with its century-old trees under which Fascist guard groups were always present.

It was not possible to spend any time on Via Telesio without being stopped, searched and even arrested, so we had to plan our action there with precise timing. Our major problem, however, was that none of us had ever seen De Martino. We needed someone who could recognize him, and, at the right moment, point him out to us. I talked to Sandra and convinced her to go to De Martino's home to ask him for legal advice. This mission was dangerous and called for great self-possession and imagination. These two qualities were by no means lacking in our lady spy.

Four partisans, Albino Abico, Giovanni Aliffi, Bruno Clapiz and Maurizio del Sale, originally Gappisti and later enrolled in the S.A.P., were shot against the wall at 26 Via Tibaldi, Milan, on August 28.

Albino Abico wrote to his family before dying: "Dearest mamma, papa, brother, sister and all my comrades, I am without a doubt near to being executed. However, I feel calm, serene, and of a tranquil mind. I am glad to die for our cause: for communism and for our dear and beautiful Italy. The sun will shine for us 'tomorrow' because *everybody* will recognize that we have done nothing evil. Be brave as I am, and do not despair. I want you to be proud of your Albino who has always loved you."

The following day, Sandra rang the bell of the house on Via Telesio, and was invited into the living room, which had windows protected by iron gratings. Several minutes later, a tall, robust man entered, surveyed her carefully from behind his thick glasses and led her into his office. After inviting her to make herself comfortable in a large leather chair, he seated himself behind his desk.

Sandra, feigning much embarrassment, quickly spoke up: "My father has sent me to talk to you about my nineteen-year-old sister. She was engaged to a high officer of the Alpini regiment. She was expecting a baby and had written to his commanding officer to request that he be granted a short leave so that they might marry before their baby was born. Unfortunately, her officer was killed on the Greek front. Now that the baby is born, my sister has become obsessed with the idea that it must bear the name of its heroic father, and she has kept all his letters, which disclose his eagerness to marry both out of his love for her and for their little one."

De Martino looked at her for some time, removed his glasses, rubbed them with care, set them back on his nose and asked abruptly: "Why have you come to me? Who gave you my address?"

Sandra had anticipated the question, and answered firmly: "My father sent me here on the advice of a friend, a medical doctor."

De Martino looked at her for some time, removed his glasses, of the meeting, and then said: "Let me have the letters of your sister's boy friend, and tell your father to come here in person the next time. Perhaps one day your nephew will carry the name of his heroic father. Those who have fallen for our country certainly deserve the right of recognition."

Sandra rose. The man courteously accompanied her to the reception hall as if to emphasize that he had been very indulgent, and that he would gladly see her again.

We now knew the face of the spy, but to execute him presented many risks. We faced them resolutely.

On Wednesday, September 1, two Gappisti were stationed at the beginning and end of Via Telesio. A few minutes before the scheduled appearance of De Martino's car, I arrived arm-in-arm with Sandra. We walked along together slowly, conversing like lovers. A big car appeared. Sandra, recognizing the man with his thick glasses, gave the signal. The two Gappisti walked toward each other along the sidewalk, timing themselves so that they would arrive in front of Number 8 at the same moment as the car.

We had calculated the timing exactly; it was not the first time that we had executed a similar maneuver. De Martino got out of the car, accompanied by his escort, took three steps on the sidewalk and was felled by three bullets. The escort, taken by surprise, did not react immediately. When he finally started to shoot at the fleeing Gappisti, it was too late.

In the Milan newspapers of September 5 there was a notice from the head of the province:

"Effective immediately: all people on bicycles are forbidden to travel in groups. All bicyclists must dismount one hundred yards before reaching inspection posts and must not remount until they are at least one hundred yards away."

❉  ❉  ❉  ❉  ❉

In the afternoon, I met Azzini on the Corso Sempione. He was walking slowly. I did not even give him a chance to greet me. "Where are you coming from?" I asked quickly.

"A search party has thrown up road blocks."

"A search party? Were you on Via Ponzio where they killed a comrade and seriously wounded Antonio this morning?" Azzini lowered his head. He did not answer, but his face expressed confusion, bitterness, and sadness.

"The action failed on Via Ponzio," I told him. "The Gappisti defended themselves, but Romeo Conti is dead. This is what it cost us. We must now think about other things. We have another plan."

For several days, I had been thinking about a plan to strike a cafe located inside the Milan Central Station. This cafe, at which beer was served, had been converted into a recreation lounge for Fascists and Germans. Naturally, access was difficult for those not in military uniform. It would be easier for a Gappista in disguise if he were accompanied by a young lady like Sandra.

The technician had already prepared the materials, using graphite delayed-action explosives. The customary fuse would be too easily identifiable with its traces of smoke. The laboratory was about ten minutes walk from the station.

Azzini listened to my explanation of the plan. "I'll go along with it," he said. And then he added, "You probably think that I'm scared! No, sir, I'm not scared, but. . . ."

"Everything should work out perfectly."

"There will be retaliations, victims. . . ."

"Retaliations? Oh, yes, there will be some, and they will be more severe than ever now that the enemy feels less secure. For precisely this reason, we must hold him by the throat."

He looked me in the eyes, "I understand."

It was I who now kept silent. We had all asked ourselves the same questions Azzini posed, at least a thousand times in front of the fallen, the dead, and the innocents who had been sacrificed. These questions were only a test of our dedication and loyalty towards the hundreds and hundreds of comrades who were still fighting, gun in hand, in every corner of Italy.

He aroused me from my thoughts. "When shall we meet? And where?"

We met on Via Copernico, not far from the technician's laboratory. Narva, who was to accompany Azzini, was with us. Before keeping the appointment, I had gone to the laboratory, and had hoisted the sack onto my shoulders. When I arrived on Via Copernico, Azzini, in Fascist uniform, awaited me. I passed him the sack. We walked together toward the station.

Giulio, the technician, left us at the foot of the staircase. Narva moved ahead alone, in front of Azzini. I shook his hand and left.

Azzini climbed the stairs, slightly bent over from the weight of the sack, and moved directly toward the recreation lounge which was at the head of the staircase. Before disappearing, I remained for a few moments watching him, while he climbed the steps calmly and surely, a cigarette between his lips. I joined Sandra who was responsible for keeping an eye on the coming and going of the pedestrians on the outside.

When Azzini arrived at the recreation lounge, he found it full of Germans and Fascists. Several were clustered in the entryway outside the lounge, and some were seated on the parapet of the stairway. A little distance away, three little children were chasing one another in circles. Azzini entered the lounge, and placed the sack on the floor in a corner. The heat was suffocating, and there were hordes of people laughing and talking loudly. Azzini wiped the sweat from his forehead and looked at his watch. It was time to get out.

But while he was leaving, he again noticed the three little children playing, laughing, oblivious to any danger. He strode over to them, took them by the hands and led them out of the lounge.

In front of the station pharmacy, Sandra was following the action so that she could report to me if anything went wrong. Just then, while Azzini was walking away with the three children, the bomb exploded, thrusting a shower of splinters into the air all around him. The bomb had exploded ten minutes in advance of the time set! Azzini was shocked. He looked at his watch, and shuddered.

The Germans who had been seated on the parapet of the staircase were thrown to the floor by the explosion. Others ran away. Thick clouds of black smoke came out of the lounge. Two or three wounded militiamen appeared at the door of the cafe, shouting in pain. Azzini was by now outside with the three children. Odd comments were heard among the people who were crowding the station at that hour.

"A bomb exploded in the knapsack of a German."

"A train loaded with explosives blew up."

Many accused the Germans of carelessness in the transportation of explosive materials. The Germans, meanwhile, were shouting, "Partisans! Criminal outlaws!"

Reinforcements arrived; they surrounded the station and made the people leave while the dead and wounded were carried outside.

Armored trucks blocked the entrance to the station, stopping everyone who tried to pass. Sandra got away just in time. Hearing the explosion from the cafe where I was watching, I realized that the bomb had exploded ahead of time. I feverishly calculated —ten minutes to arrive at the place, two or three to deposit the sack and to leave. Even if the bomb had exploded within eighteen minutes, rather than the thirty planned, Azzini would still have had time to get away, provided he had not stopped or had not attracted attention to himself.

A little later, Sandra arrived, but she could not tell me whether Azzini had gotten safely away from the recreation lounge. She had stopped in front of a newsstand for the first ten minutes and had not kept an eye on the lounge. I told her to go to Azzini's house the following morning, to find out if he was safe.

One of those absurd ideas which cross the mind in moments of anxiety and disturbance was developing in my head. I feared that Azzini had thought that he had deliberately been sent to his death as punishment for having missed the encounter on Via Ponzio. It was absurd, but I was anxious to see him, to speak to him, so as to remove all doubt.

When I met him later that afternoon, he was in a happy state of mind.

The Fascist press then published the lie that the little children had been killed and that the lounge had been converted into an infirmary. It also bragged about a secret weapon. The Communist Federation of Milan responded, "The news of a secret weapon which the Nazi Fascists have boastfully been spreading is an utter lie."

Three days passed. Fascist police strategy was ineffective, but fate brought about Azzini's capture by members of the Muti Brigade as a "deserter."

Arrested, he was taken to the barracks on Via Rovello. They cross-examined him carefully. The same commandant of the Muti rabble, Colombo, directed the interrogation. "Are you a partisan? Speak! Are you an outlaw? Speak, you devil!"

Azzini did not speak. The boy had become a man, a partisan. Tortured for seven long days and nights, he resisted. He maintained his silence in the face of insults and torture. Eventually, in broad daylight, he somehow succeeded in escaping through the same door he had entered as a prisoner marked for sure death.

## CHAPTER 12

# *A Secure Element*

Aldo[1] was in charge of distributing arms. I had orders to get in touch with him. He was waiting for me at twilight on the corner of Corso Sempione and Via Canova, reading an unfolded newspaper. "Let's go," I said to him. We made our way toward a quiet place.

"I waited for quite a while!" he exclaimed, a bit annoyed.

"I had to take time to make sure that everything was safe around here," I answered.

He continued: "We are well-armed; we work well together; our boys are dedicated, honest, and serious. Now it is up to us. We cannot lose any more time with arrangements. . . ."

He talked, but at the same time seemed quite willing to listen. I said, "The struggle is now more bitter; we must be united, well-prepared and organized with adequately trained people."

"And that is exactly what our leaders, Longo[2] and Secchia, would like us to keep in mind," he interjected. "We must find some way to convey this to the group. I'd like to get together with them as quickly as possible. . . ."

I stiffened. This man with his sleeked-down hair had irritated me at first; now, he aroused my suspicions. There was something too verbose about him even though we had been assured that he was O.K.

---

1. Giovanni Jannetti.

2. Translator's note: Luigi Longo, recent head of the P.C.I. (Communist Party of Italy).

"You are Visone, are you not? The famous Gappista of Turin? They have been very very interested in my contacting you. . . ."

Secchia, Longo and Visone—the questions he had been asking me from the start were all directed toward these three names. "Perhaps even an idiot can be useful," I thought, but I could not shake off my suspicion.

"I shall telephone you within a few days," I said. "We shall work out arrangements for the arms shipment." He seemed disconcerted by the coolness of my manner when we parted.

✳   ✳   ✳   ✳   ✳

The place set for my meeting with Piazza, the head of the Command, was the Piazzale Susa. There were several diverse but urgent problems to clear up, but one particularly concerned me—Aldo. I quickly came to the point. "Where did you pick *him* up?"

"What do you mean by that? Aldo is a fighter. Is something wrong?"

"Yes. I had to meet with him twice. I have been hoping for arms as well as some participation from his group. I have received no arms, and his group is inert. I don't even know whether it actually exists. And as to him, he is very well-briefed on me and is full of questions about Longo and Secchia."

"I think you're being overly-dramatic. Aldo has consigned arms to the C.L.N. (Committee for National Liberation) and has procured false documents for many of our partisans."

"But you did say he is a fighter? What has he done?"

"Although not in our formations now, he has asked us to place him. It is up to you to verify that he and his group are good combat fighters. In any case, they *are* making an effort against the Germans."

"It could be, but I don't trust him."

I found myself on the street in the dark, and the silence of the imminent curfew made me feel alone and restless. Perhaps it had been that man, his eagerness to know, his disturbing questions: "Where is Longo; where is Secchia; are you Visone?" Perhaps I was simply depressed. Yet, for some time, our activities had not been going well. Professor Quintino Di Vona, a teacher, as modest as he was good, had been seized and handcuffed at 7 o'clock in the morning in front of his own house in the village of Inzago. Doctor Boselli, a woman dedicated to her profession, had been arrested twenty-four hours later by the SS while she had been waiting to keep an appointment with Aldo. Virgilio Ferrari, a specialist on tuberculosis and head of the sanatorium at Garbagnate, had been seized.

A landslide had fallen upon us. The enemy was arresting, deporting and shooting us everywhere. Friends who had not yet even participated in clandestine battle were being arrested and jailed. That August, we suffered a frightful number of losses; an average of ten arrests a day. In a somber and tragic incident in Balilla di Monza, the SS rounded up and tortured a group made of old Gappisti—young students who had spoken hardly a word to anyone; lawyers, doctors, businessmen who had given or had promised help. . . . Too many arrests had been made for us to believe that the cause was our general inexperience in underground battle. There was someone who knew about us, who had tipped off the Germans about the time, place and people involved in each operation. The enemy was attacking with confidence.

We now suspended all meetings which were not absolutely indispensible; we tried to isolate all those who were in possibility of danger. But we could not stop all our activities. The struggle had to continue.

❀　❀　❀　❀　❀

I was to meet Aldo at 5 o'clock on September 12 on the Piazza Argentina, to pick up a package of fire-arms. I felt restless. My name was known. There was unusual movement by the SS throughout the city. My discomfort increased. The meeting was extremely important; it had to take place. If the enemy had been informed, he would be watching for two men.

I decided to change the format of the operation. It might be wiser to have a woman meet Aldo alone. Sandra could keep the appointment with Aldo instead of me; she would be given the package of fire-arms, ammunition and explosives, and she would leave it at the apartment on Via Macedonio Melloni, which belonged to Signora Maria Sacchi, where I ate my meals. Narva would follow at a little distance, going first to the meeting place and then to the base.

It was a warm, beautiful day. The two girls were in a happy frame of mind, enjoying their youth, vitality, and the admiration of passers-by.

I accompanied Sandra a little way along the street. A taxi was available, but I didn't want a taxi driver remembering and recognizing us. I passed up the trolley car to avoid leaving her alone too quickly. From Via Macedonio Melloni, we reached Porta Venezia; we had a long walk together before parting.

Now alone, Sandra stopped in front of a shop window, and in the reflection, noticed her hair was slightly disordered. She adjusted her hair, put some powder on her face and quickly moved on to her appointment on Piazza Argentina.

Narva smiled at her. She smiled in return, and whispered as she passed close by her; "Wait for me; I'll get the package, and we'll get out of here quickly." Narva gave her a slight nod and continued chewing on the squash seeds she had just bought.

The elegant figure of Aldo stood out in front of a large, half-opened doorway. Sandra approached him as if she did not know him. She would utter the pass-word as though she were asking directions and would continue walking if the other person did not have time to answer with the counter-word.

Aldo turned to her even before she started to speak, and as she half completed the prearranged phrase . . . "to get to via Galilei," he interrupted her, quickly responding, "the first street to your right, the first doorway to your left . . . Where is Visone?"

"He could not come."

Aldo made a gesture of anger. Then his expression changed, and, almost stammering, he murmured, "We're surrounded, we must get out of here. . . ." Instead of moving away from her, he grabbed her by the arm. It was absurd. Then, as though he had suddenly remembered the rules of guerrilla warfare, he broke away from her, almost running. Sandra was aware of a heavy step in back of her. A hand brutally grabbed her. The SS had taken her! Narva, who had left the other side of the street, was not in sight. Was she hiding, or had she gone away? She could alert the comrades, in any case. Aldo had disappeared. He had grabbed her by the arm instead of moving off and he had run off when he should have continued to walk with her arm-in-arm. The maneuver was evident. The police in the bar, where they had led her, kept on repeating the same question, "Where is Visone? When will Visone come?" Always Visone, only Visone. No one asked for Aldo. He was the traitor.

They spent interminable hours at the bar. "Where is Visone?"

Sandra remained silent. Finally, the telephone rang. The commandant of the SS answered, "O.K., we'll return."

The trap set for Visone was postponed; Sandra was taken from the bar into an automobile. They shoved Narva next to her. They had captured both of them. No one would be able to warn Visone.

It was 8 o'clock. I realized that I had not turned on the light. Three hours had passed from the time of the meeting in Piazza Argentina, three and a half hours from the moment when I had greeted Sandra at Porta Venezia. She had still not returned to her room where I awaited her.

After picking up the package of fire-arms, Sandra and Narva would have had to make a long trip on foot, avoiding the center of the city which was under heavy surveillance. But she should have returned no later than seven o'clock. Time had passed. In a while, the city would be silenced by the curfew. My worry that Sandra had been captured changed to certainty, even though I refused to admit it to myself. Perhaps, I thought, Sandra has been blocked at a checkpoint; perhaps, realizing that she was being followed, she is hiding to avoid leading the police to our center of operations on Via Macedonio Melloni.

The house was quiet, in perfect order. The opened book on the table, next to the pretty vase of flowers, was like a symbol of Sandra's personality, at once intelligent and charming. But the serene atmosphere had now dissolved into one of anxiety. The street was deserted. I vainly kept peering out the window, listening for any faint sound. I heard the clicking of a woman's heels on the sidewalk. The woman crossed the street and walked toward the entrance. She was the midwife who lived on the third floor, returning from work.

There was no time to lose. The rules of secret warfare were clear. When one lost a woman, one had to do everything possible to save her. Sandra was in the hands of the enemy. She would not talk. Of that I was certain. But I had to act to prevent the worst.

There were hand grenades and explosives, a true arsenal, in the apartment. I had to make sure it was safe. The woman who owned the house and her lady concierge officially ignored my activities, but they were part of our group, and we hid all our material here. Half an hour later, we three were shaking hands. My landlady asked, "Will we see you again?"

"I hope so."

"Watch out!"

The two women ran the same risks I did; if the police were to discover the trunks laden with arms in the attic, they would both be arrested and shot.

I left with the curfew. The enemy had not succeeded in catching up with me in Piazza Argentina, but they were certainly on my tail. I arrived at my new base, a house on Via Hayez, which also served as an infirmary.

❋   ❋   ❋   ❋   ❋

The cell in the prison at Monza was dark and silent. After the blinding lights from the lamps, after the obsessive and wearisome questioning by Captain Werner, the SS prison warden, Sandra felt herself almost protected by the darkness and silence. In a little while, she would be brought again before the ferocious inquisitors; she would again be hearing the monotonous chant, "Where is Visone?" She had obstinately answered that she did not know him and that she was on her way to the movies with a girl-friend when apprehended. But they did not believe her. They knew many things, but not everything. They did not know the address of the base, but they had been informed of the actions in which Sandra had participated. Aldo had done his work well.

"And so you wanted to go to the movies?" A question and then a blow. They had begun with slaps, then with fists as violent as blows with a club. They had hit her so hard, her vision had become blurred.

This was repeated every day for a week. When they brought her back to the cell, she could not even stand the contact of her dress against her skin. She was so battered that she could not even stretch out on the cot. She held herself upright and remained that way until she was overcome by weariness and suffering. Then she passed out for several hours.

She felt herself being shaken violently out of her inert state. They continued to shake her. She had the impression of swiftly climbing the walls of a deep well. All of a sudden, a violent slap brought her to her senses.

The jailers had left her alone for a day, to show her that they would be indulgent if she would only talk. She quickly disillusioned them. She answered as she had always answered, "I don't know anything; I cannot tell you a thing." Now, they put her in the hands of the Ukrainian, the expert with the cat-o-nine tails. He knew how to extract all the pain a human body could stand, and he knew the moment to stop just before death. This treatment was reserved for important personalities. They had made an exception for her, a novice. At the end, the captain reentered. He had learned to read every uncertainty, every weakness by observing the look in the victim's eyes. Observing Sandra's face and body, bleeding, swollen, and deformed with sores, he discovered that this young lady belonged to that very small category of those who would be killed before they would talk. He made one last test, to satisfy his conscience; "What would you say if we arrested your family, young lady?" She made no answer. The captain and the jailers went out. The door closed. Sandra felt the impulse to scream but had the strength to repress it. She did not want Captain Werner, behind the closed door, to hear her.

Pellegrini listened to my story and became graver and graver as I spoke. Not even he could maintain his usual reserve. This time, the rock was shaken. He cried, "But this is like an earthquake!" when I listed the names of the comrades who had been arrested.

"So long, Visone," he said to me, at the end, "from this moment on, you do not have to live for anybody, except for the Command."

"Naturally," I answered. But could I abandon Sandra, leaving her mother totally unaware of her situation? Sandra was more than a comrade. They were certainly torturing her. I had to liberate her.

September glowed with sunlight and color, indifferent to our tremendous war, to the tragedy of men. The magnificence of the sun was everywhere—in the sky, in the trees, on the facades of buildings, on the fields, even among the ruins.

I had an appointment with Sandra's mother for one-thirty. She was already there when I entered the little street. I walked over to her, silently. Suddenly, she whispered, "Sandra has been arrested." She had read it in my eyes. The inner anxiety which had overcome me during the day was a clear presentiment of Sandra's plight. I felt that I would not see her again, even though I tried to tell myself that there was no basis for my apprehensions. I tried to reject them, but with the empty passing of the evening hours, I was sure of it. Her appointment with Aldo was an appointment with imprisonment.

For six days the mother waited with lingering hopes; she

looked forward to any news which the comrades could bring her. Six long days, lived minute-by-minute—long and sad daylight hours and night hours filled with fearful nightmares. For six terrible days she walked in the streets, worked in a factory, continued to work for partisan defense by aiding the families of the fallen and the bed-ridden.

On the seventh day, she started to look for Sandra actively. She went everywhere—from the Casa del Fascio on Via Rovello to San Vittore. Every morning, she went through the same odious and familiar routines—places she had to frequent, doors she had to open, words she had to repeat, dull faces she had to see, deceiving responses she had to listen to.

One evening, Carlo and Lisa were with Aldo and Anna at the Odeon Ballroom. Lisa questioned Aldo, "How do you explain the fact that many partisans to whom we have introduced you have been arrested?"

Aldo grew excited: "What are you saying? For some time now certain things are being said about me. There is a nasty rumor that I am a German spy. I ask you, Lisa, not to pay attention to it."

"Do you know that your sister is the girlfriend of Captain Werner of the SS of Monza?" asked Lisa.

A moment of silence followed. Then Aldo said, "What does my sister's conduct have to do with me? Captain Werner is nothing to me." Carlo, greatly disturbed by the confrontation, had remained silent. Now he said, "Let's break up this discussion. Tomorrow I have to be in Val d'Aosta."

Aldo and Anna left. Carlo remained in the crowded hall of the Odeon. Lisa, who had gone up on the dance floor, returned hurriedly. She ran up to Carlo, and before he could say anything, he felt Lisa's hand running gently through his hair. Breathing heavily, her lips close to his mouth as though to kiss him, she warned, "Get out of here. The 'Muti' are about to arrive." Carlo stole out the emergency door; Lisa returned to the floor and resumed dancing with her companions. Just at that moment, the Republicans, whom she had seen climbing the stairs, entered the room.

✿ ✿ ✿ ✿ ✿

The latest was Moschettini, a Navy captain who had refused to surrender to the Germans on September 8. He, too, had had an appointment with Aldo. At a corner on Via Marghera, the group was surrounded by the SS. Moschettini saw Aldo for the last time, unhurriedly leaving the scene. (After being savagely tortured at Monza, Moschettini was deported to Matthausen, where he died.)

Now there was no doubt about Aldo. From San Vittore we received a crumpled piece of paper with two clear lines of writing: "Aldo betrays; he works with the Germans. He must be killed." This was Carlo's last message. He had been captured on the Rho road while on a mission.

The Germans had appeared at a curve in the road, punctually, as though by appointment. They had been expecting him; they took him into custody as they would have taken a package to a warehouse. Carlo, also, had spoken with Aldo, as had Sandro Sandri. Sandro had been surprised in his house by the SS of Monza. A few seconds earlier, he had received a telephone call from Aldo. "Watch out; they're looking for you," Aldo had said. He had tried to escape. But the purpose of Aldo's phone call had been to make sure that the prey was in the trap. Sandro had fallen into the hands of the police who had been waiting at the door.

Now every possible danger involved had Aldo's name. Busetto and Vergani were warned. The Party machinery sprang into action to throw off police investigations. Our chain of communications, which had cost such sacrifices and bloodshed, was broken.

I had to get far away from the city. I was a link in the chain. I had to break away in order to survive, to be able to continue to fight. Thanks to Aldo, the police had a photographic description of me.

I had received news that Sandra's courageous mother had traveled to Monza to face Rossi, one of the SS heads, directly. She flattered him, insulted him, prayed to him, finally forced him to admit, "Your daughter is here."

Her daughter was alive; she would be able to see Sandra. She knew she had to continue talking in this manner: showing her indignation, looking for other openings, other pretexts, demanding the reasons for her daughter's arrest and detention. At the end, Rossi was specific.

"Your daughter is implicated in matters which are completely reprehensible." The mother's look of compassion made Rossi visibly uneasy. This suggested further appropriate words to her.

"What do you expect from a twenty-year-old girl? One who lets herself be deceived by whomever pays her court, who does not listen to good advice? Who knows how many errors she had committed at twenty years of age! For God's sake, when are you going to send her home to me?"

"It's not up to me any more, but I want to be honest with you. You must not think that I am a prison warden. I'll let you see her."

She was silent and waited. She feared more deception. A quarter of an hour passed. It seemed the longest quarter-hour of her life. Finally, Rossi, perhaps because he could not tolerate the mother's presence any longer, gave the order to bring Sandra in.

She saw her daughter at the door. She had become as small and fragile as she had been as a child.

Was a surprise attack against the barracks at Monza possible? Almost as if to strengthen my hopes, we succeeded in carrying out a project to rescue Antonio from the Polyclinic Hospital, where the Fascists had put him to recuperate. They wanted him to recover so that he would talk before they sent him to the gallows. The hospital, which was located in the center of Milan, was heavily guarded, but we had a comrade inside the enemy's lines. He was Doctor Galletti, a physician at the Polyclinic Hospital and a surgeon at our little partisan hospital on Via Hayez. Through him, we got to know the routine inside the hospital perfectly and could identify the room in which Antonio was lying, guarded by three Republicans.

We discussed the plan at length, inspecting every detail, as though we were making a screen test. Five partisans arrived at the Polyclinic to visit relatives, bearing packages of all sizes to help the sick people's morale. We covered a pre-established route along the labyrinth of corridors; we finally reached Antonio's room and cut the telephone wires. The three Republicans on guard did not even try to resist. We had to stop Antonio from getting up by himself. To the applause of the other patients, we wrapped him in blankets and carried him out.

This success encouraged me to think that we could work out a plan to liberate Sandra, also. I had already made an appointment with Mario at Rho, when I received word that she had been transferred to San Vittorio. From there, she had the good fortune to be sent to the concentration camp at Bolzano, since the railroad line over the Brenner Pass was not in operation.

I knew Captain Werner of the SS by reputation. To the mother's anxious questions about the partisans who had already been sent before the firing squad, he would answer, "But madame, your son was released from custody several days ago."

Sudden outbursts of anger would upset his usually pallid and delicate face. Even his own men feared him. His technique of questioning was methodical sadism; it was prepared on the basis of information furnished him by his spies. If the prisoners remained silent, he would take a silver cigarette case from his pocket, open it, extract a cigarette, and light it. It was a ritual. The captain's eyes would follow the whirls of cigarette smoke to the ceiling. "Have you ever been in the Black Forest, comrade?" he would ask one of his assistants. Without waiting for an answer, he would describe his childhood home, far-away lands, and duels at the university. "It is the only prohibited thing which we Germans still do." His silent and motionless assistants would look impassively at the captain as he talked on and on. The monologue would change toward the end into musical subjects. Bach and Beethoven foreshadowed torture and shooting. The captain's good education prevented him from vocalizing brutal orders; he would signal with his hand and the prisoner would be dragged away. Then, the elegant, imperturbable Captain Werner would leave. The death sentences for Carlo and Sandro Sandri were given with that gesture. They were taken away to Cambiago in the night. The following morning at daylight the population learned that two more partisans had been assassinated.

✿　✿　✿　✿　✿

Anna lived on Corso di Porta Ticinese, where, using suitable caution, we were able to visit her. The daughter of an old Socialist persecuted by the Fascists, she was a partisan—and Aldo's girlfriend. We had to put her on guard.

"Do you know where Aldo is?" we asked upon entering.

Her face paled. She attempted to smile. "No. Has something happened?" We had to tell her the straight truth.

"Aldo is a German spy." Anna quickly rose to her feet and tried to deny the accusation with a brusque shrug of her shoulders.

"Do you know about Carlo?"

"No."

"He was shot."

"What does Aldo have to do with it?"

"He was responsible for Carlo's arrest."

Overcome with confusion and contradictory emotions, Anna was speechless. Then she repeated, "What does Aldo have to do with this? He is probably in jail, and you come here to tell me he's a spy." She began ranting at us in a frenzied manner. We told her as directly as possible that Aldo was a friend of Captain Werner, whose girl friend was Aldo's sister, and that Aldo had been with Carlo when the SS had apprehended him.

Anna made a last defensive statement, "Aldo will get away; he's O.K."

"Aldo is O.K. for the Germans. He was at Carlo's side, but they did not shoot at Aldo. They tortured and shot Carlo, your childhood friend. Did you ever hear us speak of Sandra? Well, two days after Carlo's arrest, the SS arrested her on the Piazza Argentina where she was meeting Aldo. They didn't even ask Aldo for his documents. Would you like to know what he did the following week? He had Sandro Sandri arrested. Do you know him?" Anna nodded, overwhelmed by the factual evidence ". . . Well, now, Sandro was killed like Carlo, at the same place and at the same moment. Either you are with us or with the Fascists. You know what you must do. You must break off all contact with every partisan you know."

It had been difficult but necessary to tell her the truth. We could understand her turmoil. One day, Aldo, an exuberant and aggressive young man, had entered her apartment on Porta Ticinese; later he had returned with a bouquet of flowers. Anna had never before received flowers from any young man.

Aldo had demonstrated his interest by getting her into a dark corner; for the first time, she felt the pleasure of being a woman.

He would come every day to relax with her on the wool-covered divan in the alcove; gently and affectionately, he would take her hands in his and speak to her of love and of politics. Her father and she had often listened to Radio London at night, leaving the water faucet running so that no one would hear on the outside. Aldo, instead, would talk aloud, as if danger did not exist, as if he had fear of no one. He had introduced her to Lisa, and they, together, had invited her to a party. There, among his friends, Anna felt overcome with admiration for the young rising star whose surge to the top seemed inevitable; she felt completely under his influence. He was a leader. He was courageous; he had no fear of open windows, of people who might be listening from the street. It seemed to Anna that all the young men and women present at the party were adherents to the partisan cause, and she fell in love with Aldo and the cause simultaneously.

We asked Anna to collaborate in helping us capture Aldo, but we did not give her any illusions about what would happen. We were hoping, at least, that she would break off contact with him. News about Anna reached us indirectly. She had obeyed the order of the Command to cut off partisan connections. Nevertheless, she had begged an acquaintance to trace down Aldo in the places where they had met in the past. She had succeeded in finding out that the man to whom she had vowed fidelity and love was married.

In spite of our warnings, Anna had attempted to communicate with a spy.

We isolated her.

Two months had passed since Aldo disappeared; he knew he was being sought after by the partisans, and he was careful to avoid being caught. One afternoon, the telephone rang in the shoe store where Anna worked. A young salesgirl lifted the receiver. "Miss, it is for you."

"Anna? How are you, this is Aldo."

The salesgirl saw Anna pale and lean against the wall.

"Hello. This is Aldo. Is this Anna?"

"Yes, this is Anna. Where have you been for the past two months?" She tried to seem cool and detached, and she reprimanded him as a fiancée would. She wanted only to believe in him. "Don't you understand," she said submissively, "after so much time, it is natural that I would want to know? Can we see each other?"

Aldo interrupted her, shouting, "Don't you understand that I am in danger? That my life depends on you? Do you want to see me killed? All I'd have to do is meet you, and the Germans who are watching you would trap me like a rat. I'll telephone you next week. Don't tell anyone that I have phoned you." She did not tell anyone.

That Christmas Eve, Anna felt empty and forlorn. Her comrades avoided her; she was isolated. Neither the freckle-faced girl at the store, nor the anonymous customers' faces, banished her feeling of solitude. The days were grey and cold. When they were not able to light a fire, Anna and the salesgirl froze, even though they wore jackets and gloves. Anna could not keep from shivering. "I can't stand this any more," she said to the girl. "I'm going to get something hot to drink at the bar. When I return, perhaps you would like to go." She went out of the store. Only a few steps away she was confronted by Aldo. Anna was so startled, she started shaking again. Aldo grabbed her by the arm before she could say a word. She let herself be pulled along in his strong grip, down a dark passage into a yard of an old abandoned warehouse, to the inside of a shed made of sheet-metal. She could hardly breathe, so mixed were her emotions of pleasure and fear. Aldo was running every risk to see her again! She did not even have time to ask him anything before he grabbed her and held her close to him.

That evening, Aldo waited for her outside the shop. It was not late, but the days were short and foggy.

"That's what makes it easier for me to get around," said Aldo. The illuminated shop windows skimmed the street with pallid and vague reflections; on the sidewalks, the people were enveloped by the fog. A figure appeared and disappeared like a game of Chinese shadows. Anna felt herself protected, hidden. "You must break up every contact by keeping on the move," said Aldo. "It's very dangerous. The Germans are spying on us and would not hesitate to shoot you, me and the others. You must promise me you'll do so."

"Don't worry. I have been living isolated from everybody for the past two months."

Aldo was moving along quickly, humming as he went. "Where are we going?" she asked.

"Don't be impatient. It's a surprise," he answered.

He led her to a restaurant inside a large hotel. Anna had a moment of anxiety. "Won't it be dangerous here?"

Aldo laughed. "You don't have any confidence in me. They're probably looking for me in some tavern, and I am instead taking my girl to dinner here in the best hotel in the city. Doesn't that seem like a good idea?"

It was a marvelous evening for her. He was entertaining, calm, as if no danger threatened him, as though his only preoccupation was the choice of wines, which he discussed at great length with the waiter.

When Anna returned home, she did not even think about the fact that the curfew had already started and that Aldo, imprudently, had leisurely accompanied her home, even though he was being sought. Nevertheless, something disturbed her. Aldo had been received in that deluxe restaurant like a regular customer. An elderly couple, obviously well-to-do, had had to wait a long time before the waiter attended to them.

Aldo had told her that he had been arrested two months earlier. The Germans, confronted by his silence even after torture, had finally liberated him. For safety's sake he had waited several days before walking around on Christmas Eve. Now he wanted to forget these painful events. "Let's not talk about tragedy, Anna. Let's think about making these hours happy together. I ask that you not mention me to anyone. Not even to your father. And you must have no relations with our people if you do not want to have me fall into a trap."

Time flew for Anna—days were spent in the shop, evenings always with Aldo, or nearly always. There were hours of happiness, some moments of restlessness, a moment of anguish when she saw a partisan near her house. For a second, she thought to tip him off that Aldo was safe. But she recalled the promise she made Aldo. The joy of being able to love him obscured her knowledge of the truth, which, deep within her, grew clearer and clearer.

On February 2, there was an announcement in the newspapers and on wall posters: "The Communist outlaws, guilty of terroristic acts against the armed forces of the Reich and the Italian Socialist Republic, Luigi Campegi, Oliviero Volpones, Vittorio Resti, Venerino Mantovani and Franco Mandelli, were shot at daybreak on February 2, 1944, at Camp Giuriati."

Around the lugubrious announcement, a dozen people stood dumbfounded. Anna was in the group. Campegi was now lying motionless on the ice crust of Camp Giuriati. He had been a friend of hers and Aldo's. Crying, she went back to the store.

That evening, when Aldo appeared, he took her to an apartment in Monza. It was an elegant apartment, with polished floors. Cushions were tastefully arranged on the divan, with the covers freshly ironed by an expert hand.

"Have you been living here a long time?" she asked.

"Only twenty days. This is my secret base. I do the cleaning myself." He was a poor liar, so sure was he of her. Anna now thought of Campegi. Suddenly, sensing her suspicions, he began to act like a scared baby. He started to cry and grabbed her. He then wanted a drink and forced her to smoke. The cigarettes and the liquor were of a foreign label; they had not been seen in Italy for two years. All of a sudden, he asked her to leave. He had an appointment.

She ran to warn the partisan command. They answered that it was her responsibility and that she must handle it. She then contacted a group of Matteottini.[3]

She made arrangements to meet Aldo on the doorstep of a small, isolated house. When Aldo entered, he was seized by his arms. He stared at Anna and then at the two men who were holding him, and shouted. "What's going on here? What do you want? Why did you come here?"

He realized very well that he was being accused.

He saw the big black barrel of a pistol pointed at him and felt the cold metal on his forehead. A small but strongly-built man held the pistol, while another searched him from behind; he extracted Aldo's wallet, took out a document and showed it to his companion. "SS identification card number 44!" he exclaimed. Aldo now knew that the three men were partisans; he remembered catching a glimpse of one at the German Command Post, and of the other, in the Todt Organization. Anna obviously knew.

"You have betrayed everyone. What do you think is awaiting you? Have you anything to say?"

The question aroused his instinct to save himself.

"What have *I* done?" he asked. For an answer, they grabbed his wallet, opened it, and showed him the grey card, pushing it right under his eyes.

---

3. Translator's note: Matteottini were partisan groups organized by the Socialists, operating chiefly in the highlands of Lombardy and Piedmont. They were named after the Deputy and Socialist Party martyr, Giacomo Matteotti, who was murdered by Fascist gangsters in June, 1924. Matteotti was killed after a fervent and effective anti-Fascist denunciation which he had delivered in the Chamber of Deputies. His murder brought about a crisis in the Mussolini regime. Mussolini was severely criticized by the Italian public and international opinion. He overrode the clamor for his resignation, going before the Senate and speaking eloquently in favor of law and order, after resigning his portfolio of Minister of the Interior and forcing General Emilio De Bono to resign as head of the police.

"What do you have to say? Do you want to answer? Or do you prefer. . . ."

Aldo was ready for this as he was for the other questions. He smiled. "You're mad! Raving mad!" Perhaps he could dissuade them; or perhaps his insolent words would provoke a spray of shot from the Sten. He had to try. The impassivity of the three disturbed him. "How do you think I was able to save so many people from the Germans? By saying that I was an Anti-Fascist? Talk to the Command about this. Ask the Professor,[4] before you do anything foolish."

"Why don't you tell us about all our people whom you have had killed?"

But he did not give up. "Now I understand. You are an isolated group. You couldn't know. I ask to be taken to the Command." This was his last try, the most risky. He had to do something. He had to break down the impassivity of these three.

The man from the Todt group came closer and pointed the barrel of the pistol toward Aldo's eyes, while another asked, "Do you wish to confess?"

Fearfully, he tried somehow to play for time. "What do you want me to confess?"

"Tell us about Di Vona!"

Di Vona was dead, and he, Aldo, was alive. "I was able to get away, and Di Vona wasn't."

"You are responsible for the arrest of Carlo, and Sandro Sandri. You are responsible for search operations at Barzio. You have the killings at Camp Giuriati on your conscience."

They knew; they knew everything, or almost everything. This last statement suggested a last opening to him.

"If the Germans had stopped you, perhaps they would have found on you notes containing plans, locations and meeting places. They found them on me when I was arrested."

"And then?"

"The Command will be able to tell you about it! I'm telling you. It was Carlo who talked. It was he. . . ." But he could not go on. They were showing him a note. . . .

"It is Aldo who has been the spy. Kill him!"

"I am no spy. You can't prove it."

---

4. Antonio Banfi.

"Carlo accuses you."

"That note couldn't be his."

"Anna has identified Carlo's handwriting. It is she, your best friend, who accuses you."

"Anna?"

Their glances met. They stared at each other for a long time. Each saw the other's intent face, the alarmed expression, trying to repress feelings, anxieties, fear and anger.

They were now alone, facing each other.

"And you, too!" Aldo finally exploded with anger and vehemence. "You think I'm guilty? Even you are on their side? And you suspect me? Tell me, when did you begin to hide your true feelings and cause me to believe you were my girl, even when I was away from you? No, don't tell me. I think I know. I believe you've been doing this for weeks. No, you've been living a double life for months. Your avowal was a double game, a deceit."

"You aren't my man, you never have been."

"Jealousy has blinded you because you discovered that I have a wife. I did love you. But I was not free. But what kind of a woman are you who would abandon me in a moment of danger? Even criminals have not been abandoned by their women."

Pallid and furious, Anna retorted, "No, I did not have the right to protect you. Nor would your wife. I could not be partner to your betrayals. To you, the freedom of our people was a mere game. I was not, nor could I ever be, an accomplice to one who betrayed the future of our children, of your children, Aldo! No woman could ever do that!"

"And so you believe me to be a spy?" he asked.

"Perhaps it was a weakness, you were perhaps overwhelmed by events which were so much larger than you. I have suffered, and I, myself, would have paid your debt to the patriots."

"I have not been condemned yet. They are only talking about their suspicions and doubts about me. Now they will hear about a plan I have in mind." Anna looked at him with sympathy, then with horror, shaken with the thought that Aldo was insane.

"What plan?"

"I can take charge of the German Command. I know troop displacements, informers, codes. But you must help me. You must support my efforts to convince the Command. We're talking about a delicate action, one that can only be carried out by someone who knows the instrument he is dealing with. And I am the one who knows it."

Aldo looked at Anna. She was covering her face with her hands.

Had he been a partisan, he would have understood that it was now the moment to confess. Had he been brave, he would have created a scene right on the street, shouting, making someone come to his rescue. Two hypotheses, only two, but how many more were possible in the most tragic moment of a man's life?

Who could know what he was thinking at that moment? He had been left alone. He was not tied up. He did not move. He heard six steps descend, then three more, a sound on the staircase landing, the spiked shoes of the one from the Todt organization on the wooden steps, every so often a squeak. A faint light penetrated the room. It was cold. Seating himself on an armchair, he felt as though he had been abandoned on an unknown planet. He realized that he had been condemned and that he would await the dawn for the last time. They had put his coat over him and had propped him up.

He stared at the things around him; he inhaled deeply as though amazed that he could still breathe.

## CHAPTER 13
# *Valle Olona*

We had met the enemy's terror with terror, his retaliation with reprisal, his roundup with ambush, his arrest with surprise action. We had seized the initiative, we selected targets and struck them, we vanished because we were few and fast. But the cycle of fate turned. When a partisan was recognized, with the enemy buzzing too close to him, he became a danger to his comrades. He must disappear, move into another zone where his face was unknown, to resume his work.

I had had to leave Turin after the attack on the RAI.[1] Now, after Alda's spying activities, I must leave Milan, even though Sandra was still imprisoned.

The messenger from the Command met me in the only safe place left in Milan, the cafe frequented by the Muti Brigade. He ordered a glass of wine for me, and I drank it nervously, knowing that the enemy sought me. As we walked to the door, he slipped my new address into my pocket, and hurried away.

I turned over my command in the Milan GAP to Campegi and left for Gallarate. My new orders were to report to Gianni there, and to organize the Resistance in Olona Valley, especially in Rho, Lainate, Nerviano, Fero and Garbagnate, including Milan. "You'll have something to do in your spare moments," I was told jokingly. We had a strange sense of humor during those times.

---

1. Translator's note: RAI (Radio Audizioni Italiane): Italian Broadcasting Corporation, the government-sponsored national radio-TV network of Italy.

When I left the train at Gallarate, I was glad to see a crowd of people at the station. So many people constituted a defense, a hiding-place. Among them I found Gianni. He would conduct me to the Commissioner of the partisan military zone of Olona Valley.

"How are things going here?" I asked him.

"There's a good deal to do. It will take time."

His manner of speech was abrupt. I waited in vain for a good-humored exchange, some light-hearted banter. Perhaps the situation was too uneasy, I thought.

Marco[2] was waiting for me at the inn, a cordial, clean place crowded with metal workers, railroad men and laborers. A spy in this inn would stand out clearly. The inn was an excellent place for a meeting but not for any discussion of our plans at length. We left there for a quieter place.

Our problem was not simple. We had to set up a Brigade, one which would be effective enough to interrupt the Nazis and Fascists in the Milan suburbs of Olona Valley. This zone spread out along the two highways that connected Milan and Varese with Como. It was a vast industrial area, intersected by railroad lines and a track network of vital importance to the German transportation structure in Piedmont and Lombardy as well as to anti-partisan operations.

In this flat country, interrupted by ditches, a myriad of cottages, farms, hamlets, villages and small clusters of homes, we had to be very agile, with quick, efficient attacks and lightning-swift retreats to safety. Our organization must be extended so that it would be capable of striking at a thousand points to overwhelm the enemy's capacity for repression and retaliation.

We talked heatedly until midnight. The room in which we sat was filled with a cloud of smoke, making the air almost impossible to breathe. When we finally broke up, I fell into a deep sleep in my temporary refuge after so many restless nights. I was awakened at dawn. Work was to begin immediately.

Something had been set in motion; the Fascists and Germans had tightened their organization; they had intensified their guard activity, doubling their vigilance. "Watch out for the partisans" was the enemy's order of the day in that area. They felt the pres-

---

2. Bruno Marco Faletti was Inspector of the Regional Command of the Garibaldi Brigade.

ence of an invisible danger. Nevertheless, our situation was not completely satisfactory. It was true that the meeting to assess the local partisans' effort had encouraged many young men to join our formations, but the results were not as effective as had been anticipated. I had the impression that the obstacles were not caused by immaturity, lack of training, and awkwardness, but by an overall laxness in policy direction.

My theory had a basis in fact; it explained the diversions and objections raised to any proposals for immediate action. I had further confirmation of this with regard to the Count, who, so it was said, had arms which he was holding back.

My search for the Count was not easy. Everybody knew this; everybody spoke of him, but it was impossible to get near him. I seemed to be following a mysterious phantom. Finally, I was told that the Count would meet me and that I would be contacted at the opportune time.

It was early in October. The season seemed more like winter than fall; the weather was gloomy, the air heavy with rain. I bicycled down interminable routes, following small roads and country paths before reaching one of my bases in order to avoid every possible surprise. I remained there until a few hours before my appointment.

I was to go to a home on Via Circonvallazione in Nerviano. Being unfamiliar with the area, I went over the route in advance in order to make myself familiar with it. As I awaited the time for the meeting, I reflected upon how unique this procedure was. There were four or five people who had served as liaison men and were aware of the "secret" meeting. The more ingenious patriots would have had reason to be suspicious and would have set up plans for the meeting with security, but I was on my way now, and the only protection I had was a revolver.

I approached the front door of this ancestral home with its neglected exterior which was the residence of the Crespi sisters. I rang the bell. The door opened quickly. I entered the comfortable-looking reception hall which was illuminated with a faint light. When I passed through the door, I could barely see. Everything was wrapped in heavy shadows. The drapes were lowered, the shutters half-closed, and the heavy curtains drawn to exclude the outside world. The atmosphere which pervaded the house was that of a rectory. The ladies themselves moved like shadows, murmuring "Please wait a moment," like priestesses at a rite.

These were the Crespi sisters, two courteous and elegant ladies who brought a new perspective to my experiences in clandestine warfare. I was filled with horror when I thought of what would happen if, after so many precautions, the Fascists suddenly broke through the half-closed blinds.

I did not see the Count enter, but I suddenly found myself confronted by him. This man, pallid and thin, was wearing a mantle which nearly reached his feet. A wave of anger overcame me; I was desperately seeking to procure arms for the Garibaldi Assault Brigade, and I had to lose many weeks just to arrange a meeting in this home, in the dark, with this eccentric figure wearing a long mantle, of the type the Carbonari of the nineteenth century had worn. I was on tenterhooks, but I had to accept his invitation to sit down; I was in a rush to conclude the negotiations, but I had to undergo questioning.

It was impossible for me to stay calm when I heard him ask "Are you an officer? What is your rank?" I rose quickly, red with anger. I wondered if he would go on to inquire if I had an orderly and if I was happy with the arrangement. Seemingly, all that had happened in Italy and in the world, including the events of September 8, and the partisans' revolt had had no effect at all on this man's preoccupation with hard and fast authority. We had not yet come to terms. I asked for arms for my partisans, and I received an evasive answer. The Count distrusted me, and I him, but I would have gained nothing had I broken up the conversation. Finally, I proposed another meeting. Perhaps we could arrive at a mutual agreement, and I would be able to get to the Count's little arsenal.

On the road between Pero and Nerviano, there was a house well-situated in quiet surroundings. Now the road was deserted. Usually it was crowded with workers and was traveled for hours at a time by military vehicles armed with machine guns and antiaircraft weapons. The silence was interrupted by the sound of firing in the distance. One single shot was followed by a cluster of explosions. They were ripping up the train tracks of the little train which ran to Milan.

During air-raid attacks, the train would stop and the passengers would hide in the bushes or lie flat in the ditches if there were any in the vicinity.

When the train had to halt near a settlement, those who were able would walk to their homes and busy themselves making sandwiches and providing bottles of wine to break up the wait for the other passengers. This train delay had become commonplace. Half-way along the route this evening, there was a stop in front of a small electric plant, one of the few left undamaged. The powerful electric current made its walls vibrate day and night, creating a strangely musical sound like that of a giant organ. The constant music of the electricity gave a sensation of efficiency. It seemed superior to the everyday routine of war. The caretaker, Jana, who was responsible for the maintenance of the plant also performed the duties of stationmaster. He lived alongside the electric plant opposite the train stop. These were connected by a little bridge over a make-shift artificial canal.

Life was difficult for everybody and no less so for the Jana family with their three children. Their only resources were the husband's modest salary and the yield from a little garden.

Their small income was unexpectedly augmented one day when a young man with a markedly alert face asked for lodging. The Jana family put him up in one of their rooms. This young man, named Nicola,[3] had identified himself as a salesman of ladies' hose. He was given a bed, but his work did not allow him to be there every night. "These are difficult times," said the hosiery salesman, "and I must not neglect my clientele if I wish to make a living."

The guest remained absent for days on end, but when he appeared, he seemed strangely worn out.

He would sleep for long periods at a  time, and would relax at the small table writing in his notebook. He was evidently a meticulous man who kept his accounts in good order.

The zone was not as quiet as it once had been. The night was often streaked with flashes of light, and the German and Fascist patrols frequently made sudden appearances in vehicles of all types, wandering along the country paths for hours on end.

---

3.  Nicola Salvatore was the name that he used with the family.

It was known that the rebels were now in the area. They seemed to be both nearby and far away at the same time. People tried to figure out if the shadows that silently passed in the night were those of phantom-like partisans or of people going to the inn.

One night, the area was shaken by a sudden crash. There was the clatter of broken glass, then gun shots and flashes of light, then a long silence, followed by bursts of machine gun fire, green and red rockets which dotted the countryside, and the furious barking of dogs. Signor Jana thought he knew what was happening. It was an attack on a truck or an act of sabotage on the railroad line, and he quietly enjoyed the spectacle as he looked out through a small crack of the shutters.

Nicola, however, slept soundly throughout, undisturbed by the gunfire. The following morning, the stationmaster felt jubilant. His wife counseled him to watch himself, especially with the stranger. At ten o'clock in the morning, the latter still had not shown any signs of waking. "His life is also hard," concluded Janas. Later, the blinds opened, and the salesman, methodical and precise as usual, went over and sat down at the little table to put his accounts in order. The woman described what had happened during the night. The salesman listened dispassionately, seemingly occupied only with his own affairs. "God bless him," thought the woman. He asked only one question: whether he could get to Milan by train. From what was known, the tracks were blown up near the cemetery at Mazzo, and the trains could not move through. The salesman had to settle for bicycling to the city.

In the afternoon, the repercussions to the nocturnal attack began. Trucks full of Germans, armored cars, and the Republican militia continuously moved into the area and occupied several villas. Large patrols, with their heavy steps and the somber clinking of arms, pervaded the region. The Germans and Fascists surprised groups of young boys at their work in the fields and then took them away; some of them were still wearing wooden clogs; others were barefoot. One of them carried a rake with blades of grass still clustered between its teeth. Republicans and Germans entered the houses; they looked into all the corners; they opened cabinets and searched under the beds; they also entered the little red cottage where the custodian of the small electric plant and the train-stop lived. They found nothing suspicious. One small, thin

Fascist with a pair of suspicious eyes looked under the little bridge where foul smelling water had settled. "When it smells, it means that the weather is about to change," said the woman, as if she were making an excuse on behalf of the artificial canal with its periodic miasmas.

The only one who found anything was one of the little Jana children. He had just learned to read and used every opportunity to practice. And so, when he found a half-torn piece of paper in the stocking salesman's room, he was determined to decipher the notes. When a friend of his own age could not help him, he asked his father. Signor Jana put on his glasses, read the notes, and grew pale. "It's nothing," he said, "just some nonsense." After thinking about it, he threw the paper in the stove and made sure that it burned completely. But the salesman knew nothing of this incident until many years afterward.

In this way, a sheet of paper disappeared from the diary of the Nerviano detachment. It listed the actions completed between September 25 and October 15: two incidents of railway sabotage; sabotage on the Milan-Varese highway; destruction of two high-tension pylons; an assault at the Rho parking area; and three attacks on spies, Republican functionaries and others.

In Rho, during this particular period, life seemed at a standstill. The tradesmen sold very little; people were spending cautiously and were buying only necessities. Even the movie houses were deserted. People preferred to remain at home when evening fell. Everything seemed to be moving slowly; even the head of a local parish bemoaned the small number of marriages and baptisms taking place.

In one of the cafes near the Piazza del Duomo, many young men who worked or studied in Milan often assembled to play cards and drink, even in wintertime. "Poor business," grumbled the cafe owner. Nevertheless, the young men kept him company; they reminded him of his sons, both of whom were prisoners in some unknown place; he loved the laughter and the shouting which accompanied the games. At twilight, the faintly-lit cafe became even darker with the lengthening shadows, and then all was silent; the billiard cues were abandoned on the tables between the empty orangeade bottles. Before rearranging the chairs, the owner would total the I.O.U.'s handed him during the day.

One October evening, the door was suddenly thrown open by one of the boys who frequented the cafe. He rushed to the bar almost on the run and asked agitatedly for a glass of liqueur. Someone greeted him. He made no answer. Then the door burst open again, and five Republicans crowded in.[4] The boy threw the glass onto the bar and resignedly followed them out. The cafe became more crowded than usual. Light trucks with protruding machine gun barrels circulated through the streets. "There's plenty of activity by the Blacks," pedestrians muttered as they quickened their steps. Things quieted down shortly after midnight.

The secretary of the Fascist group was seated at a table; the squad leader was walking nervously back and forth. "Here we are, an assembly of good people. Now, we must settle accounts between us. You must have patience because there's much to discuss." A sinister-looking militiaman standing near the door started to laugh, but the squad leader's glare froze him. The interrogation proceeded with order. The squad leader was stationed there. He knew how to handle the situation.

The boys were on their feet, leaning against a wall. They had been there for an hour. A short time before, the boy that they had arrested at the bar had succeeded in escaping. Someone must have told the Fascists of his escape. "You shriek at us when we grab you," smiled the squad leader mockingly, "we are the bad ones, the brutal ones. You, instead, are innocent, naturally. . . . Naturally, you don't know anything about what's happening."

He approached the young men. The first in line was a timid-looking boy with blond hair and freckles who wore spectacles. The leader faced him and asked, "What does your father do for a living?" He had an almost paternal look. "Your dad, what does he do?" he repeated, as though asking a friend.

The boy hesitated a second. "He is a railroad engineer."

"And does he make you study?"

"Yes, I am going to technical school. I'm studying to be a skilled electrician." The squad leader felt that the conversation was off to a good start.

"And you are one of our people. Are you from Rho?" He was

---

4. The partisans arrested and shot at Turbigo on October 13, 1944, were Pasquale Perfetti, Luigi Zucca, Alvaro Negri, and Alfonso Comminella. Only Cesare Belloni was saved.

addressing the rather dark boy of about twenty standing next to the blond. At first glance, he could be considered a Southern Italian.

"Yes, I'm from there, as were my parents before me."

"Where is your house?" The question was almost solicitous, as though he wanted to know if the boy lived far from the barracks and had had to travel a long way to get there.

"I live on the road to Legnano. . . ."

"In one of those new little houses on the right side of the road? But are they comfortable? They say that they're a little damp. . . ." He was surprised by the boy's cold response. "No, they're comfortable."

"Perhaps this is the toughest one of the gang," thought the squad leader. He tried the same questions with the other three boys. He asked the one on the right whether he liked soccer, and for what team he rooted. "The Rho one, naturally," answered the young boy. He had a pale face but seemed an emotional type. There was something about him that the squad leader had seen before, in older men.

"Very well, now we will have a confidential chat, one at a time. You remain here," he said to the first boy, who wore spectacles, "and the rest of you wait outside." He had to interrogate them separately in order to find the weak link among them. The other four went out. He told the boy to sit in front of the table. Behind the boy stood two militiamen. The door was closed.

✵　✵　✵　✵　✵

"They have arrested five of them." One of our couriers, arriving out of breath, brought me the news at our base, the Ghiringhella dairy farm. He named those who had been caught. The oldest was twenty. They had been continuously questioned without even a chance to catch their breaths. These boys were the first to be arrested after the dozens and dozens of operations we had completed. "Do you think they will talk?" the courier asked. How could I answer such a question? All I knew was that they were courageous and ready to fight.

Much depended on what the enemy had learned earlier. How had the enemy succeeded in taking them by surprise? "The fact is that the boys will not talk," I said, "but we must nevertheless take precautions. Do you believe that if I were captured, I would talk and give your names to the enemy?" There were a dozen of us in that little room in the farmhouse. The response was a unanimous No. "Well, now I'll tell you something. If I were captured, you should for precaution's sake leave your homes and hide out. This is what you must do now."

The five boys who had been arrested were transferred from Rho to the Resega Barracks in Legnano. The squad leader had failed to uncover anything by individual interrogation. "Where is Visone? Who are his accomplices?"

The answer had been consistent: "I don't know anything." The Fascists had had no success using the pretext, "Your friend has talked and we have given him his freedom. What would you like to do?" The Fascist office secretary was furious. These young fellows knew everything. The information on the five was precise, but they denied everything. The Legnano Command telephoned the Rho command to plan the punishment. The German Command urged upon the Republicans a quick decision and an exemplary punishment. These young men did know, and if they would talk, at least twenty other partisans could be rounded up. But they did not talk.

They were now sent to Legnano together. They knew that something terrible was awaiting them. Locked in a cell, they stared at each other. "Did they give you a beating?"

"A few slaps and a couple of punches."

"The worst is yet to come."

On the outside, we made plans to liberate them, but could not successfully attack the Resega barracks, and we did not get over to Rho in time. We did have an informer. The boys were not talking, but the tortures were atrocious.

These five had participated in our operations, taking food from their homes along with them, then bravely returning late at night to a barrage of maternal chastisements. Now, every night the Fascists scalded their feet and forced them to stretch out on the ammunition cases, heads and feet upright, the trunks of their bodies resting on the protruding metal projectiles. They forced them to drink quarts of putrid salt water. It was a dreadful week. Then, one evening, the boys were again herded together in one cell. "Rest for a few hours," their captors told them. They were getting ready for the kill. The last to be interrogated, the Rho soccer fan warned the others, "Boys, they are now going to finish us." The one who had been studying to be an expert electrician had an idea. "Let's leave a message for our parents." They scratched a message on the wall with a piece of granite, a bit larger than a small stone.

"Dear Bruno," wrote the boy, "your brother is leaving you, but he is not afraid. I am going to join Mother." Then the boys lay down on the cots.

Three trucks drove through the exit of the barracks courtyard. The loud rumble of the vehicles echoed through the narrow streets of the town. It was dark; day would not break for another hour. The truck sped swiftly along the asphalt highway and stopped when it came to the bank of a river.

The five boys in one truck were told to climb off. One, with bare feet tried to walk, but fell on his knees. The others, too, could hardly move and moaned as they limped along on their scalded feet. In front of them stood a firing squad with guns levelled. Behind them flowed the Ticino, and the cold spray made them shiver. "We are at Turbigo," one of them murmured.

The wind ruffled the hair of the five boys. It was rapidly becoming daylight. Perhaps someone would see them. Otherwise, the river would drag their bodies far away and no one would ever know what befell them. The Fascists had thought of everything.

The shots hit their targets perfectly. Five dark figures rolled over the bank and into the water. The current quickly carried them off, separated, submerged and swallowed them. While the Fascist squad were jumping aboard the moving trucks, one of the five, the soccer fan, felt a cold slap and opened his eyes. He had succeeded in saving himself. He was wounded but still had a bit of strength. He tried to untie his bound hands. While he moved his legs and shoulders in a desperate attempt to keep afloat, his body was caught by a shrub which protruded from the bank. The current forced him to roll over, and he hit something solid. It was a shore of an islet. His feet touched bottom. Resisting the pressure of the current, he pushed his feet with all his strength toward the bank of the river. He reached the bank but was unable to stand up. He dragged himself on his knees toward the bank.

He had saved himself. Only his feet remained in the water when he finally fainted. When he regained consciousness, he realized that he had lost much blood. He dragged his stiffened legs out of the water. He looked around; behind him was the narrow ridge where they had shot him and the others. On the opposite shore he saw smoke rising from a chimney. Perhaps it was a farm. That was his only hope of salvation. He stumbled into the water and swam desperately toward the other shore. He dragged himself along, grabbed hold of a stick which was driven into the shore, climbed up the deserted bank and tried to crawl toward the large farmhouse. He fainted. When he regained consciousness for the second time, a stranger was kneeling over him. The peasants of the farm had called the doctor.

❋ ❋ ❋ ❋ ❋

The humidity was intense, the grass was soaked as if it had just rained in torrents, but the sky was bright and the stars shed abundant light upon the small group moving along Indian file. Things had been going well, better than predicted. The explosives which had been placed on the railway tracks had been as effective as an aerial bombardment. Many windows had been shattered, many people's sleep had been interrupted.

If the stocking salesman would have dared to open the door of the house, no matter how cautiously, everyone would have noticed it. It would be as though he were to say, "Honorable gentlemen, I am a partisan, don't be surprised if I come home a little late this evening. Furthermore, you have heard and have seen that we have organized an excellent pyrotechnic spectacle."

Nicola took from his pocket the key that he had carefully been saving for a long time. "One time or another, this will be useful to me," he had said to himself. He was used to talking to himself, because he was alone for such long periods. The key was to the little electric plant. He had had to make duplicates of at least three other keys before he had found the proper one.

At this moment, only this retreat separated him from the German patrols searching the countryside with the help of dogs and large flash lights. The other boys, he hoped, would already be safe in the cabins or in the underground shelter. Now it was up to the hosiery salesman to hide without being discovered in his host's workshop.

He opened the door and closed it with relief. The thin metal barrier made him feel safe. Inside, a faint light helped him avoid getting entangled in the high-tension wires. He found everything neatly in order; the more powerful transformers were enclosed in little storage areas. It felt like a prison, but at that moment, he was more concerned with its positive aspects. There was a storage area for every transformer and a separate compartment for the equipment. Nicola spread out whatever rags he was able to find, wrapped a piece of cloth around a broom and made a pillow of it. He lay down on the floor, curled himself up, and tried to fall asleep.

The floor was cold and covered with oil. There was oil, or the smell of oil on the walls, in the storage areas, in the barrels, in the transformers. Now he was conscious of the steady infernal noise: the vibrating copper wires from the tension of the current. It was an unceasing concert of thousands and thousands of volts. It seemed like the sound of eternity, haunting and everlasting. If eternity had a sound, this was it.

Suddenly, the monotony was interrupted by the noise of a column of trucks or armed vehicles on the street, and from afar he heard machine gun shots. Nicola thought about his boys. They must be safe by now. He pulled the collar of his jacket up around his neck. He, also, was safe. No one would ever look for him in an electric transformer plant. He quickly fell asleep.

The following morning he woke with a splitting headache. It was seven o'clock but he could not remain hidden in this corner without being discovered by the stationmaster and his wife.

The door of the Jana house was already open. The wife was cleaning the house. Nicola had no difficulty in finding a pretext for his early return in the morning. "I was supposed to make my rounds today, but I don't feel well. I think I had better get into bed," he said.

"You don't have to stand on ceremony with us; you are part of our home," she smiled. The stocking salesman moved toward his room. Signor Jana, even though normally a timid and reserved man, approached him and shook his hand in a gesture of sympathy.

"It's a good thing they don't suspect anything," Nicola said to himself. He finally stretched out on his own bed and again fell asleep. It had been a wearing night.

## CHAPTER 14

# Chain Reactions

A salesman working in a small town must retain a certain propriety in his attire. The blue beret can be his only concession to the times. Nicola covered the Valle Olona, from Legnano to Pero and Nerviano, riding from one place to another on his bicycle and walking on foot from one cottage to another in Garbatola. He was responsible for more than just the delivery of merchandise. If one were to cross the muddy countryside around the Ghiringhella farm, one would be certain to find him, dressed tidily and conservatively, as though he had just come out of a cocktail lounge.

Once, however, he had been taken by surprise. He had just changed his clothes inside a cabin which was used for tool storage, trading his best clothes for a jacket and pants full of patches and dirty with mould, with a faded soft hat. He looked like a peasant field hand. He was standing at the door, when suddenly three uniformed men appeared at the foot of the path which led from the Ghiringhella farm to the secondary road. Although it was not yet the season for cutting fodder, the peasant was examining the blade of a scythe. The three men, who were holding sub-machine guns, rushed toward him. The peasant lit a cigarette. The Fascists shouted, "Hands up!"

They asked for his documents and wanted to know if he was the owner of the farm. "Have you seen anyone come by here?" The peasant knew that they would eventually ask, "Do you know if anybody using the name Visone is hiding on this farm?"

He asked if they were referring to the secondary road or the path in front of the cabin. "I have been here since daylight, but I did not see anyone," he said.

"Do you know where the Ghiringhella farm is?" they asked. "We are trying to find the meeting place of the partisans. There are many of us looking for them, but if someone shows us where they are to meet, we can get there ahead of them."

He looked down at his clogs. "But wouldn't it be dangerous for me?" he asked.

"Oh, don't be silly, don't worry about it, all you have to do is show us the way."

There was no choice. He could not get his clogs off and rush for the pistols in the leather bag inside the cabin. He would have to accompany them for a while and then attempt to flee. "Let's go, then," he said. And he began to move toward a group of small houses in the distance, followed by the three militiamen, who kept looking anxiously around, with guns poised to shoot. "They are afraid," thought the peasant, "they could easily lose their calm and start shooting at the slightest provocation." He continued to think as he walked along.

There were no accessible hiding places in the immediate neighborhood. And who would warn the other partisans that the meeting place was a trap? He could lead the three Republicans to the meeting place and try to warn the partisans. It might go off well as it had at other times; but perhaps it would not. It would be terribly stupid for him to try to get away from the three Republicans just for the thrill of it and then not have time to warn the partisans. He could get away and ambush the Republicans later. But now he had to proceed on his present course.

How would he be able to warn his comrades, he wondered. His own partisans were among the best-trained men he had ever had, and also the best shots. A few seconds would be all they needed, possibly even one second, because they would realize the situation in a flash and would act accordingly. But he had to give them that extra second to recover from the surprise. Nevertheless, he felt optimistic. He walked along steadily without rushing.

A half-hour had passed since the walk had begun. The three Republicans were becoming impatient. "Do we have far to go? Are we almost there?" The Ghiringhella farm buildings lay behind the house which was less than half a mile away. But Nicola had to keep the Republicans from noticing this too early. Fortunately, it was impossible to see the cluster of old Ghiringhella buildings. He heard footsteps nearby. Three little children appeared at the corner of the house and started to follow them, laughing as they ran. They disappeared as they ran around the building again, but their voices could still be heard. If the children continued to play around them, Nicola worried that they would be in danger. A hundred yards along, a woman appeared at a window and drew a sheet that hung on a line. Seeing the group approach, she instinctively shut her window and ran quickly down to the ground floor. The children were heard no more.

The peasant turned around and smiled. "Another five hundred yards, just ten minutes more, and we'll be there." They went past the house. The place was hardly visible behind a group of trees. The Republicans prepared to cover the remaining five hundred yards in Indian file.

"I hope the boys are on guard," thought Nicola. He walked on ahead. A few yards from the small chapel, he saw them. They were not aware of anything. Nicola quickly looked about. The house was just behind him; in front of it was a ditch which was hardly visible. Something moved behind a bush. The partisans could not be aware of what was happening. Nicola had blocked the Republican's view of the scene, but he was at the same time keeping the partisans from sensing the impending danger. Intentionally losing one of his clogs, he leaned over as if to put it back on his foot, but instead, took off the other one and ran crouched over, shouting, "Shoot, shoot, shoot!" He leaped into the ditch, losing his breath as he landed on his stomach. The Gappisti pistols gave the Republicans no time to act; one fell dead, and the other two dropped their guns and fled.

"Come on, let's go; They're looking for us everywhere!" someone shouted.

\* \* \* \* \*

"We must wait and prepare for the right moment," one of the men nearest the Count insisted. If they could, they would have conducted marching exercises and guard drills for my boys. They had no conception of our war; they could not grasp the mentality and the capabilities of these people who, though not all peasants, had been born and raised in the country.

Would they influence my men? What did the "right moment"

mean? Having storehouses full of ammunition, guns and provisions? But whose were these stores? They were keeping the little they had hidden. From aerial bombardments? It was not really the time to worry about that. The right moment! Trained expert people! Actual combat was the best school of warfare.

\* \* \* \* \*

At Nerviano, our activity became paralyzed with inertia. I had to find a solution which would shake up this closed and isolated little center, where those who wanted to stall were influencing everyone.

These boys were capable; they were no less courageous than those in Mazzo. I had to arouse them, to confront them with the realities. The purpose was not so much getting an immediate result, but arriving at general political participation. Speaking to the men of the Nerviano detachment, I tried to appeal to their pride. "What kind of detachment are you that limit your activity to taking care of your pistols?"

I proposed an action against the block post at Legnano; it would be a lightning blow, a very rapid encounter. I followed the thesis that favorable events did not wait for one, but had to be created.

The commandant, who had proposed to wait for a "more favorable moment," did not participate with his men. On the night of November 7, with the vice-commandant in charge, the partisans, who included Walter, Gini, Cip, Carletto, Giovanni and Renda, reached the periphery of Legnano at 10 P.M. and set themselves around the block post. From their hiding-places, they observed the Fascists for a long time as they came out of their inspection booths to inspect the papers of all who passed through.

At 11:30 P.M., they opened fire. The Fascists fired back. The alarm was given in the city. The attack was successful; two Fascists were hit, and the reaction of the survivors was ineffective. The Germans joined the fight; two of our men were wounded. We succeeded in saving one. We cleared out, following a path into open country. We had to leave behind 24-year-old Francesco Renda, injured. We found out later that the Germans tortured him before killing him without ever having known anything about him.

The operation's success brought about positive political repercussions. Public opinion was now on the side of the partisans.

They had demonstrated that the enemy was vulnerable and could be attacked successfully.

Several days later, I spoke to the men of the Nerviano detachment. This time the commandant was also present. I praised their courage but criticized their lack of preparation. This had cost Renda his life. I added that Renda had fallen heroically, but that the aim of the partisans was always to keep ahead of the enemy. The art of survival, I said, was acquired through actual experience of warfare. And if they did not acquire it, they would not be able to strike when that mythical "favorable occasion" arose. The men seemed convinced.

✱   ✱   ✱   ✱   ✱

The assaults set off a chain reaction. The Fascists hit back brutally, trying to interrupt the seige of the invisible and evasive army. Part of this chain reaction was the shooting of the five partisans at Turbigo.

Lilla Ferrari, a spy, who was secretary of the Fascist group at Arese, and who was responsible for the arrest of various resistance participants, was shot to death in one of our next attacks. The Fascists had to control the situation in the Valle Olona. It was now a hotbed of revolt. The roads and any evening activities had become hazardous, not only for them, but for the Germans, the auto columns, railroad trains, and barracks of both the Wehrmacht and the Republicans.

On October 18, twenty-four hours after her execution, they held Lilla Ferrari's funeral with a great and showy display. Beginning at dawn, the military trucks and armored cars swarmed through the streets of the town. At first, the people looked out of their windows curiously; then they closed their blinds.

The enemy tried to regain the upper hand psychologically. The funeral was a pretext for a display of force, the road to indiscriminate reprisals. Our rule which we had learned during the roughest months at Turin and Milan was to give no respite to the enemy, to be unintimidated by reprisals. It was the only way to maintain top efficiency and render the enemy's cruelty useless and ineffective. We reacted immediately to this display of Republican and Fascist force.

A large number of partisans with automatics attacked the automobile of the Fascist officer, Costa, on the heights of Pero and then disappeared in the ensuing confusion. We had to demonstrate that we were capable of acting at any moment, in any place, and against any formation, even in broad daylight.

＊　＊　＊　＊　＊

The meeting place of the three partisans who were to assist me was in the outskirts of Rho. We would divide arms and ammunition, and each of us would work in his own specialty. I arrived on time at the meeting place and waited for my comrades for two hours. Finally, I heard the rumble of a motorcycle; it was Sergio, the courier, whose job was to precede the Fascists and warn us of their arrival.

"What, are you alone?" asked Sergio. I did not have the courage to tell him the truth.

"The others are already in hiding up ahead" I said. "How are things going?"

"The bulk of them will be here in five minutes; they seem to be coming ahead pretty fast. Get going."

I was alone; possibly my companions had been captured; perhaps they had not been able to meet me; perhaps they had been afraid. I understood that. Ours was a terrible war, and we were not supermen. I, their leader, was only a man like the others; fear and anxiety did not pass me by. But if this show of Republican power were followed by a shower of bullets, the reprisals would aid our withdrawal. I knew this was a decisive moment. Here at Rho, the enemy was throwing together all of his strength; we had to answer him. Even though I was alone, I had to do something. If this activity went well, it would inject a feeling of trust and confidence in my group; it would whip them into further action.

I was in the vicinity of the Piazza del Duomo. There was only a small crowd there, waiting for the coffin which was carried between two continuous cordons of Republicans. Standing near a group of civilians, I was tempted to turn back.

The hearse had just passed in front of me, and the relatives of the spy had also just gone by. The high Fascist officers followed. I walked away from the group of civilians and approached the cordon of lined-up militia. I took out a bomb, one of the so-called "humanitarians," that make a great deal of noise, with little splintering. There was a need for noise. If necessary, I would use my two revolvers. I furiously yanked at the safety and tossed the bomb. I hurriedly walked away even before it hit the ground. The platoon of church officials which had been preceeding the casket dispersed instantaneously. Even the impeccable line of militia was thrown into confusion. There were bursts of gun-fire. People ran off in all directions. The Fascists threw themselves to the ground; they crawled away on all fours, and then ran off as fast as they could toward the entrances of the buildings in the area.

The air was now full of smoke, and it was hard to breathe. From one direction, I could hear one cluster of shots, immediately followed by ten from another direction. I could recognize the dry crackle of the German Mausers. I alone knew what was happening. At that moment, Republicans and Germans were shooting into each other.

I ran to one of our posts and asked for a Fascist uniform. I would change into it in spite of the fact that the Germans would kill me immediately were they to identify me in it. One hour had passed between the time I had thrown the grenade and Carmen's arrival. I donned the uniform and left with her. The shooting continued. The funeral had begun at five. One hour had already gone by, and still none of them had realized that no partisans were present in the square at Rho. The gun-fire was terrible. Two regiments were facing each other in a space hardly large enough for a theatrical performance.

We went the long way around so as to avoid the enemy. We stopped at various quiet safe places along the way. When we came to the road leading to the Ghiringhella farm, it was almost seven o'clock. Only then did the exchange of shots begin gradually to lessen. The town was completely blocked off. I heard the sound of cadenced steps, and a German patrol came into view. I hardly had time to grab Carmen and take her in my arms. I felt her fingernails in my face. Carmen was one of our bravest and most faithful couriers, but she did not like this sudden display of intimacy. However, she quickly understood when the patrol passed by.

"Fascist love," one of the Germans said, and laughed. We could hear the others join in the laughter as the patrol went off. Carmen accompanied me to the Ghiringhella farm. I searched in vain for a handkerchief to wipe the sweat from my brow; there was none in the pocket of the uniform.

Every night, throughout our territory, the Germans and Fascists were living in fear. We were told by our spies that many of their soldiers were deeply shaken by our offensives. They knew that every night our men would strike, but they did not know when, where, or how—whether with loads of explosives on bridges and sections of railroad track, or with attacks upon their motor columns. All they knew was that we were sure to attack. Throughout the territory, the Gappisti were talking about terrorizing the enemy; the arms which had been used against our population were now turned against the oppressor. Now, no soldier could fall asleep in the barracks, in the storehouses or in the Republican and German billets. The men guarding the factories, the motor trucks and barracks cursed the moment they had arrived in this area which at first had seemed so tranquil and unlikely a spot for trouble.

Now, we decided to attack in daytime as well as at night. We had done this before. It was important that the partisan forces enact a type of warfare which had clear political significance as well as military success. The choice of the next objective was made on the basis of a tip which came from Nerviano. In one of the Isotta Fraschini factories on the edge of the town, they were producing the most up-to-date war devices and gun-parts for the Wehrmacht.

Several partisans were given the responsibility of gathering detailed information about the factory's war activity. I decided to conduct my own investigation without telling anyone. Dressed in peasant clothing, I rode my old bicycle over to the factory. To reach it from Nerviano one had to cross the Simplon national highway and the bridge over the Villoresi Canal. I had to follow a road to the right which ran along the bank of the canal before turning into the country. This was Via Rovereto which led through a cluster of houses onto Via Duca di Pistoia. I noticed the factory; it was a large but decrepit complex with long, ugly buildings, and a large yard, fenced off and deserted. Three sides of the factory were surrounded by open country; the main entrance was on the Via Duca di Pistoia. There was also a small country road on the right side, shaded by large trees on either side; this offered possible hiding places, if needed. After exploring the area, I stopped at a small tavern some distance away, and ordered a sandwich and a glass of wine from the host, our friend. In addition, I asked some questions about the factory. "You are fortunate," I told him, "that you don't have to deal with members of the Black Brigade."

"You're mistaken," he answered, "there are Fascists around

here, but they are wearing civilian clothes. There are also Germans, but they hardly ever leave the factory." I paid up and left quickly.

The information which I had gathered was important. In the Isotta Fraschini factory, which was set up to produce bomb fuses, they were also working on parts for the detonation device of the V-1 and the V-2. The work was performed almost in secrecy inside these buildings without any obvious guard detail. Thus, the attention of the partisans and the allied information sources was not drawn to the manufacture of these delicate parts of the terrible weapon which had been devastating English cities. The Nazis had succeeded in hiding this production from our sabotage and the Allied bombings.

We decided upon an operation which would not only cause material damage to the factory but would also reveal its secret activity. "A military maneuver like that would appeal to the workers," I pointed out, in the course of a secret meeting to discuss our preparations.

Two Gappisti, with the aid of local partisans, would transport the loads of TNT along the country paths and set their explosions to coincide with the departure of the employees after their work shift.

On the afternoon of December 9, the two comrades arrived at the factory, followed a ditch, and set up the explosives; other partisans in the area were standing by, ready to help.

✷    ✷    ✷    ✷    ✷

It was 5:15 P.M. The workers would finish their shift at 5:40. The explosions were set to go off at six o'clock, at the precise moment of their departure from the factory.

Our objective was to cause damage to the main electric plant which was located apart from the other buildings. We were preoccupied with the safety of the workers who would still be working.

Hiding in the bushes near the Villoresi canal, I awaited the explosion with relative calm. The long months of clandestine activity in Turin and Milan had taught me how to wait and reflect. I reviewed the details of the action, the precautions taken, the men chosen among the experts of the "sappers' school" of Lainate and

Nerviano—the flourishing hotbed of the Gappisti—the courageous people who combined an exceptional technical capacity with strong, combative ideals.

My plan was to move toward the entrance while the enemy launched a search for the saboteurs after the explosion.

The clock was about to strike. The area was quiet. There was no one stirring. I grabbed my bicycle, leaving my hiding place, and pedalled toward Via Duca di Pistoia. Precisely at 6, three formidable explosions shook the air. A giant blue flame quickly leaped up, with a thick black cloud of smoke. The TNT had exploded in the electric plant. The short circuit produced by the explosion had set the large transformers afire. Production would remain dead for some time. It was the moment to act.

Behind me, dozens and dozens of workers were speedily riding away on their bicycles. The Simplon national highway was two hundred yards behind, and to the right lay the bridge crossing the Villoresi Canal. I left the bicycle on the bank of the canal and took out two large packages from my jacket. The Fascists and Germans were off looking for the partisans. They were probably near their places of retreat by now. They were unaware that the commandant of the 106th Garibaldi Brigade SAP[1] was right there at the center of activity.

I started to distribute handbills to the workers. Some appeared frightened, while others looked as if they were in a daze as they moved toward the center of the road. Some stared at me with a perplexed look, but several stopped to take the handbills, which contained the CLN's appeal to join the struggle. I shouted as loudly as I could, "Long live the partisans! Long live the Resistance! We shall fight together against the Fascists and Germans!"

After distributing my handbills, I ran back, cutting through the middle of a group of workers. I reached the bridge over the Villoresi Canal, crossed over to the opposite shore. The job was done. Even though many had not heard my words, almost all had taken the handbills and would read them in their homes.

It was a little before 11:30 P.M. At this hour, the military vehicles were the only ones on the dark highway. The boys were

---

1. SAP (Squadre d'Azione Patriottica—Sappisti) was a Communist-sponsored patriotic fighting force—a supplementary fighting force to the Gappisti.

groping in the dark. Leaping over a ditch, I approached the road with caution. Off in the distance, I could hear the muffled rumble of a motor. The boys made me anxious. They were new. Their inexperience and excitement could bring disastrous results.

I had an idea. After ascertaining that the area was deserted, I abandoned every caution, and, walking upright, I began calling out orders to the group as I approached them. I spoke in a loud voice, as though we were dealing with a tactical rather than a clandestine maneuver. I signaled three of the boys to approach me on my left, ten yards behind; I placed another group in the center, and assigned the rest of the small formation to a position about twenty yards further back. My orders, given in an energetic voice combined with a feeling of confidence seemed to relieve the boys' tension.

Now I suggested that they fan out behind the wall of rocks; this would serve as a protection against gunfire from the thickets. The boys spread out with apparent calm. I continued giving firm orders, like a film director; this was a sure way of instilling calm. I shouted to the boys lined up on the left, "Watch out for military vehicles. We must capture a trailer truck only if we think it is loaded with arms, not men."

The baptism of fire for these boys had to be gradual. It was best to avoid an armed confrontation. Now I faced the other two groups, "The rest of you must be ready to fire only if the enemy reacts, only if I give you orders. Have your guns ready, and don't let them jam. But no firing without orders! Understood?" They seemed a bit perplexed; perhaps they were asking themselves how they could attack a truck without quickly firing at it?

I knew we could fight the enemy effectively, even though we were few in number, if we had confidence in our strength, in our intelligence, but above all, if we had courage. The encounter about to take place that evening would be the lesson in courage and would be an example of partisan war action.

I called to Angelo, "Set yourself in that thicket. Throw a hand grenade at the truck, and stay behind the rock until it's over. When you pull the safety of the grenade as you count to five, make sure that the truck is a dozen yards from you. Is that clear?"

Angelo assured me that he understood, but he seemed a bit anxious. He had not figured upon acting alone. But I had much confidence in him. I accompanied him to the middle of the large thicket. "Remember that you'll have to move, so don't get entangled in the thicket." A truck was approaching, but it was not the one that we would attack; it would, however, serve for a general test. "Boys, stay right there. Angelo," I continued, "start counting to five, as though you have just pulled the safety." Angelo waited. The truck approached. He began to count.

"One, two . . . three," his voice trembled, four, five . . ."

"Very good," I said. "Remember to throw the grenade at the windshield. Even if it is only a short throw, it will damage the motor. Stay behind here, so the others can shoot without hitting you. When I give the signal to withdraw, move one hundred yards over to the line of trees, and we'll assemble there. Stay calm, and crawl along for the first few yards of retreat. Is that clear?"

"Very clear," they all cried.

I approached the group on my left. One boy had his pistol in his hand. "Do you know how to use it?"

"I can take it apart and put it together again in a minute," he responded boisterously.

"Let's see." He easily took it apart, but found difficulty in reassembling it. "What are you going to do if it gets clogged when you need it? Take it to a gunsmith?" The boy was humiliated. I gave him a slap on the shoulder, and walked over to the other two, who were not signaling the arrival of a motor truck properly. "What truck is that?" It was still a half mile away, but it was undoubtedly a military truck.

"It appears to be a German trailer truck," the boys answered.

"Very well, be sure you don't make a mistake. Make sure it's a military truck. And when it's twenty yards away and you're sure, signal Angelo. He'll take it from there. Do you understand, Angelo? Do you understand everything?" I continued speaking, competing with the noise of the approaching motor. "Don't shoot if I don't give you the signal. We must protect the retreat of Angelo and of the first group to the left. The group to the right must protect the center group and then disengage itself. I shall be with you. Pay attention to my orders. Clear?"

They answered loudly, "Everything is clear." Now we were ready.

I recognized the rumble of the motor and the blue rectangular lights. It was a military truck. A few seconds passed. There was some movement in the group to the left. The signal was given.

"Be calm. Handle everything coolly, Angelo," I succeeded in telling him, "and aim at the windshield." This time, I lowered the tone of my voice. I moved toward the group on my right. If Angelo missed his target, there would be a reaction from the enemy; we had to shoot quickly, not allowing the enemy one second's respite. Hopefully, it was a load of material, not of men.

These young boys were taking part in their first battle. Angelo had set himself to throw the grenade; he had cleared the foliage; he would remove the safety. The truck was fifty yards away. Angelo had never before thrown a grenade. The truck was approaching. "Be ready to fire on my orders. Follow the truck, and keep your guns aimed," I urged the boys. I could see Angelo's lightning-swift, violent thrust. "With that power," I thought, "he could even stop the truck with a stone." An explosion, a blinding flash, and the motor roared crazily. The trailer-truck covered a last stretch of roadway, and then, skidding fearfully, it turned over on the side of the road and caught fire.

"Angelo?"

"Yes?"

"Get your boys and move them off quickly to the rendezvous."

"O.K.," he answered in a more confident voice than before. To avoid any surprises, we waited for a few seconds. It was evident that it was only material which was now burning in the truck. It was time to get away. "Boys, move ahead, let's get going."

I watched them pass in front of me, covered with mud, happy, on their way to the established rendezvous. I joined Angelo. "You're O.K. . . . nice going!"

There was no time for comments. "Now, boys, move along!" We walked quickly along the country paths, keeping on the alert. "I suggest that those of you who live in town stay at one of the hiding places or at the farm of a friend. The enemy is alerted right now and on the prowl." The small formation scattered. The boys were beginning to learn the first rules of guerrilla warfare.

All the boys were together; it would be our first large simultaneous action covering the entire Valle Olona. I was sure the enemy's antennae had caught at least some sign of our preparations for the offensive. I was anxious about the absence of the usual skirmishes; there was no sign of activity in the Nerviano headquarters of the Fascist detachment, a dark, silent building, which was watched over by a pair of guards. The detachment at Lainate also seemed to be ignoring the impending threat; the large Borromeo villa at the center of the park was more silent than usual; its windows were tightly shut. The enemy's calm disturbed me. Through long experience, I knew that only the little actions escaped the enemy's attention; plans for vast-scale offensives usually reached the ears of the Black Brigades and Wehrmacht well in advance. We could not verify that there was enemy infiltration inside our lines, but I knew that some word, some innocent phrase from our boys—several of them were only fifteen years old—would be quickly picked up by the Republican informers.

It was an important time for inspection on the widest possible scale. Many men of the Brigade were bearing arms for the first time. Others had military experience, especially the detonation experts, who had already shown an amazing technical capacity, combined with a cold-blooded manner. Those who had fought in North Africa for the wrong cause were now fighting against the Nazi-Fascists. But the Brigade was mainly made up of boys.

I quickened my step. A detachment from Lainate lay in wait on the provincial road. There were clusters of thicket along the big road, and behind them, rows of trees and ditches. It was favorable terrain for quick, nocturnal surprise attacks. The reflectors of the German auto-columns would not be able to penetrate this thicket. Even though their lights were high power, the beams would not be able to reach beyond the rows of trees or scan the ditches which were protected by thickets of shrubs and bushes.

The boys were waiting, perfectly positioned, right in the middle of the thicket. They kept watching the road in both directions; the rifles and sub-machine guns were hidden in the bushes. An irregular row of poplars separated them from the road. They would be able to strike from an expanded position and then disperse quickly. Adolescents of fifteen to eighteen were in that thicket. They laughed nervously at the most trivial remarks; it seemed to be the same state of mind that students had at examination time.

We were fighting the Wehrmacht with young boys. We were attacking the SS with grammar-school students!

"Are you afraid?" I asked one of them.

"What do you mean, afraid? I can't wait to begin!"

Hardly convinced, I interrogated another tall and thin boy, a student in high school, who appeared more conscientious and mature. I did not ask if he, himself, was scared, but if he thought the others were.

"No, on the contrary, we can't wait to shoot down some Germans."

"Excuse me," a timid looking boy asked, "What time do you think we'll be finished?"

"You are in a war and you want to know what the time schedule will be?" I responded brusquely, and then stopped short because right behind me I noticed another boy holding a mess-tin, eating some bean soup as though he were on a picnic. I interrupted him and asked sarcastically, "Couldn't you have sent for something to eat from some cafe in the area?" The boy started to laugh.

"My mother prepared this soup, and she also gave me some steak and potatoes to take along with me." It was worse than I had feared! Not only did we have to attack the Germans with young boys, but the plans for this secret ambush had been revealed to the mothers of Lainate, who had prepared special dinners for their boys. Others, too, were eating; some were sharing bottles of wine.

"But did you tell your family that you were going to participate in an attack on the Germans?"

The answer was a loud and shocked "No!" The timid boy then added, "We did tell our families that this evening, after school and work, we would be going directly to a social gathering. I did not want my mother to worry about my getting home late. That is why I asked you when we would be through . . ."

Everything was now clear to me and much more reassuring. "You will be finished soon enough, boys, not much after midnight. In any case, it would be best to break up at that time." What a relief. It was incredible, but their anxiety was based upon their fear of alarming their families. It seemed to disturb them hardly at all that the Germans would soon be answering their fire.

✿　✿　✿　✿　✿

After inspecting the Lainate group I decided to look at the men of the Nerviano and Mazzo detachment. The night was bright and silent; the black sky was cold as ice.

The Mazzo detachment was the most alert. Its leader was G., and he was the coolest man I had ever encountered in partisan warfare in that area. He worked on his farm attending his livestock; he wrapped himself in a dark cape which he took off only when summer came. He had been a demolition expert, and he now managed explosives with the same confidence and decisiveness with which he stored his cheeses in the racks. He waged war the way he worked—seriously, precisely, and with the same careful attention that he gave to cultivating his own piece of land.

When he had to transport explosives, he dressed as though he were going to a party; he wore his best top coat and went off casually with his sack full of dynamite over the local roads. He greeted friends as he went, his old pipe always lit in his mouth.

During my inspection of the detachments, I met him on the banks of the Villoresi, a good distance away from the town. There we breathed our own air; we had a snack of salami, bread and a glass of wine at the local tavern. The host was one of our people; his tavern was a way-station, and the boys of Mazzo were gathered there with G.

At the prearranged hour, we made plans to cut through the cemetery toward the railroad line which was being protected by German guards and blow up several yards of track, to interrupt traffic to and from Milan. I returned to my base, which was a factory under construction, to await news about the progress of the large-scale operation in Valle Olona. Passing in front of a small chapel which was dedicated to Saint Rocco, I stopped to look at the religious painting. It was very familiar to me and contained a figure with its hand extended in a gesture of greeting. As usual, the slender candle with its blue glass shade was lit, and I tried to figure out whether this was an act of the friars' reverence or a warning signal by partisans who had deposited explosives and machine guns behind the altar. Then I noticed that the light had been moved to the right, away from its usual position. The two vases placed at the sides of the altar signaled that the arms had been collected for use on the Rho and Lainate roads as well as in the area of Mazzo. I took one last look at Saint Rocco and moved toward "general headquarters," a dugout which had, so far, survived demolition and bombardments. Up above, I heard the familiar roar of "Pippo," the airplane, which precisely at 11 o'clock every evening unloaded its bombs upon the roads and lights throughout the area.

At that same moment, my men were moving behind the bushes; the boys from Lainate examined the breeches of their guns, listened to last-minute instructions. Perhaps it was illogical, but I felt that everything would go well, regardless of the problems, the inexperience of the young men and the complexity of a large-scale mobilization. In order to insure receipt of the guns from the Count, after that meeting which had been held in the home of the Crespi sisters, I had had to lend a hand in distributing brule wine to a group of partisans who were assembled at the inn.

With a shudder I remembered the automobile trip to Lecco, our ultimate arrival at the villa to get the trunk from the custodian, the worried whispered exchanges, the German guard, our suspicious-looking appearance carrying the load, our "De Profundis," with our fingers on the triggers of our revolvers, and, finally, our surprise at having spirited the guns right out from under the noses of the Germans.

Was this a hazardous game, a melodrama concocted by that eccentric man who wrapped himself in a nineteenth-century cape? Who were the people in contact with the Anglo-Americans? Who was giving shelter to the American officers who were parachuting into the area?

It was due to good luck, to meticulous preparations and scrupulous attention to the rules of underground warfare that I was still free and that my partisans were able to fight against the enemy. Above all, it was due to the silence characteristic of these little towns with their traditional ties, their defiant and close-mouthed inhabitants. These people did not even exchange greetings with outsiders. They maintained this silence of their own free will, regardless of whether or not they had anything to conceal. To break through their reserve, one had to be on the right side of the barricade. One had to understand their pride, their commitment to the past, and their deep adherence to the peasant way of life.

There would be no reason to suspect these people. Furthermore, there were only a few seconds until midnight. I remained in the dark, waiting at the "base" headquarters, which consisted of a stool, a cot, a gun, explosives, and a cartridge box.

At that hour, with the curfew in effect, the motorcycle that I heard approaching could only belong either to our group or the Black Brigades. I distinctly heard several footsteps moving over the stones near my hiding place. I looked out through a crack, holding my gun in my hand. There were two men. At ten yards distance, the one ahead gave our pre-arranged signal. He threw a stone against the door, signalling again. They were my boys.

I opened the door. They had barely gotten in the door when the first boy gasped breathlessly, "Everything went well. All the wires of the Wehrmacht have been cut at Rho, and the boys got safely away before the Germans and Fascists could interfere."

The first courier had brought good news, and that called for an immediate celebration. A partisan command could be deprived of almost everything, but not a drink of brandy.

There were gun-shots in the distance. We came out of our hiding place, saw the continuous flashing streaks of gunfire and heard the deafening crackle of bullets coming from the direction of the provincial road. The reflectors were searching the parking area. There were deafening shots and violent flames of "panzer faust." Our boys were getting away, and the Germans could do nothing to stop them. In the direction of Mazzo, a flash of blue phosphorescent light lent a new color to the night. Were the first and second explosions combined? The garrison from the German detachment was shooting wildly, with every sort of weapon available—mortars, anti-tank guns, and machine guns.

Lines of German military vehicles had been attacked on the roads, telephone lines cut at Rho, trenches dug under the tracks of the Milan-Domodossola line, trains interrupted on the Milan-Turin line.

Now another phase, just as difficult, began. The decisions of the German Command had been made immediately. There would be curfews, search parties, announcements of doom from the Platzkommandatur. The enemy had unleashed its informers; columns of tanks and trucks loaded with soldiers had been sent out to terrorize the center of Valle Olona in an attempt to break up every contact between partisans and the population.

Every one of my men and boys had to rely upon his own inner strength. Each had to be quick enough to answer questions like, "Where were you this evening?" or "How come you returned home all covered with blood?" or "Why did you sleep in the home of a friend?" Now that the enemy was taking the counteroffensive, now, more than ever, was the moment for a battalion which had just proved itself in arduous combat to stand firm.

❖   ❖   ❖   ❖   ❖

Discipline in every army rests upon justice. And this was true of ours. The struggle for independence had its rules of behavior. The rules were not written into any particular form but were rigorously respected. A partisan was a fighter who never betrayed his companions. He could not desert without justification. Our war gave none of the customary retirement benefits. If a man abandoned us, he did so only because something unusual had happened. We had to be on the alert for this kind of situation. In every case, when a man became a potential danger to us, he automatically became an enemy.

✿   ✿   ✿   ✿   ✿

I tried to remember the physical features of one particular man who had left our ranks. His eyes had had a sly glint and a cold stare. He had given us no particular reason to criticize him. But, then, people had begun to talk. M. had been seen at C., on the same day that a robbery had taken place. The Republican newspapers had accused the partisans of robbing the peasants. I had ordered the group command to keep its eyes open. Details of additional robberies had begun to reach us; the accusations against M. became more specific.

Then had come some alarming news: M. was a spy. After having captured him, the Fascists had set him free. It happened rarely that a partisan was thus given his freedom. When this had been verified, we had had to act immediately. We had been forced to abandon all the refuges familiar to him, to break off all relations with the companions he had known, and to change the location of our arsenals. When the enemy had searched these places, he had found nothing. But M. had talked.

While the Republicans had still been searching the area, we had captured him. In his pocket we found a revolver and an SS identification card. M. had seemed nonchalant at our general quarters. I had felt that he had always been a spy and that he had even anticipated eventually coming up against partisan justice. Actually, his nonchalance had been a mask for his arrogant belief that he would be able to deceive his interrogators. When the partisan command had begun to challenge his answers, he had grown fearful and anxious.

"Why did you betray us?"

"Try to be reasonable . . ."

"Can anyone be reasonable with a Fascist spy?"

"I was forced to do it."

"Why?"

"To save myself. They would have killed me!"

"Did you want to save yourself as a partisan or as a robber?"

M., visibly shaken, was silent. Then, he began to reveal everything.

"The SS commandant told me that he could have me shot for participating in the robberies, but he added that he was aware of my contact with the partisans. I tried to deny it. They kept after me. They wanted to know who Visone was and where he was hiding. I just couldn't hold back."

M. had realized then that he had pronounced his own death sentence. He had begun arguing and imploring, and then finally shouted, "Let me be! Let me be!"

We had gone into another room to decide his fate. "I don't want to influence you," I had said, "You have to let your conscience be your guide."

"He's guilty," concluded the comrades.

The Command had unanimously condemned him to death for espionage, and the sentence had been carried out.

Two days later, the Command ordered me to go to Milan. I left my comrades of Valle Olona; I left the men, women and boys who had fought the hard battle; I left the commandants and the commissars of the 106th. I would always remember the multitude of faces and names. Sandro, commandant of the detachment, had used the engineers' office as a hideout. He had saved the lives of engineers Silvio, Mauro, Luciano, Mosca, Renato, Sante Boselli, Scalabrino, Beccarelli, and Captain Costa.

I said farewell to the brave partisans of the detachments from Rho, Nerviano, Garbagnate, Barbaiana, Garbatola, Pantanedo; I said goodbye to a number of obscure heroes.

## CHAPTER 15
# Perfect Rhythm

I returned to Milan. With Franci's help, I started organizing our forces all over again.

I found an ideal meeting place inside the Church of San Marco and Achille on Viale Argonne; I also found a location for the laboratory.

Two days later Minardi and two young girls, Olga and Grazia, joined out group. I relied a good deal upon Nigarda's group; I had remained in contact with them during my stay at Rho.

During the morning of December 16, the radio and news-papers broke the news that Mussolini would speak at eleven o'clock at the Lyric Theatre, in the heart of the city.

At 8:30, I met with Busetto. "Have you heard about it?" I asked quickly.

"Yes."

"Well, what are we going to do about it?"

We walked along together some distance in silence. I was waiting for an answer. "It's difficult to decide just like that, all of a sudden," said Busetto. "Who knows what security measures have been taken. This is an operation which demands several days of preparation. We just cannot improvise."

I was not convinced. A hundred ideas shot through my mind. Actually, I thought, it would be an operation like many others; the objective was the most important consideration.

Later, I met Conti on Corso Venezia. We walked together toward the Lyric Theatre. Our eyes kept scanning the walls, look-ing for a hidden niche. We scanned the corners, the windows. We also noticed the plainclothes men stationed all along the way to guard the Duce.

As we approached the theater, the crowd grew larger. Mussolini's words carried over a loud speaker, fell upon a crowd and a city which had suffered bombings and terror. Some listened and applauded, others kept on talking in various dialects.

We Gappisti felt temporarily helpless, and we postponed our attack until the following day. I told Conti, "Meet me tomorrow morning at eight o'clock at the Corso Garibaldi and bring Antonio and Giuseppe." Mussolini would be speaking again at the Piazza Castello.

We turned into Via Cusani from Corso Garibaldi, crossed Foro Bonaparte, and reached Piazza Luca Beltrami. Here, we encountered the same difficulties as we had the day before. We had to get through the cordons of armed guards and plainclothesmen. We followed Via Ponzone, Via Rovello, and Via San Tommaso, up to the corner of Via Dante.

"Damn it," I swore to myself, "isn't there some niche, window or even a vent where we can hide?" But time was passing and meanwhile, the Fascist procession was breaking up. We walked off in silence, followed by the raucous "Evviva!" shouts of the Blackshirts.

It had been a bitter experience, hearing all that applause for the dictator. But I knew I had to overcome my disappointment. I tried to emphasize to myself that the real Milan was not found on Via Dante, in the Lyric Theatre or Castle Forzesco.

I arranged a meeting with Franci and Marcello in the basement of the church on Viale Argonne. We discussed an attack against the assembly places used by the Nazi-Fascists. Marcello said he would be responsible for reinforcing the GAP organization with men from the Fronte della Gioventù (Youth Front). (Unfortunately, before these youths could join the Brigade, they were discovered, arrested, and subsequently shot at Camp Giuriati.)

We were about to leave the meeting when we discovered that the door was bolted on the outside. We succeeded in freeing ourselves after working for half an hour with a screw driver and a hammer.

Our plan of action had been completed. Day and night, with the help of Minardi, Selvetti, and Olga, we would attack, one by one, the assembly places most frequented by the enemy.

Our first attack was made on a military truck of the Resega Division. Near midnight on December 29, 1944, the truck was driving down Via Stephenson, returning from Turin with a load of bombs and guns. We killed seven soldiers, and seriously injured several others.

❋   ❋   ❋   ❋   ❋

On New Year's Eve, the Allied armies were on the offensive at every front. The partisans were reinforced, mostly with youths, throughout the mountains.

It had already turned dark when I arrived at the assembly place. Groups of Fascists and Germans were idly lounging about. The place was full. I went to pick up the bombs from Minardi and Olga. Back at the entrance, the Fascists and Germans were more numerous than ever. I heard the notes of a popular tune. Two Germans were arguing with a Fascist over a woman.

The argument attracted a crowd, and confusion reigned. I took advantage of the situation and moved behind the group. I lit the fuse with a cigarette and placed the little case on the ground. Suddenly, somebody grabbed me by the arm; he held on to me and mumbled in a strange Italian, "I arrive war . . ." The quarrel continued. I wrenched free from the drunkard. It was time to clear out. A few minutes later, a violent explosion lacerated the air. This was our first answer to the pathetic blusterings at the Lyric Theater.

On San Silvestro's Day, the Gappisti broke up film showings with a protest demonstration in three downtown movie houses: the Peace, Emerald, and Empire Theaters. We distributed leaflets urging on the struggle for Liberation. At the Peace, a battle developed with several Fascists of the Bir el Gobi Company; one was killed, two others wounded. During the evening, on Piazzale Firenze, other Gappisti of the Third Brigade attacked two Fascist junior officers, killing one of them.

The following day, after a call from Colonel Rauff, German Commandant of Security Police, Prefect Headquarters ordered the closing of public bars at 7:30 P.M. Riding bicycles was forbidden between 7 P.M. and 5 A.M.

We intensified our operations; we gave no respite to the enemy. On January 7, I attacked a bar on the Via Vittor Pisani, on the corner of Piazza Duca D'Aosta. It was frequented for the most part by Germans and Fascists. The Fascists, who had learned their lesson after that first attack, had set up a guard detail in front of their quarters. With the help of the technician, I had wrapped a bomb in cardboard shaped to look like an accordion. It was a dark and cloudy evening. I threw the "instrument" onto my shoulders, shuddering at the contact. Before entering the bar, I lit the fuse. I looked around, sat down, ordered something to drink, asked where the toilet was, set the package on the floor without being noticed and walked out right under the eyes of the guard. I advanced a few yards, and then, the explosion! According to the subsequent report, fourteen people were killed or wounded.

The following day, the head of the province, Mario Bassi, released an order: "In view of Article 19 of the communal and provincial law, I have decreed: (1) Effective immediately, the curfew begins at 8:30 P.M. instead of 10 P.M. (2) The public services will adjust their activities to conform to this schedule. (3) Public functions will cease and places of recreation will close at 7:30 P.M. . . . ."

I had done my best, and was feeling nervous and alone. I had asked for help, but I had not received any answer. I wrote again in protest. I finally gave up, then I thought of something. I met with Lina.

"Why did you want to see me?"

"Tell me something," I asked her, "why do you always wear the same dress? They'll be able to recognize you easily. Why don't you try to change it sometimes?"

"I would certainly do it if I could afford it."

"Look, why don't I buy you a new one? Let's go."

We walked toward a store on Corso Vittorio Emanuele. Lina selected, instead, a solid grey coat. It looked well on her, and she was very pleased. She again asked, "Why do you want to see me?"

"Well," I said, "would you like to work with me on a job?"

We quickly formed plans for a joint undertaking for the evening of January 13, 1945; we would set off several bombs in a place on Via Ponte Vetero which was frequented by Nazi-Fascists and black marketeers.

The action would be difficult, primarily because of the steady flow of Germans and Fascists.

During the evening, Lina and I picked up the bombs, which had been brought over to us earlier by Minardi and Olga. We walked along slowly together. It was a dark, humid night with overhanging clouds. Lina had put on her new coat; around her neck, she wore a scarf which had been sent to her by her mother. I walked alongside with my hand in my pocket, ready for action. Lina would remain with me until we reached the door and then move away. We would meet the next day.

Nearing our objective, we paused. We heard a scuffle of steps and the murmur of voices. A group of people seemed to be approaching us. The sound of the steps disappeared, but not of the voices, which were too low to be intelligible. Then the voices faded, too, and the only sound was that of Lina's heart beat.

"Aren't you afraid?" she asked.

"No."

What could I say to a girl who was carrying a load of bombs in her pocketbook? She gazed at me fixedly. I asked, "How come you aren't afraid? Everyone is afraid."

"Well, I'm not like others. Perhaps you'd like me better if I were afraid."

"There are moments when one is afraid," I insisted.

"Well, I'm sorry to disappoint you. I'm not lying, I assure you."

I felt her eyes piercing through me; my cheeks began to burn. I lit a cigarette: I observed the movements of her hands; I tried to concentrate on the slow rings of smoke winding around us as I exhaled. She whispered, "I think people are starting to arrive." And then she put her arms around me. I was astounded. I felt her lips on mine. Our eyes met as she lifted her head. "I had to do it," she murmured.

My eyes were half closed. My gaze fell. I was overwhelmed with embarrassment. Two Germans were entering the place. She took my hand in hers, squeezed it desperately, and anxiously pressed it against her heart. I felt her hands, and her soft cheeks on fire against my temple. I did not speak: I had all I could do to keep silent; in a moment, she pulled away from me.

She murmured a few words. I shook my head. She looked at me with a serious expression, with sweet and tender eyes. "You are a truly courageous person," I whispered. Her lips trembled. "It's easy to be courageous when you're with good company. I'm no different from anybody else."

"No, you are different. You are courageous."

There was silence. I lit a cigarette and pushed it against the bomb fuse.

"Until tomorrow."

"Until tomorrow," I answered, as she walked away.

I entered and sat down. This time, the grenade resembled a box of candy. I placed it under the table. I walked over toward the toilet and went through the door which led into the corridor. I retraced my steps to the outside. A small truck pulled up. I looked inside.

I quickly walked away and headed toward one of the streets I had followed before. I turned again and found myself in the middle of a block of houses which had been destroyed by raids. I climbed over the debris. It was cold. My pants caught in the beams, the stones lacerated my hands and knees. A violent hail of gunshot made me jump. I tripped; I was being pursued. I saw a dark shadow close to the wall moving toward me; it advanced a few steps and stopped, turning its head to look around, as though frightened. I saw another shadow, also moving along cautiously. The two shadows seemed to be exchanging a few words. I could tell they were men. They walked along together and then disappeared through a door which was opened for them. "Is it possible that we won't be in contact with other Gappisti? What will happen to us, to me, after the war? When will we win?"

Perhaps those who now were collaborating with the enemy, those who always knew how to adjust themselves to a situation, those who knew how to say "yes," would rejoin us at the end of the war. And so, what good were our sacrifices, let alone the sacrifices of those who were dying? And tomorrow? Oh, tomorrow the others—the parvenus—would move ahead. I remembered the miners and their poverty, the days without bread, the cold fireplaces, the weeks without work, the doors found locked in the evenings because the rents were not paid.

I remembered the sacrifices of many comrades, here and in Spain, and the battles, the ambushes, the interminable waiting before the assaults. I remembered Huesca.

The combination of cold, anxiety, restlessness and emotion made me feel feverish. It was curfew time. Several vehicles were whizzing by with sirens screeching at full blast. I lay flat on my stomach, pressing my forehead against the rubble to avoid the headlight beams. The shadows and silence returned. The cold penetrated my bones. I breathed deeply; I rose and again saw the street before me in the dark. I heard new voices, new motors. I slowly stumbled on, filled with uncontrollable desire to abandon that heap of rubble which had once been a house.

A piece of wood moved, making me jump. I leaned my shoulders against the wall and looked around. I heard a voice.

There were a thousand voices! I stood there petrified, my hand resting on my heart, which was beating wildly. I saw a man. He seemed drunk. I bit my finger and dug my teeth into my lips to keep from crying out. The man lay down. Calm returned, but not inside me.

It was another one of those many partisan nights through which I had lived, yet it was different from the others. I recalled the stars in the Spanish skies which had so many times been my only companions in the waiting hours of my guard-watches. I remembered my longing for home and my far-away native land, recollections of my infancy, of the mine, of the faces of many friends and comrades. Now I saw before me the face of the German in Piazza Cadorna who begged for his life while frantically showing me a snapshot of his children. I had let him live. I still felt Lina's burning kiss. I recaptured tender scenes from my distant childhood in their fleeting moments of memory. But then, the reality of the present cruelly returned. Tormented by the big city, the smell of war and the death rattle of a man in a drunken stupor, I slowly drifted off to sleep.

Was this, then, my destiny? Was I truly going crazy, I wondered, as I lay on a heap of rubble alongside the drunkard? I was bewildered for a few seconds and then began to think rationally again. "Is it possible," I asked myself, "that we must always be alone, so few in number?"

✲  ✲  ✲  ✲  ✲

"Attack to save Bilbao," had been the order of the day. The Spanish Republican forces on the march toward Huesca that day had been composed mainly of the International Brigade and of regular army troops. We arrived at Huesca in the middle of June which for months had been an inactive front. Here, the inertia of the Anarchists troops actually favored the Franco forces on the other fronts; not one shot had ever been fired in this sector. The heat, the dazzling sun, the arid earth, the dearth of water and the Anarchists' diffidence were depressing.

The liaison office considered the tacit truce natural. One day, General Lukas crossed into territory only partly hidden by wire netting, with no precautions. Lukas' auto, heading toward the command post of the zone, directly ahead of the Brigade Commander, was hit directly. Lukas, himself, was killed. The news of his death hit us like a flash of lightning. Born in Hungary, a General of the Red Army, a great writer and a great soldier, he deserved a better fate.

After a nocturnal march we arrived in the trenches on the Colle del Cigno, a hump of earth protected by two rows of barbed wire and some vineyards. There was not even a tree to shield us from the sun. A large hollow, a stream, a field of grain, a road, a village and a bell tower separated us from the enemy.

Upon our arrival, the Fascists broke the wonderful truce. The enemy, able to follow all our movements from the bell tower, opened fire on every moving target. We were forced to remain crouched in the trenches.

Then, the order to attack arrived.

The Republican planes bombarded the enemy positions; our tanks, followed by a battalion, attacked the buttress, forging ahead from Chimilas.

The artillery of Franco relentlessly hammered the tanks and the men in order to stop the assault and allow the regular forces to advance. Our battalion was blocked behind the enemy trenches, our tanks withdrew.

Buzzing through the sky, Republican planes encountered a big enemy formation. One of our planes was hit. The pilot attempted to bring the machine back to the base; the plane fell into no man's land; the aviator parachuted down. The enemy machine gun, planted in the bell tower, opened fire on the tiny dotted figure swaying under the white umbrella. We signalled so that the pilot would know our whereabouts. He plunged down upon the open earth. The machine gun continued shooting from the bell tower. Two Garibaldini crept out of the trench toward the pilot, now lying motionless on the ground. They could not advance, because the Fascists had seen them. We responded to enemy fire with all of our guns, in order to keep the Fascists from killing or capturing the pilot.

Hour after hour passed; our eyes were glued to the aviator stretched out on the ground, incredibly motionless. Perhaps he had been hit; perhaps he was dead. The two Garibaldini who had left the trench succeeded in returning. Suddenly, in the vineyard, a head appeared and disappeared. It was the pilot. He had moved, but still did not respond to our signals.

"Dandolo," a Garibaldino, shouted something at him in Russian. The pilot crept a few yards toward us and stopped again. He seemed confused. Baldassare shouted, "Tovarisch, tovarisch!" but he could not put together more than two or three articulate sentences. The pilot remained silent, immobile. "Tovarisch, tovarisch!" Baldassare shouted again. All of a sudden, the pilot started to creep toward us again, this time without stopping. He slid into our trench. He was no more than a boy, tall and robust. He smiled bemusedly, as if rebuking himself for not having immediately recognized us. He shook hands with everyone and embraced the Garibaldini nearest him before leaving for the Command.

The "tovarisch" had been gone only a few minutes when a Garibaldino shouted excitedly. I saw no enemy aircraft, but I could hear the angry whistle of their bullets. A moment later, the roar of their motors deafened us; the machines above spat fire, flying very low.

The bombardiers released the bombs, we could see them falling before hearing their explosion. Four bombers flew toward us; they made no deviation, but continued straight toward us. They were 500, 400, 200 yards away. At that point, we all began shooting at once, with rifles and machine guns; we aimed at their bellies.

As the planes disappeared in the distance, one left in its wake a tail of flames; it plummeted toward the ground, and then fell shattered on no man's land.

The men in the trench laughed, shouted, cheered, and whistled. An order of the day applauded the man responsible; he was a Garibaldino of our battalion, the modest and shy sergeant Pietro Borghi. Seated in his hole behind his victorious machine gun, intently scrutinizing the sky, Borghi broke into laughter when two Garibaldini informed him of the honor. Perhaps he did this in order to hide his embrarrassment.

Evening came. Finally we could move, walk, stretch our legs. The enemy continued shooting at random in the darkness.

The next day we would go on the offensive; we were excited and restless, as we were at every vigil. We looked forward to a big day. The well-entrenched enemy had already released a considerable amount of fire. The night passed slowly, exasperatingly. The sky was full of stars. Their white light illuminated the wide plain which lay before us, bare, without any shelter, with its fields of corn, vineyards, and little river. The night, the darkness and the obscurity were more and more our friends. Few of us could sleep. We were all thinking of the same thing, of the companions who had died the day before, and of those who would die the next day.

At this moment we were alive and together; others had been alive and together with us the day before. I wished that night would never end, that the darkness would last, that it would continue to protect us from death.

The dawn.

I ran onto the plain; others were running along with me; I had no idea of what I was shouting. Perhaps all soldiers in all battles shout when they are running to the assault.

Shouting made me realize that I was still alive, made me run on; it obliterated the explosion of the bombs.

Others were shouting; others were running; I hardly noticed them. All hell had broken loose! Bursts of gunfire raked the earth to the front and on all sides of me; the thuds of the bombs lacerated the air. I heard shouts, moans, sobs. Many were falling, but I had no other thought but to run. We were retreating. It was now daybreak; the night had ended. The order to attack resounded anew; again we left our trenches and holes—and again were smothered by the fire of the inexorable machine guns. I stopped for a second; I stared at the men who were falling to earth like empty sacks. Two armed tanks were on fire in the corn field. Near me a wounded man was shouting and cursing; another lay doubled over on the ground, trembling, crying and calling for his mother. A veteran with white hair, staring straight ahead, overtook me as he shouted to himself, "Go ahead, quickly, go ahead, run!"

One of our tanks was hit at the river and caught fire. I advanced with head lowered, but as we ran ahead, our numbers dwindled, more soldiers fell. The hail of machine bullets sprayed fountains of earth about us. The river was near by. The enemy machine gun barrage continued to spray an incessant rain of bullets. I ran between the wounded, rolled down the bank, crossed the little river, and threw myself on the bank of the other shore. There were only four of us who had made it. And we could not continue the assault with only four men.

A young Spanish courier joined us. He announced that reinforcements were arriving. He raised himself, then suddenly fell, hit in the face. His body rolled into the water.

Thomat. He was there, too, right in back of me. "We must retreat," he shouted. These were the orders of Raimondi[1], who was in command of the battalion. Battistelli had been seriously injured.

There were many dead and even more wounded. "Where is the machine gun of the first detachment?" asked Thomat.

"Up ahead."

"Up ahead! That's impossible."

I insisted it was there. Thomat ordered me to go and get it. I crawled out from the protection of the river bank. Following a path made by the corn stalks, I advanced one hundred yards. I almost crawled onto the back of a dead Garibaldino. Cerbai and the machine gun were still ahead. I encountered other wounded, shouting and crying. I could not stop; I crawled along. There was the machine gun, along with Cerbai and another Garibaldino. They were the only ones remaining of the squad of eight men. Cerbai cursed. Crawling between dead and wounded, we dragged along the machine gun. I pulled a Garibaldino by the arm. He had a fractured leg and a broken shoulder. We moved slowly, ten yards at a time. I dragged him to the river, where Cerbai had preceded me with the machine gun. We waited for the evening in order to continue. The dark would save the wounded. It was night; we left the river, and finally got back to the trenches between the vines. Sixty men out of one hundred on our muster roll were missing.

✻　✻　✻　✻　✻

A rat, nibbling at something, brushed up against my feet. I was shivering from the cold; I could do nothing. The man stretched out nearby disturbed me and made me anxious.

A bell rang: 2:15. I wished I could go to sleep and wake up in the morning. I heard the uncoupling of a trolley car. I attempted to rise. My feet, back—my entire body was in pain. With an effort, I stood up, brushed myself off, and walked away, passing in front of the unknown man. He was still sleeping.

---

1. Raimondi (Agostino Casati) substituted as Commander of the Battalion for Libero Battistelli, who was gravely injured. Battistelli, Republican writer and lawyer had hastened to Spain. After joining the "Roselli" column and commanding an artillery group of the "Ascaro" Division on the Argon front, he had joined the Garibaldi in April. He died gloriously on the Huesca front.

✿　✿　✿　✿　✿

After the Camp Giuriati and Arcore massacres, the Piazza Command was not long in issuing the order to throw every effort into a counterattack. The enemy was given no respite, nor were we in Piazzale Firenze. The SAP assaulted the Fascist barracks; an officer and two Fascists were killed by the "Walter" group which had recently joined the GAP. On February 3, 1945, the men of this group executed a marshal and a sergeant of Affori, who had been found to be spies and jailers. Other young men joined the partisan forces of the GAP. One of the new squads managed to derail a train; the "Walter" detachment destroyed five large military trucks, killing two German soldiers.

In the course of this unceasing counterattack, a plan was devised to attack "Leon d'Oro" (Lion of Gold), the restaurant on Corso Garibaldi. This was the eating place for the Muti Brigade stationed on Via Schiapparelli. The Fascists had tried to transform their center into a fort, by stocking it with cases of munitions and intensifying the watch. The plan of attack had to be studied in great detail. I ordered Minardi, Olga and Pellegrini to determine the best way to penetrate the Leon d'Oro, and to make the necessary arrangements. February 4, 1945, was set for the day of action.

The squad would act under Franci's orders. Albino Rossi, Albino Trecchi (who was now in the Third Aliotta Division, operating in the Oltrepo of the Pavia region), and Lina Selvetti would go with him.

I met with Franci at 5 P.M. and a half hour later, with Lina Selvetti. I decided to take direct charge of the command. Later, Franci looked at me incredulously. "What does this change of plans mean?" I remained silent. "Is it that you don't trust me?" The simplicity of his words eliminated any desire on my part to argue with him.

"Very well, I'll tell you. You know it's not a matter of distrust. I only wanted to convey to all of you the importance of this mission." I watched the four of them walk away.

✿　✿　✿　✿　✿

Minardi and Olga were surprised by the explosion. They looked at their watches. "That one was ahead of schedule!" exclaimed Olga, terrified. Her words were lost in the curses and the shots.

That evening, I waited in vain for Franci on Piazzale Susa. I left very much disturbed. I did not go to my regular address but to a secure refuge, the house of Signora Amelia Rossi, on Via Merzario. She was the wife of an engineer who had been deported to Germany. Signora Baroni, who always provided me with refuge when I needed it, lived in the same building. I passed a sleepless night there.

The following morning, I was on the street at dawn to meet with Minardi. Everything was dismayingly clear. "The bomb," he said, "exploded ahead of time. And so, it wasn't possible to get close."

"And the young people?"

"Nothing, I haven't heard a thing."

Franci's family was worried and in the dark about everything. They implored me to give them information. I promised them I knew not what in my confusion.

The following day, I sent a comrade, Tatanis, who knew both Franci and Lina, to the morgue. I waited on the Piazza Guardi until eleven. I knew that we would never again see Franci or the young girl.

How could this have happened? A technical defect of the bomb? A spy who had recognized them? Perhaps someone had hit the bomb with a bullet and had caused it to explode. Or had Franci lighted the fuse before he should have? These were all questions without answers.

Lina Selvetti had been only twenty-four years old. In September, 1943, she had been among the first of the young female partisans in the Valtellina. I remembered when she had kissed me and then said, "I had to do it!"

Albino Rossi, a glorious fighter of Oltrepo, was another. He had asked to be transferred to the third GAP Brigade because he "wished to contribute more." He had been seriously wounded in the action against the rest home. He had borne up under excruciating pain and when he had fainted at the hospital he had murmured, "For liberty, for independence," to the nun assisting him.

There was also Albino Trecchi, a twenty-two year old, another partisan from the Oltrepo. He, too, had asked for a transfer to the Gappisti. It had cost him his life.

And Luigi Franci, immediately after September 8, had helped English prisoners to escape to Switzerland. A generous and enthusiastic person, he had kept himself busy hiding patriots, collecting money and medicines, and distributing underground newspapers. He too had asked to "do more;" he had insisted upon enrolling in the GAP. He had been a great help in manufacturing bombs and in procuring quantities of urgently needed explosives and arms. But he hadn't been satisfied. He had wanted to get into direct action against the Nazi-Fascists.

✿   ✿   ✿   ✿   ✿

During the years before the war, working in white coveralls at the Caproni airplane factory meant escaping a destiny of having to emigrate to Ethiopia. And from 1937 onward, the chances for avoiding Ethiopia were even greater. Whoever considered disembarking at Massawa was, instead, told to leave the ship at Tangiers, to embark once again for some port on the Iberian peninsula. And then? The rest was written into the books on the war in Spain. Working at Caproni still meant security, a sure job in a factory where the most modern equipment—hydroplanes, bi-motors and recordbreaking aircraft—were constructed in a pre-assembly line and artisan atmosphere. Moreover, the name was prestigious and would remain so even after its decline. No one ever dreamed that this decline could happen.

Working at Caproni, as in other factories defined as being "in the national interest," permitted the worker to escape the general uncertainty prevalent elsewhere. The work force was the pick of the young Italian workers. It was so precious a group that even the *regime* had to close an eye to certain escapades and abstain from "cleaning up certain little corners." The regime depended upon the workers at Caproni for its own prestige. If many of them were anti-Fascist, they were, on the other hand, most able workers. And so they were pretty well left to themselves.

With the war, times became more strenuous. Bombs were falling outside. Inside, discipline was tightened. On April 25, it seemed that the incursions were brusquely interrupted. On September 8, while the members of the house of Savoy were escaping to Pescara, and the rich of the North to Switzerland, the workers occupied the factory; they seized two hundred machine guns and began to resist. But Milan fell, and the workers of Caproni could not wage war by themselves. They slowly resumed their activity in the factory. The two hundred machine guns were shipped to a secure place, first to Via Manzoni, the headquarters of the Libera-

tion Committee (Comitato di Liberazione), and then to Cernob-
bio, where they were used by one of the first partisan groups.
Colonel Cesarini now returned to Caproni. Physically, he was a
giant, but morally, a mad beast. He was the essence of arrogance
and terror. He made a display of his violent temper, leaving no
doubt of his brutality. He supervised every arrest and personally
signed the punitive papers for every repressive act. He was insolent, full of hatred, boorish, a chauvinist drunk with power. This
man, who before the war had come to the factory to take charge
of internal discipline, now was back as the incarnation of revenge
and retaliation, the essence of Republican Fascism.

He had hardly arrived, when he ordered a listing of anti-
Fascists who had been outspoken during the Badoglio period.
Many of them were already members of the Patriotic organization that had started operating inside the factory. Colonel Cesarini
began a relentless program for the Republicans, forming the nucleus of the Black Brigade's permanent supervision of the factories, surveillance of the workers, and systems for arrests. In
addition, this nucleus organized espionage within the ranks of our
organization, which was engaged in sabotage, recruitment of
fighters for the mountain formations, and apprehension of spies
and jailers.

Giovanni Cervi, an engineer and director of "Giustizia e Lib-
ertà," (Justice and Liberty), was taken to San Vittore one foggy
morning in October, 1943 and killed at the Arena. He was Colonel
Cesarini's first victim.

The assassination produced an atmosphere of hate. It was as
though they had killed a relative of every one of the workers. The
assassin, the man who had tipped off the firing squad, was in the
factory, moving from department to department, followed by his
henchmen. The workers decided to go on strike; at least four thousand remained absent from work.

The reprisals began. The Fascists took note of the absences
in each department. If a worker was not seen at work for a day or
two, this meant that at night, a team of the Black Brigade would
call at the worker's home and lead him off to prison. From prison,
many would be sent to Germany; others would be shot or hanged
on some piazza or on some street corner. We would find out by
looking through the newspapers to read the names of the "bandits"
who were killed.

Meanwhile, the Fascists had to stand guard around the exit

gate, where there was always a member of the Muti Brigade or someone whom we suspected of being a spy. They were on the alert for anyone seeking news of a companion. And if they had the impression that his interest was excessive, another order for arrest would be issued, and the next day, another locker inside the factory entrance would be emptied.

The thirty members of the Muti Brigade who worked for the Colonel were relentless in carrying out their responsibilities in the Caproni factory, but this could not stop the workers from their activities. After the October strike, additional strikes developed in November and December. In November, one of the thirty Republicans stationed at the Caproni factory was felled by several pistol shots on Via Aselli. This was the work of one of the Caproni Gappisti; he had vindicated the engineer, Cervi, and many others who had been deported and imprisoned.

Terror was massive. Hundreds of workers were deported in a tragic follow-up of reprisals. Others were forced to leave the factory. If they went into the mountains, they became partisans—soldiers in a growing army. The 196th Garibaldi Brigade was composed of workers from the Caproni factory; it blew up an electric station, sabotaged several airplanes and, right under the eye of the Republicans, strewed three-pronged nails on the roads to blow out the tires of the Nazi-Fascist automobiles. By March, 1944, the arrests, deportations and expulsions from the factory of many of the partisan leaders not only impeded strike activity, as massive as it was, but made the situation more difficult. The Fascists were not only making isolated arrests but they were taking lives as well. From that moment, the chief goal of the clandestine movement in the city was to eliminate Cesarini. This man had succeeded in spreading terror. It had become almost impossible to unleash our harnessed energy because of the constant surveillance and continuous reprisals. The fight continued but under extremely arduous conditions.

Cesarini was at the apex of his power. He was the authoritarian voice of the Republican Federation; he was the boss of the Caproni factory, ordering his men about as he wished; a patrol followed him everywhere, both in the factory as well as at his home.

The last months of 1944 and the beginning of 1945 were the low points. Houses were without heat, hunger was everywhere.

Lugubrious notices of mass executions covered the walls. The Muti firing squads alternated with the SS and the Republican Air Command at Camp Giuriati and in the city streets. A suspect had only to fall into the hands of the oppressors to be shot. The enemy was aware that time was closing in on him; the spilled blood reinforced his hatred. A gun shot could come from any window; death could issue from the hand of a Gappista silently waiting on the corner of a street. Fear increased the enemy's cruelty. Bodies of patriots hung from lamp posts; reprisals became more heartless than ever. At the Caproni factory, Cesarini was in a fury.

☼   ☼   ☼   ☼   ☼

Through the usual secret channels, I was told that a comrade of the regional Lombard Command was expecting to see me on Sunday afternoon in a certain bar which I knew. The proprietor was an unsuspected militant. We would meet at his place, ostensibly to play a game of cards and smoke a cigarette together. Everything seemed normal, but while I was waiting for Sunday to roll around, I learned from new reports that several Garibaldini had been arrested. Names were not listed. The Republican police were careful to hide any clues which would reveal to us the weak link in our chain. I had a feeling that the news was concealing something. It hinted of a partisan assault that had been thwarted by the security forces of the Republic of Salò; but not before there had been several arrests. There was no mention made of the precise locale, only a general reference to the city of Milan. Usually, when news of this nature was published, the story concluded with an announcement that one or more mass executions had taken place. There was not even a hint of this in the story. My suspicion was that the arrests were the result of a man-trap. As the first order of business, caution required me to examine the invitation to meet the comrade from the Command; I found everything in order. There could not possibly have been infiltration there. My examination was thorough. I retraced the communications link which had brought me the message to meet Alberganti. On Sunday, I examined the neighborhood more minutely than usual before entering the bar. At least, from outward appearances, there was no sign of police or Republicans in civilian clothes.

Inside, the atmosphere was quiet. People were playing billiards with a seriousness and concentration typical of peace time and drinking cups of coffee-substitute or glasses of wine. The odor of cigarettes was everywhere. In a corner, an old man was rolling them for the customers, using leaves of the plane-tree, saved I knew not how, perhaps from the winter before, and heavy paper. One could hardly breathe because of the smoke.

Alberganti was quietly standing near the telephone with a glass of beer in front of him. He was an old acquaintance from the days of confinement at Ventotene. We were both old hands, and so we lost no time in proprieties. We were both preoccupied—Alberganti, because he knew what had happened, and I, because I had no information. The arrests mentioned in the newspaper had not taken place, but an important assault had failed, and what was worse, those who had been in charge of the assault had retreated after placing their lives in jeopardy. Having been discovered with guns in hand by the Republicans, they might just as well have concluded the action, and thereby eliminated some Republican sympathizers. Those who had participated would have been executed, whatever course they followed. No one was arrested because no one's life had been spared. "No," said Alberganti, "the stakes were politically too high and it is the third time that the attempt has failed."

With these words I understood that the fourth attempt to remove the Caproni executioner from circulation would fall upon me. Naturally, the Command was letting me decide whether or not it could be done, and whether I wanted to take on this responsibility. I was given a week in which to think about it. Rather than risk another meeting, I decided to come to a quick decision right then and there. I accepted. Alberganti slapped me on the shoulder and walked away. I remained awhile, and was just about to go out the door when a voice suddenly shouted at me. My hand leaped into my pocket. I grabbed hold of my pistol, but it was not necessary; it was the waiter, complaining that Alberganti had not paid his bill. I burst out laughing. Seeing Alberganti again after so many years had reminded me only of his courage. Now I remembered that he always had been a bit of a tightwad. I left a good tip, so as not to leave any lingering bad impression.

Of all the assignments I had ever received, this was one of the hardest. It was better that I handle it alone. I sent word to my Gappisti comrades that there would be no action for a while. I suggested that they make good use of the time by reading and studying, as Gramsci[2] had advised. I didn't know whether they would heed my advice, but on the other hand, they did not have many distractions, since the rules of clandestine warfare required that they remain in their houses in a sort of voluntary incarceration, so as to be noticed as little as possible.

I, too, stayed at home, staring at a map of the area where I was to perform Operation Cesarini. On the corner of Viale Mugello and Corso XXII March the sketch showed a delicatessen, directly in front of the trolley stop. On the other side was an old unoccupied warehouse. On paper, the plan of action seemed to work, but when I went to inspect the location, I realized that the area was completely in the open. After the action, I would either have to run onto Viale Mugello, on Piazza Grandi, which was usually teeming with police, or escape through Via Campania, a wide, straight roadway, where I would be exposed to the gunfire of Cesarini's guards and the other Republicans who frequently crossed there.

I had to admit that my plan was full of loop-holes, an unforgiveable condition for a Gappista of long experience. I passed a rather disturbing night. The following morning, as soon as I woke, I returned to the area. I bought a small piece of mortadella in the delicatessen; then I went over to a bar on the corner of Via Campania for a cup of coffee. I somehow felt calmer. The area was completely open, but the old abandoned warehouse did offer an excellent escape. And another solution came to mind when I noticed a water department employee just about to descend into a manhole. In a desperate situation, I could try to remove the manhole cover and find a safe underground escape. I moved toward the manhole and stopped to light a cigarette right alongside another worker who was assisting his companion in his descent. I was lucky. He asked for a light. I threw away the used match, took a box from my pocket, and calmly lit the worker's cigarette for him. We exchanged a few words about the weather, agreeing that, this being March, it was a bit early for regular spring weather; he chatted about how hard he had to work. At the end of the conver-

----

2. Translator's note: Gramsci, Antonio (1891-1937) Communist deputy, writer and editor of the weekly, *Rivoluzione Liberale*, a spirited anti-Fascist journal of the early Mussolini era.

sation I learned that in case of necessity I could certainly go down that manhole, move along a few hundred yards, and reappear on the street through the next manhole.

However, the old abandoned warehouse offered the best escape. A secondary exit led onto another street; there were large windows through which I could climb, and beyond that, there was a gate which was easy to open. In addition, there were no watchmen on duty. I had to find a set of keys for the doors. A locksmith who was a comrade would provide this.

I awoke during the night. In the street, there was the hum of voices, perhaps those of the military. I pulled aside the curtains; they were soldiers. Being awakened again stirred up my anxiety and tension. What time was it? The light of dawn came through the curtains. Something leapt inside me. I saw Cesarini's face, a symbol of power and of evil. He had entered the factory and was beating up the defenseless. This picture merged with the memory of a dawn of long ago on Spanish soil.

At seven the following morning, with the keys jingling in my pocket and my eyes fixed on my watch, I rode my bicycle with a comrade to Via Mugello. I got off just before arriving at the delicatessen, a few feet from the trolley stop. It was 7:20. I felt impatient, but calm.

There were people on the streets. In a little while, the workers would be rushing along to their offices and factories, and the trolleys would begin to fill. Men and women were already queuing up at the trolley stop. Cesarini appeared from the direction of the Piazza Grandi. I had seen him only a few times, but I knew it was he. There was always someone like him, an enemy that had to be fought, whether in Spain, France, Italy or here in Milan. This one had been responsible for the deportation of hundreds of workers and technicians (practically all of whom had ended up at Auschwitz). He had also been responsible for the imprisonment and shooting of comrades and friends.

Now he was coming to his own end, along with his escort, two militiamen with sub-machine guns. I didn't have to move. He was approaching me directly with his overbearing stride, as though he thought no one would dare to obstruct his walk. But I was on the street, I, the son of a Piedmontese worker who had moved away to France, in order to escape the arrogance of the Cesarinis of those days.

I blocked his way.

His face filled with amazement when he saw my two revolvers pointed at him. He couldn't believe that anyone would dare to stop him.

I shouted loudly, so that the workers around could hear, "Cesarini, you're through deporting workers from the Caproni factory." I fired. He attempted to move his hand to his holster, but it was too late. He was already on the ground alongside one of his escorts. The other one tried to fire his sub-machine gun, but not in time. My guns were now emptied.

I shouted, "Justice is done! Rise up against Fascism!" The people who had thrown themselves on the ground at the sound of the gunfire rose and cheered. Several shouted, "Cesarini has been killed. Evviva!"

I had to get away before it was too late. The street was clear. I didn't have to escape through the old warehouse. I hopped onto my bicycle and furiously pedalled away. I saw a captain of the Air Corps standing in front of me brandishing a revolver; I pointed my gun at him, and the hero of Salò dropped his revolver and ran. I got away with no further trouble.

Justice was done. The workers on the trolley carried the big news to the factory which was only a short distance away: "The executioner of Caproni, the assassin of hundreds of workers, has been killed!"

\* \* \* \* \*

After the arrest of the members of the Campegi group, who were shot at Camp Giuriati, four more Gappisti were killed in an assault.

And so, we had to obtain reinforcements for the Brigade. It was not easy. One could not make a full-fledged Gappista in one day; you had to build him up.

During those weeks, we heard about a Milanese detachment of the SAP, which was composed of workers from the Mabo and the Cabi-Cattaneo factories. They had already disarmed Republican militia and German soldiers and had engaged in some sabotage activities. Now Bruso, Novelli, Roncaglione, Romano, Giuseppe Colombo, Cesare Colombo, Alfredo Sinistro, Giancaro, Mantovani, and Orsi, who commanded a brigade in Valle Olona, had joined our ranks, and so we secured our reinforcements. Novelli was given the command of the detachment; Bruso was appointed the commissioner. They had demonstrated in more than one action that they were loyal and courageous boys.

Reinforced by Novelli's group, the Gappisti were now in action everywhere, from Affori, where they were engaged in a real battle, to the center of Milan, where a Nazi was killed.

February 22, 1945, marked the twenty-seventh anniversary of the Soviet Army. Red flags were unfurled on the smoke stacks of Milan factories, political graffiti appeared on the walls, and here and there little groups gathered. On February 28, three Gappisti, eluding the vigilance of the sentinels, set off a bomb at Affori, on the Milan-Turin railroad line, interrupting traffic for several hours. The month of March was approaching, and liberation was in the air; it was heralded not only by partisan deeds but also by discussions between people riding the trolley cars or lining up for the distribution of rationed goods.

Everybody cursed Fascism when they heard the sounds of the Black Brigades. The women, standing in front of shops, damned the war, Fascism and Hitler. One heard the phrase, "It's almost over," even more frequently, or "It's only going to last only a bit longer." Spies and informers were still busily operating; many citizens were still being imprisoned or deported to Germany. But people were less fearful. Above all, the workers in the factories responded to every Fascist provocation, openly displaying their opposition to the regime by organizing workers' meetings inside the offices. Strikes and demonstrations defending people's rights to live freely with ample food were taking place everywhere. The order of the day was, "Get finished with the Nazi-Fascists." Members of the Fascist hierarchy who still tried to intimidate the workers in many of the factories were interrupted with shouts, "Death to Fascism, Out with the Germans! Enough of the War!"

On the first of March, I met Ugo Clocchiatti, who informed me of Curiel's death, near Piazzale Baracca. The news of Curiel's death travelled around the city quickly. "They have killed Curiel, the founder of the Youth Front, the director of Unità!"[3]

I had known Curiel at Ventotene in 1940. I remembered his slender figure, his affability, his habit of always carrying a book. I

---

3. Unita—The official Newspaper of the Italian Communist Party.

had often met him with Frausin,[4] the worker from Trieste, who was burned alive in 1944 by the Germans. I had seen Curiel again in July, 1944, on via Marcona, with Dozza. I had watched them from afar, without approaching them. Curiel had known, perhaps more than anyone, how to understand and work with the young, how to spur them on to open warfare—only in this way, he had said, could the young people formulate their ideals, and continue the battle for liberty and democracy on a more meaningful level.

The death of Curiel acted as an additional motive for the third GAP Brigade to intensify the attacks. The Gappisti were mobilized twenty-four hours a day. The Fascists and Germans, suspicious of everything and everyone, felt the end approaching and locked themselves in their barracks. When they did go out, they moved in groups, cautious and armed to the teeth. But the initiative was now ours.

Our activities in March, 1945, included the executions of Colonel Cesarini; Angelo Contini, the junior officer of the GNR,[5] an unarmed Wehrmacht marshal who had distinguished himself by his repressive measures in the Lambrate quarters; the noted squad leader, Romualdo Papa; several officers of the "Resega;" and the commandants of the groups who had made their reputations during the last of the fierce roundups of partisan brigades in the mountains. In addition, a well-known spy whose activity had cost the lives of numerous patriots was attacked and nearly killed; Fascist headquarters on via Delfico were bombed; arms were captured in the home of a notorious Fascist on Strada Novate Milanese; and various Fascists of the X Mas were disarmed.

Incessant Gappisti actions were an aid to the worker uprisings. On March 28, the workers in more than one hundred Milan factories went on strike. The order of the day was, "Enough of the war. Out with the Germans. Death to the Fascists!"

Militiamen of the Muti squads, soldiers of the Black Brigades and SS troops lined up in front of the factories. The workers

---

4. Luigi Frausin, born in Muggia in 1894, was killed by the Nazi-Fascists in August, 1944. He was condemned to twelve years imprisonment by a special tribunal. He organized the resistance movement in Venezia Giulia.

5. GNR (Guardia Nazionale Repubblicana)—Republican National Guard —Fascist militia.

feared them no more. Numerous demonstrations were organized in spite of repressions, threats, and arrests. And while the workers demonstrated, the partisans of the third GAP and the SAP attacked: industrial collaborators, spies, militiamen, Republicans, German officers, soldiers, SS torturers—all were cut down in full daylight on the streets, in their homes and in front of barracks. And the barracks themselves were attacked by fast-moving two- and three-man squads. Pistol shots and bomb explosions augered the end of tyranny.

Giancarlo, a very young Gappista, fell in one of the last actions. Small, thin, of insignificant appearance, slow to express himself, Giancarlo had been very astute, sensitive and courageous; he and Mantovani had attacked a barracks in full daylight, had thrown grenades and fired their Stens at a group of black-uniformed militia who were standing in front of the door which was protected by sand bags. They had continued firing even when the Fascists had begun to return the gunfire; they had blocked those who tried to leave and forced back those Fascists who appeared at the windows. Then, the two boys had attempted to flee on their bicycles. Mantovani had succeeded in getting away. Giancarlo's chain had broken, and he continued on foot. Even as he was surrounded, he had continued to fire, until he was hit. He fell to the ground, and with the Sten, still forced his pursuers to seek refuge in doorways; rising again, he started to run; again he had fallen to the ground, feigning death. He held a grenade in his hand. He pulled the safety catch. When a group of Fascists approached him, he threw the grenade. Eventually captured a few minutes later, and carried inside the barracks, he was promised to be set free if he would reveal names. "If you don't talk, you'll never see your family again."

After three hours interrogation, during which the Fascists had yanked at his wounds to torture him, Giancarlo was carried outside, and leaned against the wall in front of the barracks. While the black-uniformed brigade pointed their guns, Giancarlo shouted, "Long live the partisans! Comrades, move forward!"

These seem like sentences reconstructed from legend. But this was how Giancarlo had actually died. We were told of it by the same black-uniformed men who had killed him, when, a few hours later, we made an assault upon the barracks on Via Cadamosto to avenge Giancarlo. Before dying themselves, they gave us an account of the heroic death of our comrade.

Insurrection was in the air. On the 24th of the month, the streets of Milan were teeming with people. Fascists and Germans still moved here and there in well-armed groups or in armored trucks, but their faces revealed their fear. They did not know what to do. Many Fascists now wore civilian clothes and were seeking to escape. 'Surrender or perish," read the latest message. And those who did not surrender, did perish. There was no escape for the man who, whether a spy, a jailer or a killer, did not surrender his arms.

April 25 was the day we had long been awaiting. It was the day for which we, together with all of the people, had prepared. That day, April 25, 1945, there were even more people on the streets than the day before. The entire city was running, shouting, rising up. Fascists and Germans attempted to carry on a last resistance, but in vain. For hours on end, the GAP and SAP squads, while waiting for the mountain formations to come down into Milan, rushed from one quarter to the other, eliminating the last strongholds of Fascist resistance, arresting Fascist officials, forcing the surrender of the German groups. Twenty-four hours before, we had been few in number. Now we were many.

We had been able to exist, fight, and win because, behind us, supporting, helping, hiding, feeding and informing, had always been that mass of people, who now raced through the streets embracing each other and embracing us, as they shouted, "Long live the partisans!"